The Great Philosophers

Stephen Law is Senior Lecturer in Philosophy at Heythrop College, University of London, and the author of *The Philosophy Gym*, *The Philosophy Files*, *The Outer Limits* and *The War for Children's Minds*. He is also the editor of the Royal Institute of Philosophy journal, *Think*.

The Great Philosophers

The Lives and Ideas
of History's Greatest Thinkers

Stephen Law

Quercus

First published in Great Britain in 2007 by Quercus

This paperback edition published in 2013 by

Quercus
55 Baker Street
Seventh Floor, South Block
London
W1U 8EW

A CIP catalogue record for this book is available
from the British Library

ISBN 978 1 78087 747 1

10 9 8 7 6 5 4 3

Text designed and typeset by Ellipsis

Printed and bound in Great Britain by Clays Ltd, St Ives plc

Contents

CONTENTS

Introduction

If you are entirely new to philosophy, the first question you are likely to ask on picking up this book is – what *is* philosophy? Where lie the boundaries of the discipline to which these thinkers belong? What makes them all *philosophers*?

These are not easy questions to answer. As a first stab at defining philosophy, we might try: all these thinkers are concerned with questions that are both significant and deep. One way in which they are deep is that they reach beyond the point where the empirical or mathematical sciences might conceivably provide us with answers. For example, questions about moral value, or about why there is something rather than nothing at all, would seem to fall into this category.

That initial answer would not be *quite* right, however. There are philosophical questions that science – or at least empirical observation – may be able to settle fairly conclusively. Some would suggest this is true of the question of the existence of the Judeo-Christian God, either because they think there's very good empirical evidence for his existence, or because they think there's overwhelming evidence against. Yet whether God exists remains a philosophical question.

Others tend to place more emphasis on philosophy as an *activity* rather than a subject area. It is certainly true that within the Western philosophical tradition, a questioning, critical approach rooted in reason is usually considered to be one of the hallmarks of philosophy. But of course, even if taking such an approach is a necessary condition of doing philosophy, it is not sufficient. Philosophy is not the only discipline to adopt a rational, critical method.

Perhaps the right answer to the question: 'What is philosophy?' is that philosophy is what Wittgenstein calls a *family resemblance concept* (see page 25). If we look at a variety of different philosophers, we will find overlapping similarities, but there need not be any common, defining feature that makes them all philosophers. If philosophy is a family resemblance concept, then perhaps the easiest way to grasp what philosophy is would be to look at a fairly wide range of examples. You can do that by reading this book.

The book is written for those who want a succinct introduction to some of the key ideas and arguments of the world's greatest philosophers. My hope is that it will stimulate you to think and question, and, in some cases, to turn to the writings of the philosophers themselves.

Anyone who writes a book entitled *The Great Philosophers* can't do so without placing their tongue partly in their cheek. Does this book contain all and only those philosophers that are 'great'? Undoubtedly not. Indeed, many would question whether all of the thinkers included are even philosophers.

What I present here are important philosophers and thinkers that I personally consider among the most interesting and significant. Rather than attempt any kind of overview of the work of each thinker, I have in many cases focused instead on one key idea or line of argument – one that I happen to find of interest. My aim throughout has been to transmit some of my own fascination with their ideas and arguments to you.

The Buddha

C.560–C.480 BC

The release from suffering

*'It is just thirst or craving, which gives rise to re-
peated existence, which is bound up with impas-
sioned appetite and which seeks fresh pleasure now
here and now there ...'*

THE BUDDHA ON OUR ATTACHMENT TO TRANSIENT THINGS

The Buddha is dismissive of attempts to answer many of the
great philosophical questions, such as whether the universe has
always existed. He considers such questions unanswerable,
preferring to focus on the *practical*. The Buddha is interested
in acquiring the wisdom necessary to achieve a very concrete
result – the removal of *suffering*.

The philosophy of the Buddha involves a theory about the
nature of human existence and how we might achieve release
from suffering. He does not recommend that we passively
accept his pronouncements as a matter of 'faith'. Rather he en-
courages us actively to test them for ourselves against our own
experience.

The Buddha's diagnosis of the root cause of our suffering, and his recommended cure, are encapsulated in his four 'noble truths':

The four truths

The first truth is that life is suffering. We see pain, frustration and misery all around us. Our suffering – both physical and mental – may be punctuated by brief moments of happiness, but the suffering soon returns. Why?

According to the Buddha, because we have a mistaken conception of both ourselves and the world. We think of ourselves as possessing an enduring core or essence. We also suppose that the world is comprised of enduring, substantial things possessing essences of their own. But the truth is that the world is fundamentally one of transience and impermanence. There is no robust essential core to either ourselves or the world. Being ignorant of this, we try to cling on to things: to ideas, to external objects and even to our own identity. We crave and attempt to maintain a grip on what we believe will make us permanently happy. But we are inevitably frustrated. We are grasping at air and, therefore, what happiness we achieve is always short-lived.

The second truth is that this ceaseless attempt to grasp at transient things traps us in an endless cycle of suffering, of birth and rebirth. What is reborn is not an enduring, substantial self – for we possess no such essential core. A person is best thought of, not as an *entity*, but as a causally interrelated bundle of ceaselessly shifting psychological and physical features that pass through countless cycles of suffering.

The third truth is that we can release ourselves from this treadmill of suffering. If we let go – if we cease trying to grasp what is not there – our suffering will cease. For many Westerners the thought that there is life beyond the grave – that we might be reborn to live again – is reassuring. But for the Buddha, rebirth is something we should seek to avoid. In fact, if the Buddha is correct, the craving for such a permanent, enduring self is actually one of the root causes of our suffering.

The fourth truth is the Buddha's eightfold path: a plan for living that will help us to achieve nirvana. We need to acquire the right view, right intention, right speech, right action, right livelihood, right effort, right mindfulness and right concentration.

Is Buddhism a religion?

The teachings of the Buddha gave rise to a movement called Buddhism that has a number of different schools. One interesting question that might be raised about Buddhism is whether it can rightly be described as a religion. Those who deny that it is a religion might indicate the following:

1. The Buddha denies that there is a God.

2. The Buddha does not offer, as many religions do, a belief system that must be accepted on faith. Buddha emphasizes the importance of individuals testing his claims against their own experience.

On the other hand, those who claim Buddhism is a religion might point out that:

1. Buddha asserts that certain gods or god-like beings exist.

2. Like many other religions, the Buddha offers both a moral code and a transformational goal.

3. While the Buddha emphasizes that we should test his observations against experience, the degree to which they can be tested is debatable. The thought that 'life is suffering' is vague and open to interpretation, and it is hard to see what might count as evidence against it. Karl Popper (see page 170) might well accuse Buddhism of being 'unfalsifiable'. Nor is the claim that we are repeatedly reborn well supported by the evidence.

The Buddha and Western philosophy

At various points the Buddha's philosophy bears a close resemblance to the thinking of several major Western philosophers. Here are two examples:

The Buddha and Hume The Buddha claims that what we think of as an enduring self is in fact merely a bundle of transient features, a view that closely parallels Hume's (see page 158).

The Buddha and Schopenhauer Another obvious parallel is in the work of Schopenhauer (see page 200), who was familiar with Eastern philosophy and with Buddhism in particular. His view that the world is one of terrible suffering brought about by a ceaseless striving, clearly mirrors the Buddha's view. The Buddha believes release can be achieved by attaining nirvana. Schopenhauer believes we can attain it temporarily through, among other things, contemplating works of art.

Biography

Born c.560 BC. At the age of 29, Siddhartha Gautama, the son of a provincial ruler, left his home province in northern India (now part of Nepal) to seek enlightenment. It is said that he found it at the age of 35 while meditating beneath a fig tree. Gautama then became known as the 'Buddha' or the 'awakened one', and he spent the remainder of his life encouraging others in the search for enlightenment through his teaching. He died c.480 BC.

Confucius

551–479 BC

The golden rule

'Never impose on others what you would not choose for yourself.'

Confucius, like the Buddha, also offers a very practical philosophy, containing much concrete advice. He believes that a harmonious and stable society requires a number of key ingredients, including:

1. *Shared values and traditions.* Confucius teaches that common values and traditions function as a cement that helps bind people together into communities. He recommends that people come together to engage in *li* – the study of ritual forms of propriety and respect.

2. *A concern for others.* Confucius proposes a version of the golden rule – that you should never do to others anything you would not want done to yourself.

3. *People responsibly fulfilling their allotted social and familial roles.* Sons and daughters have certain duties to their parents, and government ministers have duties that they must discharge properly. To fulfil their allotted roles people need the appropriate *virtues*. A government minister for example should be both trustworthy and exercise due respect towards the ruler.

Confucius believes in leading by example. A leader who discharges his role responsibly will be more likely to command the loyalty of his subjects, who in turn will be more likely to emulate him and fulfil their own allotted roles properly. Confucius says, 'If the ruler is virtuous, the people will also be virtuous.'

Confucius's version of the golden rule

I am going to focus here on Confucius's golden rule. The golden rule appears variously in many religious and ethical systems. Sometimes it takes a positive form, as in the Christian injunction: '*Do* unto others as you would have them *do* unto you.' Others, including Confucius, formulate it as a prohibition: '*Do not* do to others what you would *not* want done to you.'

Counter-examples to the rule

Despite its popularity, the golden rule attracts a number of counter-examples.

Suppose a fat man is on a diet. He wouldn't want anyone to offer him a fattening meal. But then Confucius's golden rule requires that he should not offer such a meal to others, even if they are starving to death – hardly the moral conclusion to draw.

Or suppose a doctor would prefer not to be told if she were herself diagnosed with a fatal illness. Confucius's rule entails that she should refuse to provide similar information to her patients, even if they want it. Again, surely not the right conclusion to draw.

A different interpretation of the rule

But perhaps we have misinterpreted the rule. Maybe we should interpret it as saying, not that we shouldn't do to others what we, *given our actual situation and desires,* wouldn't want done to us, but instead that we shouldn't do to others what we wouldn't want done to us *if we were in their position and had their desires.*

This alternative reading of the rule allows us neatly to side-step the first two counter-examples. In this reading, the fat man on a diet is not prohibited from feeding the starving, as he certainly would wish to be offered food if he were starving himself. And our doctor is no longer prohibited from informing her patients that they are fatally ill if they want to be told the truth.

Other counter-examples

Unfortunately, if we interpret the rule in this other way, we run into more counter-examples. Take the punishment of wrong-doers. If we were cruel and unrepentant murderers found guilty by a court of law, then no doubt we wouldn't want to be pun-

8

ished. It seems to follow, then, that we shouldn't punish such murders. Confucius's golden rule now has the consequence that we can only punish those murderers who *want* to be punished. But that is ridiculous, surely?

Even if we set the problem of punishing wrongdoers to one side, there are other counter-examples. Consider someone who wants to drive recklessly and dangerously at huge risk to others. Given that, if we were in this person's position and had their desires, we wouldn't want anyone to stop us driving recklessly, it appears to follow that we shouldn't stop *them* driving recklessly. Yet clearly they should be stopped.

The golden rule as a reminder

So it seems that *whichever way we interpret Confucius's golden rule, we run into some fairly obvious counter-examples.* Why, then, has the rule been taken so seriously by so many sages down through the centuries?

Perhaps we should view the rule, not as a strict prohibition without exceptions, but as an ethical reminder. When we weigh up what course of action to follow, it is easy to forget how deeply our action may affect others, particularly if they are some distance from us. The golden rule reminds us to take a step back and consider our actions from the point of view of those most likely to be affected by them. If a political leader orders the bombing of another country without reflecting on the impact such an action will have on the lives of its inhabitants, we would rightly consider it a badly made decision.

If we think of the golden rule as telling us, not what we should or should not do, but what we should carefully consider when deciding what we should or should not do, it becomes far more plausible.

Biography

Born 551 BC, in Qufu, Lu (now Shandong Province), China.

It is a curious fact that many of the greatest philosophers were very young children when their fathers died. Confucius is one example – his father died when he was three, leaving the family in poverty. However, Confucius was well educated by the state, and he became a teacher.

Confucius was concerned by the social and political disorder of the time, and developed a practical philosophy to deal with it. He sought political office and became a minister of justice. It is claimed that, while in office, Confucius was successful in reducing crime.

Much of what we know about Confucius's thinking derives from the *Analects of Confucius*, a collection of fragments assembled long after his death in Lu in 479 BC.

Major works

Analects of Confucius

Parmenides

C.510–C.450 BC

The perception of reality

'How could what is perish? How could it have come into being? For if it came into being, it is not; nor is it if ever it is going to be. Thus coming into being is extinguished, and destruction unknown.'

The poem *On Nature* begins with Parmenides being taken by chariot to the palace of a goddess, who teaches him about the way of truth and the deceptive way of opinion and appearance. The poem subsequently sets out a number of arguments intended to show that nothing ever changes, moves, comes into existence, or ceases to be.

Nor is there plurality – that is to say, a multiplicity of 'things'. Ultimately, there is nothing but the Parmenidean one – a timeless, changeless whole. Everything else, including the observable cosmos, belongs to the way of opinion and appearance – it is an illusion.

A principle about thought and talk

We begin by taking a closer look at one of Parmenides's key claims – that it is impossible to talk about – or think about – what does not exist. As he puts it:

That which is there to be spoken and thought of *must* be.

Parmenides supposes that the act of talking and thinking about something is parasitic, or dependent upon there being a something for us to talk and think about.

If we add to this Parmenides's further claim that anything that exists can be thought or spoken of, it follows that *that which can be thought and spoken of and that which exists are the same.*

But...

You might well question Parmenides's claim that we can only speak of or think about that which exists. What about elves, unicorns, Santa Claus and Pegasus? We can speak of and think about them, can't we? Yet they don't exist. So Parmenides's central claim seems mistaken, doesn't it?

Still, even if we don't agree with Parmenides, we can at least concede that it is, at first sight, *puzzling* how we are able to speak or think of something if it's not there for us to think or speak about. Even today, many philosophers acknowledge that the significance of thought and talk about at least *some* entities is 'object-dependent'.

Applying the principle

Parmenides then takes his principle (that that which can be thought and spoken of and that which exists are the same) and uses it to argue that there is no plurality, no movement, no change and no coming into existence or ceasing to be.

1. *Coming into existence and ceasing to be.* Take the thought that an orange has come into existence. This involves the thought that an orange exists now, but did not exist before. But this requires that you think about what does not, or did not, exist. Because Parmenides thinks he has already established that we cannot think of what is not, it seems to follow, then, that we cannot think of things coming into existence.

For much the same reason, Parmenides believes we cannot think of things being destroyed, either. The thought of an orange being destroyed requires the thought that it exists at one time, but does not exist at a later time. But again, that involves thinking of what is not, and so is a thought we cannot have.

Parmenides concludes that, while we have the impression of things coming into and passing out of existence, this impression is deceptive.

2. *Movement.* Parmenides supposes that for something to move, it must move from one place, where it is now, to another place, which is currently empty. But an empty space is one where there is nothing, and nothing is not something we can

think of, so we cannot even entertain the thought that things move. Therefore: movement cannot be real.

3. *Change.* Parmenides has already argued that things cannot come into and go out of existence. But change, it seems, requires that states of affairs come into and go out of existence. For example, in order for a traffic light to change from green to red, one state of affairs – its being red – must cease to be and another – its being green – must come into existence. Parmenides, therefore, also rules out change.

4. *Plurality.* How Parmenides supposes the conclusion that there can be no plurality follows from his principle is less clear. One suggestion is that in order for there to be a plurality of things – more than one thing – there must be at least two things, each of which is not the other. But to say of something that it is not something else is to talk of what is not – that is to say, of nothing. And that, as we have seen, Parmenides thinks impossible.

The principle that we can only talk or think about what exists has cropped up repeatedly throughout the history of philosophy, and has been applied in a variety of different ways. See the chapter on Russell (page 258) for related arguments.

Biography

Born c.510 BC, in Elea, Italy, Parmenides is one of the most important of the pre-Socratic philosophers. From an illustrious family in the Greek colony of Elea, on the south coast of Italy, he was well known and respected, not least for drafting legislation to which the citizens of Elea had to swear an oath.

All that survives of Parmenides's works is a poem, *On Nature*, of which we possess only fragments. In the poem, Parmenides argues against the philosophies of Pythagoras and Heraclitus. His central philosophical claim concerns the nature of reality. The world as it is presented to us is deceptive. Time, change, motion and plurality are all illusions, according to Parmenides. Our senses, having access only to the world of appearance, can't provide us with knowledge of this reality. True knowledge is obtained solely by the intellect – by pure reason. Many of these same ideas were later to feature in the philosophy of Plato (see page 27).

When he was about 65 Parmenides travelled to Athens where he met the young Socrates (see page 21). Plato's dialogue 'The Parmenides' dramatizes this meeting.

Major works

On Nature

Zeno

C.490–C.425 BC

The paradoxes of motion

*'In a race, the quickest runner can never overtake
the slowest, since the pursuer must first reach the
point whence the pursued started, so that the slower
must always hold a lead.'*

ARISTOTLE PARAPHRASING ZENO

Zeno is best known for his paradoxes, some of which are designed to show that Parmenides was right to deny the reality of
motion. Here we look at three paradoxes concerning motion:
the dichotomy, the arrow and Achilles and the tortoise.

1. *The dichotomy.* Suppose a runner wishes to get from the
start to the finishing line of a race. To reach the finish, he must
first run to the halfway point. That might not seem to be a
problem. He can spend half the time available to him reaching
the halfway point and the other half reaching the finish. But to
reach the halfway point he will need first to complete the first
quarter of the race. This too he can achieve by allocating half
the time he has allowed to reach the halfway point to complete

the first quarter. However, before completing the first quarter of the race he must complete the first eighth, and to complete the first eighth he must first complete the first sixteenth, and so on without end. But then, in order to complete the race, our runner must cover an *infinite* number of finite distances, and that is impossible, as, no matter how many of these distances he covers, *there will always be another to complete.* There is no last and final distance to cover. Therefore the runner can never complete the race.

Of course, this argument can be repeated for any given distance. To cover any given distance, our runner would have to first cover an infinite number of finite distances, and, as he cannot do that, *he cannot cover any distance at all.* Therefore, our runner cannot move. Indeed, nothing can. Zeno concludes that movement is impossible.

2. *The arrow.* Consider an arrow flying from a bow towards a target. The time taken by the arrow during its flight is made up of moments or instants. At each of these instants, the arrow is at rest. But if the arrow does not move at any instant, it does not matter how many of these instants pass – the arrow will still not move. The appearance of its movement must, therefore, be deceptive.

3. *Achilles and the tortoise.* The fleet-footed Achilles is chasing the slow tortoise. Let's suppose that Achilles moves at 10 metres per minute, and the tortoise at 1 metre per minute. The tortoise starts off 9 metres ahead. To catch the tortoise, Achilles must first travel 9 metres to the point where the tortoise was. But of course, in the meantime, the tortoise will have moved 0.9 of a metre ahead. So Achilles must now make up this 0.9. But as he does so, the tortoise moves ahead a little more – a further 0.9 of a metre. And so on. Each time Achilles moves to catch up with the tortoise, the tortoise again moves farther ahead, and so, no matter how many times Achilles plays 'catch up', he will never catch the tortoise.

Notice that both the dichotomy and Achilles and the tortoise rely on the thought that, in order to complete the entire task (finish the race or catch the tortoise), the runner must first complete an infinite number of finite tasks – but that is something he cannot do.

Paradoxes

Why are these three arguments called paradoxes? In a paradox, we are presented with an apparently sound argument based on seemingly true premises that nevertheless lead us to a conclusion we feel sure is false. Faced with such a paradox, we can either (i) reject one or more of the premises, (ii) question the logic of the argument (question whether the conclusion follows), or (iii) accept the paradoxical conclusion.

Zeno himself believed we should accept his conclusions. The runner never completes the race, the arrow does not move and Achilles never does catch the tortoise. Indeed, movement does not take place. Of course, it's true that things *seem* to move. But, according to Zeno, appearances are deceptive.

Most philosophers since have instead tried to show either that Zeno's logic is faulty, or that his premises are not all true, or both. Quite where Zeno's arguments go wrong remains a matter of controversy.

Solutions to the paradoxes

Here are some proposed solutions to the paradoxes. Whether or not they are adequate I leave for you to judge.

The arrow Aristotle questions whether time is composed of indivisible instants or moments at which the arrow fails to move. If time is not composed of such instants, then Zeno's argument is based on a falsehood.

The dichotomy and Achilles and the tortoise Both these paradoxes rely on the thought that the runner must complete an infinite number of smaller tasks before completing the main task. In the dichotomy, for example, for each distance the runner must cover, there is always another distance to cover first. So he can never cover the whole distance.

But of course the infinite number of tasks that must be completed does not require that the runner cover an *infinite* distance. One half, plus one quarter, plus one eighth, plus one sixteenth, and so on to infinity, will never add to more than one. True, the runner has to complete an infinite number of tasks before he completes the whole task. But simply by covering, say, one metre, he *does* succeed in covering an infinite number of finite distances (half a metre plus a quarter metre plus an eighth of a metre and so on). And covering one metre is something he can easily achieve.

But perhaps this move, as it stands, begs the question. How can a runner cover one metre, if in order to do so, he must first cover a half metre, then a quarter metre, then an eighth, and so on, there being *no final distance he can cover that will bring him to his goal*?

Biography

Born *c.*490 BC, in Elea, Italy, very little is known about Zeno other than that he was a friend and follower of the philosopher Parmenides (see page 11). Zeno defended Parmenides's doctrines that change, motion and plurality are impossible, and that the appearance of these things is therefore misleading, developing several ingenious arguments to support this end. He died in Elea *c.*425 BC.

Major works

Only fragments remain

Socrates

469–399 BC

The method of counter-examples

'. . . before we began to see and hear and use our other senses we must somewhere have acquired the knowledge that there is such a thing as absolute equality; otherwise we could never have realized, by using it as a standard for comparison, that all equal objects of sense are desirous of being like it, but are only imperfect copies.'

PLATO EXPLAINING SOCRATES

In Plato's Dialogues, Socrates wanders around Athens, engaging all and sundry in philosophical debate. Typically he starts with a question, asking, 'What is beauty?', 'What is justice?', 'What is friendship?', 'What is courage?', putting these questions to people who think they know the answers.

For example, Socrates asks the soldier Laches, 'What is courage?' Laches answers confidently that courage is standing firm in battle. Socrates then submits this answer to close critical scrutiny. He demonstrates that, in fact, the answer cannot be correct.

One of the techniques Socrates employs is the *method of counter-examples.* When Laches defines courage as holding fast in battle, Socrates points out that a soldier who stood fast in battle out of reckless and foolish confidence, putting himself and others in danger, could surely not be described as courageous. Laches has to concede that this is indeed a counter-example to his definition, and is forced to try again.

The elusive common feature

Socrates wants to know what is the one thing that is common and peculiar to all acts of courage that makes them courageous. What is this elusive common denominator?

We have seen that, in the case of courage, Laches suggests it is standing fast in battle. Socrates points out that an act might possess this feature, yet not be courageous – merely foolhardy. But then what *is* the one feature possessed by and only by all acts of courage? What is that one feature that makes them truly courageous?

Because, in each case, those questioned always fail to identify such a feature – they fail to identify what is truly essential – Socrates concludes that they really don't know what courage, justice, friendship and so on essentially are. People *think* they know, of course. But Socrates has, it seems, revealed our ignorance. Which is not to say that Socrates himself knows the answers – he claims to be ignorant of them too.

Why imaginary counter-examples will do

Notice, by the way, that, when applying the method of counter-examples, even an imaginary counter-example will do. Take the counter-example Socrates offers to Laches – the example of a soldier who stands firm out of foolish confidence. It doesn't matter whether Socrates is aware of any actual cases of soldiers standing firm for that reason. In fact it doesn't matter whether any soldier *has* ever stood firm out of foolish confidence. Even if Socrates's example were entirely imaginary, it would still remain a valid counter-example to Laches's definition. This is because Laches's definition is supposed to identify what is *essential* so far as courage is concerned. It is supposed to identify what it is that makes *any* act courageous, be it an actual, *or merely possible*, act. But if that is right, then even a merely possible example will do.

The Socratic approach to answering 'What is X?' questions – to develop answers by testing the questions against actual or imaginary cases – remains popular with philosophers to this day.

Wittgenstein on Socrates

One of the assumptions made by Socrates – the assumption that there must be *one thing* common and peculiar to all beautiful things in virtue of which they are beautiful, *one thing* common and peculiar to all courageous acts in virtue of which they are courageous, and so on – is questioned by Ludwig Wittgenstein (see page 276).

Wittgenstein points out that some concepts are what he calls 'family resemblance' concepts. If we look at the members of a family, we may be struck by the way they resemble each other. But, despite a strong similarity, there need not be any one feature that they all share. Some may have the big nose, others the joined-up eyebrows, others the shell-like ears, others the piercing blue eyes, and so on. There may be an overlapping series of similarities, but there need not be any one feature they all have in common.

Wittgenstein suggests that our concept of games is similarly a family resemblance concept.

Consider for example the proceedings that we call 'games'. I mean board-games, card-games, ball-games, Olympic games, and so on. What is common to them all? -- Don't say: 'There must be something common, or they would not be called "games".' – For if you look at them you will not see something that is common to all, but similarities, relationships, and a whole series of them at that. To repeat: Don't think, but look! – Look for example at board-games, with their multifarious relationships. Now pass to card-games: here you find many correspondences with the first group, but many common features drop out, and others appear. When we pass next to ball-games, much that is common is retained, but much is lost... I can think of no better expression to

characterize these similarities than 'family resem-
blances'; for the various resemblances between
members of a family: build, features, colour of eyes,
gait, temperament, etc. etc. overlap and criss-cross
in the same way.

If Wittgenstein is correct and many of our concepts are family resemblance concepts, then Socrates's assumption that all examples of beauty must share a common feature might well be mistaken. And of course, our inability to identify this common feature will then reveal not our ignorance, but Socrates's error.

Biography

Socrates was born in Athens in 469 BC. Despite no recorded works, Socrates is one of history's most influential philosophers. He is also something of a mystery. What information we have comes via Aristophanes, Xenophon and Plato. Of these three sources, the most important is the philosopher Plato (see page 27), who was profoundly influenced by Socrates, and whose *Dialogues* feature Socrates as the main character.

A rotund, ugly fellow, Socrates enjoyed engaging anyone and everyone in philosophical debate. His commitment to philosophy meant that other matters – including personal hygiene – invariably took second place. He was often dirty and barefoot and had very few possessions.

Socrates's aim was not to tell others the truth – he often

claimed to be ignorant of it himself – but rather to help them discover it for themselves as best they could.

The trial and execution of Socrates, famously dramatized by Plato, has inspired many thinkers and artists across the ages. Considered to be a dangerous and subversive influence, Socrates was eventually arrested and charged with refusing to acknowledge the gods of the state, introducing new ones and corrupting the young. Condemned to death by drinking hemlock, he refused a chance to escape and, surrounded by his friends, embraced death with great dignity in 399 BC.

Plato

*c.*428–*c.*348 BC

The theory of forms

'Philosophy begins in wonder.'

Down through the centuries, many philosophers, theologians and artists have been struck by the thought that what we seem to see around us is not the 'ultimate' reality, but that the real world is somehow hidden. They have suggested that, if we could only pull back the curtain that divides us from this reality, we would be confronted by something extraordinary.

One of the most vivid and dramatic examples of this kind of thinking can be found in Plato's writings – in his theory of forms. The theory is one of the most famous in philosophy, and has had a powerful effect on the shape of philosophical thinking over the last two millennia. While comparatively few philosophers might now be described as Platonists, Plato's theory remains endlessly fascinating, and continues to be a source of not only philosophical, but also religious and artistic inspiration.

Introducing the forms

What is the theory of forms? According to Plato, those objects that we seem to see around us – chairs and tables, trees and mountains, ants and planets – are not what is ultimately real. They are mere shadows or reflections of the truly real objects – the *forms*.

Take trees, for example. According to Plato, each particular tree is a fleeting reflection of a form: the form of 'tree'. There is also a form of the table, a form of the chair, and so on. These forms differ from the particular tables and chairs we observe around us in a number of important ways:

1. The forms are *more real* than are the particulars that 'partake' of them. Indeed, particular trees derive what existence they have from the form of the tree. If there was no form of the tree, there could be no particular trees.

2. Unlike their particular instances, the forms are *perfect*. Again, consider trees. No particular tree is ever entirely perfect. It always possesses some flaw. The form of the tree, by contrast, is perfect in every respect.

3. Plato points out that particulars often exemplify both a property and its opposite. Take equality, for example. No two particulars are ever perfectly equal. Two glasses of water will never exhibit perfect equality. There will always be *some* inequality present: one glass will contain a tiny bit more water

than the other, or will be of a microscopically different shape. Or take the property of being small. A particular that is small – an ant, say – is always small in a qualified way. While an ant is small compared with us, it is large compared with a speck of dust. So again, we find that when it comes to particulars, smallness is always present with its opposite: largeness. Plato believes that the *forms* of smallness and equality, by contrast are always *unqualifiedly* so. There is no inequality present in the form of equality, nor is any largeness present in the form of the small.

4. The forms are eternal and unchanging. Particulars come and go. A particular tree grows, then dies, then rots and is gone. The form of the tree, by contrast, is eternal. It neither comes into being nor ceases to be. Nor do the forms change. Our ideas change, of course. Take our idea of beauty – it is constantly evolving. Not so long ago, being pale and buxom was all the rage. Now being thin and tanned is considered more desirable. According to Plato, while fashions may change, true beauty does not. The form of beauty is both changeless and timeless.

If Plato's forms exist, where are they? They are not located within the physical world. Nothing within sensible reality is ever perfect and everything is in a constant state of change. So the forms, if they exist, must exist on a higher plane. The forms, according to Plato, constitute an eternal, changeless, perfect reality – a domain more real than that revealed by our senses.

Knowledge, the forms and the soul

Plato argues that not only is the realm of the forms true reality, but that ultimately, the forms are also the only source of knowledge. True knowledge, argues Plato, cannot change. Our *beliefs* change, of course. We might believe that Paris is in Germany, and then later on believe it is in France. But genuine knowledge can't change in this way.

Plato argues that if knowledge cannot change, then true knowledge must be *of what is unchanging*. As the world revealed to the senses is in a constant state of change, it follows that the senses cannot provide us with knowledge. True knowledge can only be of the unchanging realm of forms.

So how do we acquire knowledge of this higher realm? According to Plato, each of us possesses an immortal soul. This soul was once acquainted with the realm of the forms. Because we were once presented with the forms, we are now able dimly to *recollect* what they are like.

So we are, if you like, born with knowledge of the forms. The knowledge is innate. But it is not easily accessed. In order to begin to recollect more clearly, we need to engage in philosophical inquiry. We must shun the senses (which reveal only an illusion) and apply our powers of *reason*. It is philosophical inquiry that ultimately produces true knowledge: knowledge of the forms.

Shadows on the wall

Plato's theory is highly abstract. To dramatize it and make it more accessible, he develops an allegory. Suppose that, at the very bottom of a cave, a group of prisoners lies in chains. Shadows pass back and forth upon the wall in front of them, but because this is all the prisoners can see, the prisoners take these shadows to be reality.

One day, one of the prisoners is released and is led upwards, where he sees a fire. Because he is accustomed to the dark, he is at first blinded by the light of the fire, but as his eyes start to adjust he begins to recognize what is before him. In front of the fire, people are passing carrying models, or statues, of animals and other objects. The prisoner now realizes that it is these objects that are the true source of the shadows cast down onto the wall below. He now recognises how he had previously been misled. What he had taken to be reality was nothing more than a shadow world. The real objects had been hidden from sight.

The prisoner is then led upwards again, towards the entrance of the cave. As he steps outside, the brightness of the light again blinds him. After a while he begins to make out the landscape and, ultimately, the sun in the sky. He comes to understand that the sun is what ultimately governs everything around him.

The prisoner is now led back down into the dark

depths of the cave, but because his eyes have become accustomed to the light, he stumbles. When he finally reaches the other prisoners and tells them of his amazing journey upwards and of how they are being deceived, they mock him. '*You* are the one who is blind', they say, having noted how he now stumbles. The prisoners remain seduced by the shadowplay on the cave wall and consider the tales of a 'higher reality' to be ludicrous.

Plato's allegory is not difficult to interpret. The shadows on the cave wall represent the world available to our five senses. Just like the prisoners, we are seduced by what we immediately experience around us. We take it to be reality. Above the prisoners' heads, the objects casting shadows onto the wall represent the higher realm of the forms. The sun outside the cave represents the *form of the good*: that which is the origin of everything. The prisoner's journey upwards represents the path of the philosopher who, freed from the hypnotic grip of the senses, comes to understand what reality is truly like. Of course, just like the philosopher Socrates, Plato's own mentor, the prisoner is shunned. Those who have not enjoyed the insight philosophy brings remain seduced by appearance. Just like Socrates's accusers, the prisoners grow increasingly irritated by the one wise person among them who insists on telling them the truth.

The one-over-many argument and the form of the good

Plato's theory is dramatic. But why should we suppose it is true? What grounds have we for supposing that the realm of forms actually exists?

One of Plato's key arguments for the forms is often referred to as the *one-over-many argument*, set out below:

Consider beautiful things. They all have something in common, of course. They are all beautiful. Now this 'something' they share is clearly not identical with any particular beautiful thing. We have already seen that each particular beautiful thing could be more beautiful than it is, whereas beauty itself surely cannot be anything other than perfectly beautiful. And while beautiful things come and go – the beautiful flower withers; the beautiful woman ages and dies – beauty itself does not change. So it seems that beauty itself must be a further something – something that exists *in addition to* all the particular beautiful things that there are. This additional 'something' is the form.

If this argument is cogent, it can be applied over and over again to establish the existence of a form of equality, a form of the mountain, a form of smallness and so on for every property that there is.

However, even after we have applied the one-over-many argument to establish the existence of a form for every property a particular might possess, we can still apply it one more time: we can also apply it *to the forms themselves*. The particular forms also have something in common: they are all forms. So it seems we can deduce the existence of a further form: the form of the forms.

This ultimate form – the form of the forms – lies at the apex of a hierarchical structure. Towards the bottom are particular, sensible objects – a particular cow, a particular bed, and so on. These objects cast shadows and create reflections. These shadows and reflections derive what existence they have from the particulars, of which they are mere fleeting, imperfect copies. But the physical objects are themselves mere fleeting copies of the higher forms, to which they in turn owe their existence. Finally, at the top of the pyramid, we find the form of the forms, upon which the forms in turn depend for their existence. The form of the forms is that which all the other forms have in common. What they have in common is existence and perfection. So, the form of the good is the ultimate source of all existence and perfection. It is also, claims Plato, the ultimate source of all knowledge

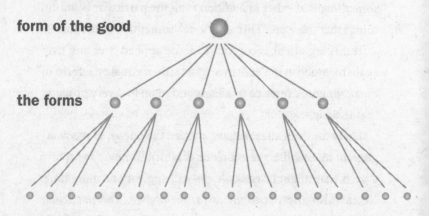

form of the good

the forms

particulars

Plato's influence on Augustine

One of the reasons Plato's theory has had such a lasting impact on Western culture is that many elements of it have been embraced and adapted by Christian thinkers. Augustine (see page 44), in particular, took many of Plato's ideas and wove them into the fabric of the Christian intellectual tradition. Plato's thinking on the immortality of the soul, Plato's conception of a world beyond the sensory and Plato's God-like form of the good have very much shaped Christian thinking on God, the soul and an afterlife.

Two difficulties with Plato's theory

We have outlined Plato's theory, and looked at one of the arguments that might seem to support it: the one-over-many argument. There is, however, a well-known objection to that argument, one with which Plato himself was familiar. In the dialogue *Parmenides*, Plato puts the objection into the mouth of the philosopher Parmenides (see page 11).

The problem is this. Let us suppose that the one-over-many argument is cogent. It is reasonable to suppose that, whenever things have something in common – because they are all beautiful, all trees, all small, or whatever – there then exists a further entity which is the 'something' they have in common. This 'something' exists in addition to all the particular things that exemplify it. It is what explains or accounts for this commonality.

But now notice that if, say, the form of beauty *is itself beautiful*, then both the particulars and the form all have something in common. In which case, we need to introduce a *second* form of beauty to account for *this* commonality. But then if this second form of beauty is in turn beautiful, we will have to introduce a third form of beauty, and a fourth, and so on without end.

It appears that, if the one-over-many argument is cogent, it establishes not the existence of one form for each common property, but an infinite number of such forms. Surely this is to prove too much? Plato denied there are such forms. Yet if we reject the conclusion that there is an infinite number of such forms for each common property, we must then reject the one-over-many argument that led us to it. In which case, we cannot use the argument to establish the existence of even one form for each common property.

It requires the existence of deeply unpleasant things too, such as mud, faeces and mucus. The 'Platonic heaven' of the forms does not sound quite so heavenly once we populate it with the forms of disgusting things. But if the one-over-many argument works for justice, truth and beauty, why not for mud, faeces and mucus?

Biography

Born *c.*428 BC, Plato is the most widely known of the ancient Greek philosophers. An Athenian of noble birth, he was brought up by his mother and stepfather. Plato's writing primarily takes the form of dialogues within which the philosopher Socrates appears as a character. The real Socrates (see page 21) was an enormous influence on Plato. He was deeply affected by the trial and execution of Socrates in 399 BC, and left Athens in disgust. After travelling in Italy, Sicily and Egypt, Plato eventually returned to Athens to found his Academy in 377 upon some land he had inherited on the outskirts of the city. The Academy was, in effect, the Western world's first university. Many great intellectuals were schooled here, including Aristotle (see page 38).

It is likely that on his travels to Sicily Plato encountered the work of Pythagoras. He died c.348 BC.

Major Works

The Dialogues:

Apology

Phaedo

Republic

Laws

Aristotle

384–322 BC

Form

'And indeed the question which, both now and of old, has always been raised, and always been the subject of doubt, viz., what being is, is just the question, what is substance?'

Aristotle's thinking on form can be introduced by contrasting it with that of Plato, with whom he profoundly disagreed. For Aristotle, form and matter cannot exist independently of one another.

Particulars and universals

Let's begin by looking at the distinction between *particulars* and *universals*.

A universal is a type or kind of thing: for example, *dog* is a universal. Under the universal dog we find particular dogs such as Fido and Rover. *Red* is also a universal. Under the universal red we find particular red things, such as this poppy in that man's lapel, or that ripe strawberry his wife is eating.

Plato's forms

Plato (see page 27) believes that *universals exist in addition to, and independently of, particulars.* They are entities in their own right that exist in a timeless and changeless higher domain. Plato calls these abstract entities *forms.* So if Plato is correct, the form of the dog exists in addition to all the particular dogs that exist, but it inhabits this higher abstract realm.

According to Plato, particulars are mere imperfect, fleeting reflections of their higher forms. If all the particulars were destroyed, the perfect forms would continue to exist. So, even though the dodo is extinct, the form of the dodo still exists – within the higher Platonic realm.

Plato argues both that *true knowledge is knowledge of the forms* and that *the forms can only be known through reason and reflection.* According to Plato, our five senses, having access only to the imperfect realm of fleeting particulars, can only confuse and mislead us.

Aristotle's forms

Aristotle rejects the Platonic theory of forms. One of the key differences between the thinking of Aristotle and Plato's thinking is that *Aristotle denies that forms can exist independently of particulars.*

According to Aristotle, each of the particular things we see around us is a fusion of *form* and matter. What Aristotle calls the form of each particular thing is that fundamental and essential feature of it that explains why it has the attributes it does.

So, for example, a particular swan is a synthesis of form and matter. It is because this particular swan possesses the *form of the swan* that it has this sort of beak, those sorts of feathers, that sort of size, and so on.

In Aristotle's view, the basic realities are concrete particulars such as this swan or that table – what Aristotle calls *primary substances*. Neither form nor matter can exist on their own. For matter to exist it must take on some form or other. And for the form of, say, dog, to exist, it must be realized in some particular, material dog. So, in Aristotle's view, now we have killed all the dodos, the form of the dodo is gone too.

Aristotle on knowledge of forms

Aristotle also rejects Plato's theory of knowledge. Like Plato, Aristotle aspires to knowledge of the forms of things, but, unlike Plato, he supposes that these forms are located right here in the world we see around us. So we can use our five senses to arrive at knowledge of the forms. Unlike Plato, Aristotle emphasizes the importance of *empirical* investigation.

A baking analogy

Plato's theory of form is, in effect, a 'two worlds' theory, with the universals in one world and the particulars in another. Aristotle's theory is more economical in that he places both universals and particulars within just the one world, the material world in which we find ourselves.

It is here that form ultimately resides, not in some mysterious other realm.

The following analogy is sometimes used to explain a key difference between the two philosophers' thinking on form. Suppose we roll out some pastry dough and make some little pastry men by pressing a cookie cutter into the pastry. These particular pastry men will then take on, if somewhat imperfectly, the cookie cutter's form. If we then eat the pastry men, the particulars have ceased to be. But the 'Platonic form' shared by the pastry men – here represented by the cookie cutter – will remain (in the kitchen drawer).

In Aristotle's view, by contrast, each particular is a fusion of matter and form. Suppose we fashion some pastry men by hand. Their Aristotelian form is not, as it were, a further 'something' that exists independently of them, as on the cookie cutter model. Their form resides wholly in the pastry men. We have matter – represented by the pastry dough – that has taken a certain form – in this case, a man-shape. And so, when we eat all the pastry men, their form vanishes along with them.

Biography

Aristotle was born in 384 BC, in Stagira, Greece. His father, a court physician, died when Aristotle was young, leaving his son to be raised by a guardian. At 17, he was sent to Plato's Academy in Athens, where he remained for 20 years, first as a pupil, and then as a teacher, until Plato's death in c.348 BC.

When Speusippus succeeded Plato as the head of the Academy, Aristotle left (possibly in protest at having been passed over). He returned to Athens in 335 after having tutored the young Alexander the Great in Macedonia. On his return, Aristotle founded his own philosophical school, the Lyceum, where he taught for a further 12–13 years.

After the death of Alexander in 323, anti-Macedonian feeling erupted in Athens, and Aristotle, with his strong Macedonian connections, found himself facing trumped-up charges of impiety. He fled to a family house in Chalcis where he died a year later.

Virtually all of Aristotle's work was lost to the West after the fall of the Roman Empire. What we do have we owe to the safe-keeping of Arab philosophers such as Averroës (see page 60). The small legacy of Aristotle's work that remains is largely in the form of notes – writings through which, unfortunately, little of his famed eloquence and style shine forth. Aristotle studied not just philosophy, but also science and mathematics. While Plato was dismissive of empirical investigation, Aristotle thought it important, and compiled a great deal of observational data. He was also a great classifier – ordering things into categories and sub-categories. Indeed, it was Aristotle who sub-divided philosophy under the general headings that we are familiar with today, such as epistemology and metaphysics. He died in 322 BC, in Chalcis.

Major Works
Physics
Metaphysics
Nicomachean Ethics
De Anima

Augustine
AD 354–430

The problem of evil

*'…were it not good that evil things should also exist,
the omnipotent God would almost certainly not
allow evil to be…'*

Christians, Jews and Muslims have traditionally conceived of God as being all-powerful, all-knowing and all-good. One of the most difficult puzzles facing anyone who believes in such a being is explaining why there is so much evil and suffering in the world. Why would such a God allow wars, pain, disease and natural disasters?

If God is good, surely he wouldn't allow such suffering to exist. If he is all-knowing then he knows it exists. And if he is all-powerful, he can prevent it. So, doesn't the existence of this immense suffering, as well as many other 'evils', provide us with very good grounds for supposing that there is no such God?

Theists have struggled with this problem for centuries, and have devised a number of ingenious solutions – though the extent to which any of these solutions are successful is debatable.

Here is Augustine's attempt to explain suffering and other evils.

Two problems of evil

There are at least two problems of evil. The first is the *logical problem of evil*. It begins with the thought that the claim:

(i) There exists an all-powerful, all-knowing and all-good God;

is logically inconsistent with the claim

(ii) evil exists.

The argument then proceeds as follows. Clearly, (ii) is true. Therefore (i) is false.

Note that the amount of evil in the world is irrelevant to this argument. It rests on the thought that God's existence is logically incompatible with the existence of *any evil whatsoever.*

But perhaps this version of the problem of evil is not so great a problem. In order to deal with it, it would suffice to show that an all-powerful, all-knowing and all-good God might allow *some* evil, perhaps for the sake of a greater good.

A second problem, known as the *evidential problem of evil*, says, not that (ii) is logically incompatible with (i), but that (ii) provides *good evidence* against (i). The amount of evil now becomes relevant. Even if we acknowledge that an all-powerful, all-knowing God might have created a world with at least *some* suffering in it (perhaps for the sake of some greater good), surely he would not have created a world containing *this* much suffering?

We can sharpen the problem by noting that God will presumably not allow any *unnecessary* suffering to exist. There must be a good reason for every last ounce of it. However, when we start to consider the enormous amount of suffering in the world – including the millions of years of animal suffering caused by natural events that occurred before humans even made an appearance – doesn't it become overwhelmingly improbable that every last ounce of suffering can be accounted for in this way?

Two kinds of evil

Discussions of the problem of evil usually make a distinction between natural and moral evils. Moral evils are produced by moral agents. They include the suffering that results from humans plundering, murdering and destroying the environment. Natural evils, on the other hand, are caused by natural events and disasters such as earthquakes, tidal waves and diseases.

A simple free-will explanation

One of the standard explanations of suffering is an appeal to free will. We are not helpless automata, but free agents capable of making our own free choices and acting upon them. As a result of God having given us free will, we sometimes choose to do evil. We start wars, for example. A great deal of suffering can result from having free will. However, it is better that we have free will. Free will is a very great good that far outweighs the evil it sometimes causes.

One problem with this explanation of evil is that it explains only moral evils, not natural evils.

Augustine's free-will explanation

Augustine presents a version of the free-will explanation that attempts to account for the suffering brought about by diseases and natural disasters. He begins with the biblical story of the Fall of Man. God created a perfect world in which Adam and Eve had free will. Unfortunately, they chose to disobey God and sinned, with two key consequences.

First, it brought about the corruption of human nature, so that every subsequent generation inherits this 'original sin'.

Secondly, it brought about the corruption of God's creation. It is here that we find the root cause of today's diseases and natural disasters. Such evils did not exist before the Fall. They too are the consequences of a human act of free will.

So yes, we suffer. But this suffering can be explained. We have brought the suffering upon ourselves through our own sin. True, God could have prevented our suffering, but only by denying us free will, which is a very great good. So, the world is, on balance, better than it would have been without free will, despite the consequences.

And of course God does also hold out to us the offer of

redemption and release from the suffering that we have caused ourselves. Notice that, in effect, Augustine *explains natural evil by supposing that it is really moral evil after all.*

Two objections

Augustine's attempt to deal with the problem of evil remains popular. Many Christians continue to accept it. But it does face some obvious objections:

1. *No Adam and Eve.* Perhaps the most obvious objection is that Augustine's explanation rests on a belief that science has shown is false – that we are the descendants of the biblical Adam and Eve. If they never existed and the Fall never took place, then they cannot be used to explain the suffering caused by diseases and natural disasters.

Nor, of course, can they be used to explain the millions of years of animal suffering that are now known to have occurred prior to the existence of humanity.

2. *The role of sin.* Another objection focuses on the role that sin plays in Augustine's free-will explanation.

The claim that earthquakes, tidal waves and disease are caused by human sin is highly implausible now that we understand the laws and mechanisms that produce these phenomena. If God made the world, he made it a world governed by laws of nature. Given these God-given laws, it is clear that *earthquakes are going to happen anyway, whether humans sin or not.*

Here is one very obvious problem with Augustine's contention that natural disasters are caused by human sin.

But, in any case, *even if* Adam and Eve did exist, and *even if* earthquakes are a result of their sin, why did God allow, say, thousands of children to be buried alive in the Pakistani earthquake of 2005? The youngest of them had not yet sinned, had they? The suggestion that their death is somehow justifiable because they were 'born in sin' seems outrageous. Sin is not inheritable in that way. Here's an analogy. Suppose that, in an attempt to line his own pocket, a builder knowingly produces a dangerously weak building. After the builder dies, his own children come to be schooled in the same building. Suppose that, on discovering the building is about to collapse because of the father's greed, a court decides it would be just if the building were allowed to collapse on his children. Would that be just?

Obviously not. It would be wrong to allow these children deliberately to suffer the awful consequences of something their father did. They do not inherit his 'sin'. But then, similarly, why isn't it equally wrong for God to allow children to be crushed to death because of the sin of their long dead relatives? Surely an all-powerful, all-knowing and all-good God would not allow such a thing to happen?

Of course, we should remember that Augustine's solution to the problem of evil is just one of a whole range of solutions that have been developed down through the centuries. Even if

Augustine's attempt to deal with the problem of evil fails, it doesn't follow that better solutions cannot be constructed.

Biography

Born AD 354, in Hippo (now Annaba, Algeria), Augustine spent much of his life travelling. He wrote an autobiography detailing the development of his thinking. The *Confessions* are frank, and include details of his sexual adventures. Apparently, Augustine used to pray, 'Lord make me chaste, but not yet.'

One of Augustine's most important philosophical achievements was to take the philosophy of Plato (see page 27) and Plotinus (AD 204/5–270, a Greek philosopher who developed the Platonic tradition) on the one hand, and the Christian belief system on the other, and marry the two together – but the marriage is not one of equals. While Augustine thinks philosophy important, its role is secondary to religious revelation. Where philosophy fails to fit in with Christian dogma, it is philosophy that must change. So successful was Augustine in seamlessly incorporating Plato's philosophy into Christian thinking that many Christians are unaware that significant parts of their belief system derive not from the Bible, but from ancient Greece. He died in 430, in Hippo.

Major Works

Confessions
City of God
Retractions

Anselm

1033-1109

The ontological argument

'Faith seeking understanding.'
ANSELM'S MOTTO

How *reasonable* is it to believe in God? Many of the best-known arguments for God's existence are based on experiences or observations of one sort or another.

For example, some believe religious experiences – visions and other supposedly revelatory phenomena – provide excellent grounds for supposing God exists.

Others consider religious miracles are good evidence of a benevolent and supernatural force at work in the world. They might point to, say, the crutches hanging outside the grotto at Lourdes as evidence of the existence of a benevolent God.

And of course, many suppose that certain observable features of the universe – the complexity of living things, the seemingly 'fine-tuned' character of its fundamental laws, and so on – also provide evidence of a cosmic designer.

Perhaps some of these observations and arguments do

indeed provide us with at least some grounds for supposing that God exists. The problem is that the evidence seems to fall well short of being conclusive.

Take religious experience, for example. Even the firmest of religious believers will usually admit that very many religious experiences must be, at least to *some* extent, delusional – namely, the religious experiences associated with the many *other* religions that this believer rejects in favour of his own. But once this concession is made, it raises the worry that they may all be delusional.

We also know that miracles, religious and otherwise, can be faked. And while the universe may perhaps show signs of intelligent design, that by itself does not establish that the designer is specifically the Judeo-Christian-Muslim God.

Indeed, doesn't the further observation that the world, while possessing many excellent features, nevertheless also contains staggering amounts of acute and seemingly pointless suffering – both human and animal – provide us with fairly good grounds for supposing that, even if there is some sort of cosmic creator, this being is not particularly concerned with the well-being of the inhabitants of the Earth? In which case, this cosmic being is presumably not God.

So while there are plenty of arguments for the existence of God based on religious and empirical experience, these arguments are not always as strong as some would like them to be. Can we do better?

Anselm's proof

Anselm of Canterbury thought so. He believed that *it is possible to prove conclusively the existence of God through the use of reason alone*. Yes, we might try to appeal to observational evidence and experience to justify belief in God, but we need not take that route because we can instead establish, *just by reflecting on the concept of God*, that God exists. Anselm thought his rational demonstration could and should convince even those who are sceptical about God's existence. He thought only a fool would remain unpersuaded.

At first sight, Anselm's argument is simple and elegant. He begins by characterizing God as *a being greater than which cannot be conceived*. That God, if he exists, is such a being seems clear. If you conceive of a being, yet can also conceive of a still greater being, then the being you first thought of cannot be God.

Armed with this concept of God, we can now argue for God's existence as follows. We can at least conceive of such a being. That there exists a being greater than which cannot be conceived is at least a hypothesis we can entertain. But, adds Anselm, as it is greater to exist in reality than merely in our imagination, this being must really exist.

Here is the argument laid out more formally:

- God is a being of which nothing greater can be conceived.
- I can conceive of such a being.

- It is greater to exist in reality than merely in the imagination.
- Therefore the being of which I conceive must exist in reality.

This argument is called an *ontological argument* (though that label is not Anselm's – it is Immanuel Kant's, see page 79). An ontological argument attempts to establish the existence of God by reason alone. Though several philosophers have subsequently offered ontological arguments of their own, including Leibniz (see page 137) and Descartes (see page 104), Anselm's is the original and, arguably, the best.

The ontological argument was once very popular, but few philosophers today – and I include among them the majority of philosophers who believe in God – consider the argument cogent. Still, while few philosophers find the argument convincing, there remains no consensus as to exactly *what* is wrong with it. To finish let's look at three criticisms.

Gaunilo's island

Even in Anselm's day, the argument had its critics. A monk called Gaunilo in the abbey of Marmoutiers, France, pointed out that we could, by means of a similar line of reasoning, apparently 'prove' that a perfect island exists – an island as perfect as it is possible for any island to be.

Gaunilo's argument is this: Can we not conceive of a perfect island – an island perfect in every conceivable way, from the purity of its streams to the sublime contours of its landscape? It seems we can. But if we can conceive of such an island, and it is greater to exist in reality than in imagination, then the island we are conceiving of must exist. If it didn't exist, it would not be as great as it could be.

On the seemingly safe assumption that there is no such island, it seems we have no choice but to accept that there is something wrong with the argument that appears to establish that there is such an island. But if there is something wrong with this argument, isn't there also something wrong with Anselm's analogous argument for the existence of God?

Anselm knew of Gaunilo's criticism, and replied to it, although his response is widely considered to amount to little more than bluster. One move we might make in defence of Anselm's version of the argument is to insist that, actually, we cannot conceive of a perfect island. We might think we can, but we are mistaken. An obvious problem with this move, however, is that it merely invites the same response to the claim that we can conceive of a perfect being. Perhaps we merely *think* we can conceive of such a being. I'll return to this suggestion at the end of this chapter.

Kant's criticism

The philosopher Kant offers one of the best-known criticisms of the ontological argument. According to Kant, Anselm's mistake is to treat existence as a further property that we might conceive of something possessing, in addition to various other properties such as, for example, being tall or all-powerful. Existence is not such an extra property. If you imagine a pile of money, and then imagine it existing, what you are conceiving of doesn't change at all.

But if existence is not a property that can be added to our conception of a thing, then Anselm's argument fails, since it is not, as the ontological argument requires, a property that might be included in the concept of God.

Kant's diagnosis of what is wrong with the ontological argument, while ingenious, is not universally accepted. In particular, it is debatable whether Kant is right to deny that existence is a property.

Let's suppose, for the sake of argument, that Kant is mistaken and existence is indeed a property that we can add to our conception of a thing. Unfortunately for Anselm, the argument then runs into other difficulties, such as the following:

Can we conceive of God?

Suppose I define a wibble thus:

> Something is a wibble if, and only if, it is: (i) red, (ii) spherical, (iii) weighs one ton and (iv) smells of fish.

Are there any wibbles? I have no idea. Maybe there is a wibble floating in a harbour somewhere (functioning as a buoy, perhaps).

Now suppose I define a wooble thus:

> Something is a wooble if, and only if, it is: (i) red, (ii) spherical, (iii) weighs one ton, (iv) smells of fish and (v) exists.

The difference between these two concepts is that we have added the property of existence to the latter. Of course, Kant would deny that we can do this. He would insist that the concept of a wibble and the concept of a wooble are the same. But let's suppose Kant is mistaken. Let's suppose we are dealing with distinct concepts.

Notice that, in order for something to be a wibble, it need not exist. An object that is merely imaginary can qualify as a wibble. For something to be a wooble, on the other hand, it has to exist. If it doesn't exist, it is, at best, not a wooble, but a wibble.

I can conceive of a wibble. But can I conceive of a wooble? Not if there are no woobles. I might *think* I am conceiving of a wooble, but if there are none, the most I can be conceiving of is a wibble, as what I am conceiving of will not possess the further property of existence (though I may think it does).

Similarly, if existence is one of the properties built into the concept of God, then I cannot prove God exists by supposing I can conceive of him. If there is no God, then I cannot *really* conceive of him (just as, if there are no woobles, then I cannot really conceive of them, though I may think I can).

So, even if we reject Kant's view and allow that existence is a further property that we can build into our concept of a thing, it seems Anselm's argument *still* fails. It fails because the argument now *begs the question.* One of Anselm's premises is that we can conceive of God. But as his concept of God includes existence, in order to know that we can conceive of such a being, Anselm would need first to have established that there is a God. But that is what his argument is supposed to establish.

In other words, Anselm's argument is circular. The most it establishes is that, if God exists, then God exists. But that is something with which even an atheist can agree.

Biography

Born 1033, in Aosta (now in Italy), little is known of Anselm's early life, but he travelled widely in his early 20s before entering the school attached to the Benedictine Abbey at Bec in Normandy in 1060. Bec was an influential and wealthy monastery and an important centre of learning at the time. Anselm's obvious talents as both a religious thinker and a spiritual leader led to his becoming the Abbey's prior in 1063 and, in 1078, the abbot. Under his leadership, Bec's reputation as an intellectual centre grew. While there he wrote the *Monologion* (1076), the *Proslogion* (1078) and four philosophical dialogues. In 1093 Anselm travelled to England and was appointed Archbishop of Canterbury by William Rufus who had succeeded William the Conqueror, holding this position until his death.

These were potentially difficult times for any leader of the Church of England. William Rufus, a cruel despot, insisted on the primacy of royal authority over religious authority. As a result, Anselm found himself exiled for visiting Rome without having gained royal permission, and was later exiled a second time by William's successor Henry I.

Anselm described his philosophical enterprise as 'faith seeking understanding' (*fides quaerens intellectum*). He died in Canterbury in 1109.

He was canonized in 1494.

Major Works

Monologion

Proslogion

Averroës

1126-98

The harmony of religion and philosophy

'Two truths cannot contradict one another.'

Averroës fuses Greek ideas – and particularly Aristotelian ideas – with Islamic thinking. Like Aquinas, who followed him, he believes that there is but one truth, a truth upon which both religion and philosophy converge. There can be no conflict between the truths of philosophy and those of religion, for 'two truths cannot contradict one another'. Philosophy and religion are merely different ways of reaching the same truth.

The incoherence of philosophers

The 11th-century theologian al-Ghazali published a famous book called *The Incoherence of Philosophers* in which he argued that philosophy should not be applied to religious matters and that the Greek philosophers should be ignored because they were pagan. Ghazali's book was very influential and prompted widespread distrust of philosophy in the Islamic world.

His work *The Incoherence of the Incoherence* was Averroës's answer to al-Ghazali's book. Averroës attacks the author's attempt to show that reason cannot demonstrate key metaphysical truths.

Averroës aimed to rehabilitate philosophy and the ancient philosophers. The Koran, he points out, directs us to reflect and think. We should also, he argues, be prepared to turn to the work of those who have thought philosophically, whether they happen to share the same religion or not. Averroës insists that, where ancient philosophers such as Aristotle have shown something to be true, we should accept that it is true. Indeed:

> All that is wanted in an inquiry into philosophical reasoning has already been perfectly examined by the ancients. All that is required of us is that we should go back to their books and see what they have said in this connection. If all that they say be true, we should accept it and if there be something wrong, we should be warned by it.

The existence and character of God can be established by reason, thinks Averroës. He offers two versions of the argument from design. The universe, he observes, is perfectly adapted for humans. Everything in it is geared towards us. There must, therefore, exist a God who has fine-tuned it for us. Moreover, animals, plants and so on have such ingenious constructions that they must have been invented. And where there is invention, there is an inventor.

So philosophy can indeed establish religious truth, thinks

Averroës. But what if philosophy and scripture should appear to be in conflict? Averroës believes that, if there is conflict, it must be merely *apparent*. He insists that where philosophy and religion diverge, religious scripture should no longer be interpreted literally, but *allegorically*.

Allegory and scripture

Averroës suggests that the idea that certain parts of religious texts should be understood allegorically rather than literally was already widespread among educated Muslims, and indeed Muslims more generally. It is the extent to which sacred texts should be understood allegorically that was a matter of dispute. Averroës argued that the idea of heaven as involving our having a kind of individual, embodied existence within a garden-like environment should certainly be understood allegorically, as should the suggestion that God created the world out of nothing (Averroës, following Aristotle, believed philosophy had established that the world must be eternal).

Philosophy is not suitable for all

While Averroës supposes that philosophy is a tool for discovering the truth, it is not a tool that everyone is competent to use. This is why religion is important. Religion also represents the truth, but in a manner that is more intelligible to the masses, for whom its stories and images make more immediate sense.

It is not a good idea, thinks Averroës, to teach the higher meaning of sacred texts to everyone – only the most literal of interpretations that should be made available to all. That certain passages are really allegorical should be revealed only to those sufficiently well educated that their faith will not be undermined.

Biography

Ibn Rushd or Averroës (as he is known in Christian Europe) was born in Cordoba, in Islamic Spain, at the time it was remarkable for its intellectual freedom. Averroës followed his family's tradition in becoming a judge and legal scholar, but he was also a physician and a philosopher in the broadest sense – studying biology, astronomy and the other sciences.

In 1182, Averroës was appointed court physician under the Caliph of Cordoba, Abu Yaqub Yusuf. Struck by Averroës's ability to explain philosophical points clearly, the caliph commissioned him to write three commentaries on the works of Aristotle (see page 38). Aristotle would soon be translated into Latin and so become available again to the Christian West. (Most of Aristotle's work had been lost to Christian Europe since the sixth century, and what was available had largely been ignored.) Averroës's commentaries on Aristotle's work were clear and insightful, and were equally embraced by Christian thinkers struggling with the newly discovered Aristotelian texts. Aquinas (see page 65) was so impressed by Averroës's commentaries that he refers to Aristotle as 'the philosopher', and to Averroës simply as 'the commentator'.

Averroës's enthusiasm for philosophy and the work of ancient, non-Muslim thinkers such as Aristotle was disturbing to more conservative Islamic thinkers, and particularly to the less well-educated public. He was reviled, and even physically assaulted when, after the old caliph died and was replaced by his son, the new ruler eventually found it politically expedient to accuse Averroës of heresy. As a result, Averroës was banished and his philosophical works burned. He was soon pardoned, but died shortly after.

Interestingly, Averroës has been far more influential in the Christian than the Arab world. This is partly because of his role in making Aristotle accessible to Christian Europe, and partly because the more liberal, philosophical tradition within Islamic thought, of which Averroës represented the apex, was about to go into decline. He died in Marrakesh in 1198.

Major Works

The Incoherence of the Incoherence

Commentaries on Aristotle

Thomas Aquinas

1225–74

Sexual ethics

*'Some truths about God exceed all the ability of
human reason … But there are some truths
which natural reason also is able to reach.
Such as that God exists.'*

Aquinas's thinking remains hugely influential within the
Roman Catholic Church. In particular, his ideas concerning
sexual ethics still continue to shape its teaching. It is on these
ideas that we focus here. In particular, I will look at Aquinas's
justification for morally condemning homosexual acts.

When homosexuality is judged to be morally wrong, the justification often offered is that homosexuality is, in some sense,
'unnatural'. Aquinas develops a sophisticated version of this
sort of argument. The roots of his version lie in the thinking of
Aristotle (see page 38), whom Aquinas believes to be scientifically authoritative. Indeed, one of Aquinas's over-arching aims
was to show that Aristotle's philosophical system is broadly

compatible with Christian thought. I begin with a sketch of Aristotle's scientific conception of the world.

Aristotle's vision of the world

Man-made objects typically have a purpose. A knife is made for cutting, a telephone for speaking to people at a distance and a car for transporting people. In the case of knives, telephones and cars, it is clear what their purpose is, as we made them for that use. But what about naturally occurring things? Might they, too, have a purpose?

Clearly, some natural things do have a function. Legs are for walking and running, teeth are for biting and chewing, hearts are for pumping blood. But what of clouds, pebbles and mountains? Are they, too, *for* something?

Aristotle believed that here, too, a purpose can ultimately be found. Clouds exist to produce rain, rain to water plants, and plants to feed animals. In his view, the natural world forms a rational system within which *everything* has a purpose. Nothing just *is* – it is always *for* something. And the ultimate end to which everything is, finally, directed, according to Aristotle, is *man* – 'nature has made all things specifically for the sake of man'.

The addition of God

This Aristotelian vision of a purpose-driven world – a world that, if we apply our powers of reason, we are able to fathom and comprehend – was well known and much admired by many medieval Christian thinkers. They considered that it involved only one major omission: God. Aquinas took Aristotle's view of a purpose-driven world and added to it the thought that *the purpose each thing possesses is given to it by God.*

God's entire creation, according to Aquinas, is imbued with divine purpose. By examining the world carefully – by uncovering the *essential natures* of things and the *laws* determining what they are for – we can discern God's plan and intentions.

Aquinas extends this view to cover even humanity – we, too, are made by God for a purpose. By examining our essential natures and revealing what we are for, we can discern what God intends us to be. We can arrive at knowledge of what is in keeping with, and what is contrary to, God's intentions, and therefore what is morally good and bad.

The claim that morality can, as it were, be 'read off' nature in this way is called the theory of 'natural law'.

John Stuart Mill on what is 'natural'

John Stuart Mill (see page 205) argues that what is natural and unnatural for humans is no indication of what is morally right or wrong:

> Conformity to nature, has no connection whatever
> with right and wrong... To illustrate this point, let us
> consider the phrase by which the greatest intensity
> of condemnatory feeling is conveyed in connection
> with the idea of nature – the word unnatural. That

> *a thing is unnatural, in any precise meaning which can be attached to the word, is no argument for its being blameable; since the most criminal actions are to a being like man, not more unnatural than most of the virtues.* **On Nature**

In fact we might go further than Mill does and point out that virtuous behaviour often requires that we struggle against our natural inclinations. Many of us seem to be more 'naturally' disposed to vice than to virtue.

Mill concludes that even if homosexuality were unnatural that would still not give us the slightest grounds for saying that it is wrong.

Aquinas on sexual ethics

You can now see how Aquinas's version of natural law theory is likely to have repercussions for sexual ethics. Many parts of our bodies have a purpose. These purposes are, according to Aquinas, God-given. It was God who gave us legs so that we can walk, a tongue so that we can taste and speak, and so on. But then someone who uses their body, or any part of it, contrary to the manner God intended, contravenes natural law. To thwart the natural functions that God has given things is to act against God's will. That makes it wrong.

The God-given role of semen

Aquinas notes that semen plays a role in reproduction. That is its purpose, he supposes. So any activity that involves thwarting the natural function of semen must be contrary to nature, and thus morally wrong. 'It is evident', says Aquinas, 'that every emission of semen, in such a way that generation cannot follow, is contrary to man. And if this be done deliberately, it must be a sin.'

For Aquinas, as homosexual acts between males involve thwarting the purpose God has assigned to semen, such acts are 'contrary to nature'. If we act in this way, we frustrate the will of God. We sin.

If Aquinas is correct, it follows that masturbation, oral sex and contraception are sinful too. This is, of course, the current position of the Roman Catholic Church on all these sexual activities.

To date, the Roman Catholic Church continues to oppose the use of condoms even in places like Africa, where they might save countless lives by reducing the spread of HIV and AIDS (though there are signs that the Church may be about to shift its position on this). The roots of the Church's justification for continuing to forbid the use of condoms lie, at least in part, in Aquinas's medieval blending of Christian theology with Aristotle's science. The use of condoms involves thwarting the natural reproductive function that God has assigned to semen.

An initial objection: walking on your hands

One of the more obvious worries you might have about Aquinas's justification for condemning homosexual acts is:

doesn't it commit him to condemning morally all sorts of behaviour that is, in fact, entirely blameless? Take walking on your hands. There is nothing morally wrong with that, surely? Circus performers and acrobats do it all the time. No one, not even the staunchest Catholic, condemns them. Yet our hands are not designed to be walked on. So why doesn't Aquinas condemn the activities of acrobats?

Aquinas's response

Aquinas is ready for this objection. He admits that it isn't *always* wrong to use a body part contrary to its natural function. Walking on your hands is not a sin, because, as Aquinas puts it, 'man's good is not much opposed by such inordinate use'. It is acceptable to use a body part contrary to its natural function if this helps man as a whole, or at least doesn't frustrate the natural purpose of that whole. Walking on your hands does not frustrate the purpose God has given man, and so it is morally acceptable. But homosexuality does frustrate this purpose. Man is designed by God to procreate as indicated by nature and the Bible. Homosexuality thwarts this God-given purpose and that makes homosexuality morally wrong.

Is homosexuality 'unnatural'?

The claim that homosexuality is 'unnatural' is largely an empirical question. There is a growing body of evidence to support the view that a minority of the members of many mammalian species are exclusively homosexual. For example, studies of Longhorn sheep reveal that about 10 per cent of rams will *consistently* choose to mount other rams rather than fertile ewes, even when both are freely available.

A powerful drive towards homosexual activity – indeed, towards *exclusively* homosexual activity – would seem to be something that God, if he exists, has given to a minority of the members of many mammalian species. Is it not plausible, then, that God might have given this same inclination to some members of our own species (the sexual activity of about 1–3 per cent of whom also seems to be exclusively homosexual)?

If so, then the idea, popular among some religious people, that homosexuality is an unnatural tendency that individuals have as a result of their own free choice, doesn't hold water.

Objections to Aquinas's sexual ethics

Many other objections have been raised against Aquinas's sexual ethics, including the following:

1. Just as occasional bouts of walking on your hands won't prevent you from using them for their intended purpose, so occasional bouts of homosexual activity do not prevent a man from using his sexual organs to reproduce normally. Just as I might use my hands 'normally' most of the time, but occasionally engage in a bout of hand-walking, so I might use my sexual organs procreatively for the most part, while also engaging in the odd homosexual fling. It is not immediately clear how

Aquinas's argument, at least as outlined above, allows him to justify condemning homosexual activity *per se*, rather than just *exclusively* homosexual activity.

2. Aquinas's justification is dependent upon several claims that many no longer accept. These include:

(i) The claim that God exists. If there is no God, then the suggestion that things possess purposes that are given by God is false. Aquinas's argument has rational force only if he can show that there are good grounds for supposing God does exist. Whether there are such grounds is contentious, to say the least. In the absence of good grounds for supposing God exists, we lack good grounds for accepting Aquinas's conclusion.

(ii) In any case, even if there is a God, the claim that those purposes found in nature indicate what God desires is questionable. Few scientists now accept that the universe and all the species in it were created more or less simultaneously by God just a few thousand years ago, as Aquinas believed. If what Aquinas took to be natural functions, roles and dispositions laid down by God at creation were in reality laid down by natural selection over millions of years, then the functions, roles and dispositions that have evolved by natural selection need not be good. Natural selection favours attributes that enhance the ability of organisms to survive and reproduce. And what enhances that ability may well not be morally admirable. For example, we may have evolved a natural disposition to dominate and subjugate others. Such a disposition may well have survival value. But just because this tendency is 'natural' for humans in no way entails that it is morally good. Nor does it entail that God approves of it.

Philosophy is sometimes accused of being a discipline with its head in the clouds and having no relevance to everyday life. However, if philosophy can show that the moral justifications offered for condemning, for example, the use of condoms are, in fact, intellectually bankrupt, then philosophy might prove very useful indeed. It might even contribute towards saving countless lives.

Levin on sexual orientation

Michael Levin, Professor of Philosophy at City College and the City University of New York, and co-author of *Sexual Orientation and Human Rights,* has argued that someone whose sexual activity is exclusively homosexual is behaving in a way that is both unnatural and abnormal. Such a person is 'misusing' his penis – using it in a way that thwarts that purpose for which it is clearly designed:

> *Someone playing a melody on his teeth as a xylophone is not misusing them so long as he chews*

> *his food at mealtimes, but let him paint miniature landscapes on his teeth, avoid eating to keep these paintings spotless, recoil at the thought of chewing, and nourish himself intravenously – then he is misusing his teeth. This is why homosexuality is abnormal, while male homosexuals are misusing their penises...*

Of course, even if Levin is right that homosexual activity or, at least, exclusively homosexual activity, is abnormal and unnatural, that does not yet give us grounds for saying that it is *morally* wrong.

Biography

Aquinas was both philosopher and theologian and was unquestionably one of the greatest medieval thinkers. Born in 1225, in Roccasecca, Italy, into an aristocratic family, Thomas Aquinas was educated at a Benedictine Abbey before attending the universities of Naples, Cologne and Paris. In 1252 he took up a post at the University of Paris and taught theology.

At the heart of Aquinas's thinking lies the belief that religion can be reconciled with philosophy and science. Like Averroës (see page 60), Aquinas argues that if religion is true, and reason leads to the truth, then reason and religion must ultimately converge. Indeed, Aquinas supposes that reason points to the existence of God, and he offers his own five arguments for God's existence – his 'five ways'.

But while Aquinas believes that religion and reason will converge on many of the same truths, he also supposes that there are truths knowable only to one or the other. The Christian doctrine of the Trinity, for example, is something Aquinas believes reason cannot establish. Here, the faithful must rely on revelation. By contrast he also accepts there are scientific truths that only reason can reveal.

One of the oddest incidents in his life occurred when he joined the Dominican order – a move his family opposed. Just as the families of victims of some modern cults do today, his brothers kidnapped Aquinas and confined him within the family for a year in an attempt to release his mind from the Dominicans' grip. Their actions failed.

Aquinas's output was vast – more than eight million words – but on 6 December 1273, four months before his death, he had a religious experience after which he never wrote again (leaving his *Summa Theologica* unfinished). He explained, 'All that I have written seems to me like straw compared with what has now been revealed to me.'

Aquinas died in 1274, in Fossanuova, Italy, and was canonized in 1323.

Major works

Summa Theologica
Summa Contra Gentiles

William of Ockham

C.1288–C.1358

Ockham's razor

'Plurality ought never be posed without necessity.'

Sometimes two theories will predict exactly the same observable consequences. Here's a simple illustration. Suppose that, at 7 o'clock. each morning I take a walk along the beach. And each morning I discover another set of footprints already there – shoe size 10. I might come up with two theories to account for what I have observed:

Theory 1. Each morning a person with size 10 feet walks down the beach before 7 o'clock.

Theory 2. Each morning a person with size 10 feet – and with an invisible, intangible fairy sitting on their head – walks down the beach before 7 o'clock.

These two theories both explain what I have observed. Not only that, but they make the exact same predictions about what I would observe were I to rise earlier and track down the mysterious morning footprint-leaver. Which theory is best?

Clearly, theory 1 is preferable to theory 2. It is more likely to be true. But why? Because it is *simpler*. Why complicate matters with the fairy?

Here's another example. Why does the universe exist? Why, indeed, is there anything at all? Here are two explanations:

Theory 1. The universe was created by a god.

Theory 2. The universe was created by a god, who created a second god, who in turn created the universe.

These two theories predict the very same observable consequences – the existence of the universe. Yet the first theory is clearly preferable to the second. Why? Again, because it is simpler. Why introduce the additional god?

In short, it seems that, when we are presented with competing theories that make the same predictions and which both fit the evidence, we should choose the simplest of the two. This principle is known as *Ockham's razor*.

Why a razor?

Why call Ockham's principle a razor? A razor might be used for trimming fat, of course. Similarly, we might use the principle to trim off unnecessary entities. However, in medieval times a razor was actually also used as an *eraser* – as a tool for scraping mistakes off parchment. It seems likely that this is the origin of the label. Ockham's principle can be used to *erase* or *rub things out.*

Different versions of the principle

Ockham's razor is variously formulated, and these formulations fall broadly into two main categories, depending on the kind of simplicity they recommend. One version says:

Choose the theory that involves the least number of *entities*.

However, the principle is also regularly interpreted as saying:

Choose the theory involving the *least number of basic principles or hypotheses.*

Different theories may be preferred depending on which interpretation of the principle we choose. After all, one theory might have very few principles but posit a great many entities, whereas its rival might have many principles but posit very few entities. If both theories have the same observable consequences, which are we supposed to prefer?

Scepticism and the razor

Let's finish with an example of how Ockham's razor might be applied within a particular philosophical debate.

On page 107 we look at Descartes's hypothesis that the world you seem to see around you is an illusion conjured up by an evil demon. There are, in truth, no tables and chairs, seas and mountains, or cats and dogs. You don't even have a physical body. There's just your mind, and the mind of an immensely powerful demon intent on deceiving you into thinking that a physical world exists.

You now have these two hypotheses to consider:

Theory 1. The world you seem to experience around you is real.

Theory 2. The world you seem to experience is an illusion conjured up by an evil demon.

Both hypotheses account for everything you have experienced up to now. They also make the same predictions concerning what you might expect to observe. In which case, concludes the sceptic, *they must be equally reasonable.*

But of course, now armed with Ockham's razor, we might well question that conclusion. Are the two hypotheses equally reasonable? What if one is simpler than the other?

We might suggest, for example, that the first theory is simpler. In effect, the second theory posits two worlds. It posits a real world – containing an evil demon – in which a second illusory world is generated. As the first theory invokes just one world, it is therefore simpler.

The trouble is, we might also argue like this: the first theory invokes very many entities – tables and chairs, mountains and seas, and so on – whereas the second invokes just two: your mind and that of the demon. Therefore the second theory is simpler.

You can now see one of the difficulties we can face when applying Ockham's razor. Even if we interpret the razor as applying to entities, *what is to count as an 'entity'?* Ockham's razor is undoubtedly a valuable philosophical and scientific tool. However, it is not always obvious precisely how it should be applied.

A popular principle

Ockham himself did not devise Ockham's razor. The principle was already well known in medieval times. Aquinas (see page 65), for example, presents a version of it:

> *If a thing can be done adequately by means of one, it is superfluous to do it by means of several; for we observe that nature does not employ two instruments where one suffices.*

The reason the principle has become associated with Ockham is that Ockham made particularly frequent use of it.

The principle can be formulated in a number of different ways. The version usually associated with Ockham is:

> *Entities should not be multiplied beyond necessity.*

However, these words do not, in fact, appear to be Ockham's. Ockham himself said:

Plurality ought never be posed without necessity.

Note that although philosophers regularly apply Ockham's razor, it is, of course, also popular with scientists. Isaac Newton says:

We are to admit no more causes of natural things than such as are both true and sufficient to explain their appearances.

Biography

Born *c.*1288, in Ockham, Surrey, William of Ockham (or Occam) is one of the most important medieval thinkers. Little is known of his early life – he studied theology at Oxford from 1309 to 1321, but never completed his Masters degree. He was a Franciscan, and became deeply involved in a dispute between the papacy and the Franciscans. In 1327 the Franciscan Minister General (administrative head of the order), Michael of Cesena, was summoned to the papal court (then located in Avignon, not Rome) on charges of heresy, having argued that Jesus and the Apostles lived in poverty (as did many Franciscans but not, of course, the Pope and his retinue). Ockham was asked to investigate the matter, and did so, concluding that the Minister General was correct and that it was in fact the Pope who was guilty of heresy for continuing to assert what he had been shown to be false. Ockham, Cesena and other Franciscans fled Avignon into exile. They found refuge under the protection of Ludwig of Bavaria, where

Ockham continued his career and remained for the rest of his life. Ockham was excommunicated in 1328 for leaving Avignon without permission. He died c.1348 in Munich, Bavaria, now part of Germany.

Major works

Four Books of the Sentences

Sum of Logic

Quodlibeta Septem

Niccolò Machiavelli

1469–1527

Advice for rulers

*'A prince, especially a new one, cannot observe all
those things for which men are esteemed, being
often forced, in order to maintain the state, to act
contrary to faith, friendship, humanity, and religion
. . . [But] a prince ought to take care that he never
lets anything slip from his lips that is not replete
with the above-named five qualities, that he may
appear to him who sees and hears him altogether
merciful, faithful, humane, upright, and religious.'*

Machiavelli's great work *The Prince* takes the form of practical
advice to a new ruler. Machiavelli argues that, while rulers may
wish to be loved, and while it is often supposed that they ought
always to behave fairly and justly, a prince cannot, in reality, afford the luxury of Christian morality.

Human nature

The problem, suggests Machiavelli, is *human nature*. Human

beings are, by nature, selfish, greedy, cowardly and untrustworthy. If a ruler is loved, but not feared, he will soon fall victim to the unscrupulous:

> *[O]ne can say this in general of men: they are ungrateful, disloyal, insincere and deceitful, timid of danger and avid of profit ... Love is a bond of obligation that these miserable creatures break whenever it suits them to do so; but fear holds them fast by a dread of punishment that never passes.*

The same is true of the leader who shackles himself with customary Christian virtues. Many suppose that a leader should be a paragon of virtue and goodness, and that this is what legitimates his power. Machiavelli, by contrast, insists that sometimes, in order to protect and maintain his state, a prince must 'act contrary to faith, friendship, humanity, and religion'. He must be prepared to lie, cheat, steal, torture and murder if necessary. Again, the prince that is not prepared to do so makes himself weak and vulnerable.

A handbook for princes

It's worth remembering that Machiavelli's advice is aimed specifically at rulers. He is not necessarily recommending that everyone be prepared to act contrary to faith, friendship, humanity and religion. It is the specific situation in which *rulers* find themselves that justifies such ruthlessness.

Nor is Machiavelli recommending a prince engages in cruelty for cruelty's sake. It is only when circumstances make it necessary that Machiavelli advocates throwing off the bonds of customary morality. Indeed, he supposes that a ruler who is needlessly and gratuitously cruel is less likely to be successful than one whose cruelty is carefully targeted.

Machiavelli particularly admired Cesare Borgia. Once Borgia had invaded Romagna, he put the vicious Remirro de Orco in charge. De Orco's cruelty quickly quelled any resistance, but Borgia considered it might eventually become counter-productive. So to ingratiate himself with the people of Romagna, Borgia then had de Orco killed, hacked in half and left on public display.

The importance of appearance

While Machiavelli recommends utter ruthlessness where necessary, he is aware of the importance of appearance. Yes, rulers should be prepared to cheat, torture and murder when necessary, but they should aim always to appear as paragons of Christian virtue. It is particularly important, he thinks, that rulers appear to be *religious*:

> *[A] prince ought to take care that he … appear to him who sees and hears him altogether merciful, faithful, humane, upright, and religious … There is nothing more necessary to appear to have than this last quality, inasmuch as men judge generally more by the eye than by the hand … Every one sees what you appear to be, few really know what you are…*

Not everyone has supposed that Machiavelli is entirely sincere. Might not *The Prince* be, in effect, a work of satire, exposing the truth about how princes really behave – about their ruthlessness and immorality? That is how philosopher Jean-Jacques Rousseau (see page 169) views Machiavelli. Comparatively few contemporary philosophers interpret Machiavelli this way, however. It does seem that Machiavelli intended his work to be taken at face value.

Whether or not we admire Machiavelli's philosophy, it certainly presents a challenge to the views of many political thinkers down through the centuries, particularly those who have stressed the importance of moral virtue to those in political power. Machiavelli's suggestion that the reign of the wholly virtuous and lovable is likely to be short and ineffective is not so very implausible.

Biography

Born in Florence, Italy, in 1469, Niccolò di Bernardo dei Machiavelli was the son of a lawyer. Relatively little is known about his early life. He lived in Florence and is thought to have attended its university. Machiavelli lived through politically tumultuous times. The city-states of Italy were being invaded by foreign powers, including Rome by the soldiers of the Holy Roman Empire in 1527, the year of Machiavelli's death. Machiavelli entered government as a clerk and ambassador in 1494, the same year that the ruling Medici family was thrown out and Florence became a republic.

In 1512, the Medicis, with the help of Pope Julius II, re-captured Florence and dissolved the republic. Machiavelli was soon accused (apparently unfairly) of plotting against the Medicis and was imprisoned and tortured. He was eventually fined and released. Retiring to his farm in Sant'Andrea in Percussina, Machiavelli then worked on his political writings, including his masterpiece, *The Prince*. Machiavelli wrote the book in part to gain favour with the Medici family, dedicating it to Lorenzo de' Medici. Unfortunately, Lorenzo ignored it, though Machiavelli did eventually manage partly to reingratiate himself with Florence's rulers. He wrote a *History of Florence*, commissioned by Cardinal Giulio de' Medici, but died in 1527 before being fully rehabilitated. Florence became a republic again in 1531.

Major works

The Prince
Discourses on the First Ten Books of Livy

Francis Bacon

1561–1626

The modern scientific method

*'Men have sought to make a world from their own
conception and to draw from their own minds all
the material which they employed, but if, instead of
doing so, they had consulted experience and observation, they would have the facts and not opinions
to reason about, and might have ultimately arrived
at the knowledge of the laws which govern the
material world.'*

Bacon was instrumental in developing the modern, experimental scientific method. The young Francis was not much impressed by the scholasticism that had dominated his education
at university. The scholastics' approach made scientific inquiry
largely an armchair enterprise. They spent the majority of their
time pondering the works of Aristotle and constructing syllo-
gistic arguments, and put little effort into actually observing
the world around them.

Bacon considered this approach stultifying, and developed

an alternative method of scientific inquiry firmly based on experiment and observation. He recommended scientists collect data and perform experiments in order to determine when phenomena are present and when they are absent.

Bacon himself conducted a number of such experiments, discovering, for example, that the rays emitted by the sun and by flames contain heat, whereas those emitted by the moon and stars do not.

The ultimate aim of science, thought Bacon, should be to establish the fundamental laws governing nature. He anticipates Popper (see page 170) by stressing that scientists should strive not only to prove their hypotheses by experiment, but also to *disprove them*. There is great value not only in finding evidence to support a hypothesis, but also in conclusively ruling a hypothesis out.

Bacon also emphasized the importance of developing the right *institutions* for scientific research. Science, Bacon believed, is primarily a communal activity while research is a group effort. He attempted to set up a college specially equipped with laboratories in which scientists could together apply the new scientific method. Unfortunately, the necessary royal funding couldn't be found. However, a group of natural philosophers began to meet in the mid-1640s to discuss Bacon's ideas and this eventually led to the foundation of the Royal Society in 1660.

The four idols

In the *New Organon*, Bacon explains why he believes that, before scientists apply his new scientific method, they should engage in a little intellectual personal hygiene, ridding themselves of the four 'idols' that, he supposes, are otherwise likely to distort their thinking. These idols are tendencies or defects of the mind that can prevent it from developing a true understanding of nature. Bacon places them under four headings:

1. **The idols of the tribe** These are innate tendencies that we all share, and include:

(i)   the tendency of our senses to deceive us about what is really there (Bacon recommends the careful use of scientific instruments to correct these failings),

(ii) our inclination to impose more order and structure on nature than is really there (in the same way that we tend 'to see' faces in the embers of a fire or creatures in clouds),

(iii) our inclination towards wishful thinking, and

(iv) our tendency to jump to conclusions before sufficient careful investigative work has been done.

2. **The idols of the cave** Unlike the idols of the tribe, these idols can vary from person to person and are the result of our particular cultural background. We have, for example, a tendency to view phenomena in terms of our

pre-existing points of view. We also tend to have an excessive reverence for, and tendency to defer to, the opinions of our own particular 'authorities' and 'experts'.

3. **The idols of the market place** These are obstacles to understanding and reasoning that arise from *interactions* between men, and particularly from *language*. Bacon warns against the use of vague and obscure jargon. He would undoubtedly condemn as idols of the market place the pseudo-scientific gobbledegook spoken by some modern New Age thinkers. Bacon believes a tendency to use language rather too casually and imprecisely can cause problems throughout the sciences. In particular, he believes scientists have a tendency to imagine and name things that do not exist.

4. **The idols of the theatre** We are attracted to the grandiose and theatrical, and this can lead us away from the truth. Those theories and dogmas with which we are already familiar may take on a special lustre and we may become entranced by them, as we are by, say, a play. Scientists also have a tendency to try grandly to explain everything on the basis of a few observed cases or in terms of a single insight. The suggestion that, for example, almost everything anyone ever does can be explained as a result of early childhood experiences undoubtedly demonstrates the tendency that Bacon has

in mind. Yes, sometimes a childhood experience can have a powerful effect on a person's later behaviour, but someone who inflates this observation into a complex theory accounting for human behaviour *in general* would surely be guilty of over-dramatizing the importance of a comparatively modest insight.

Spiders, ants and bees

Bacon offers an engaging simile to illustrate how he believes science should progress. The traditional metaphysicians, says Bacon, are like spiders spinning elaborate webs that float in the air, and all from material produced from within their own bodies. The empirics – such as alchemists – are, by contrast, like ants, busily collecting material together but never producing anything from it. Scientists, says Bacon, should be like bees, which not only gather together new material, but also digest and transform it. The job of scientists is not only to amass data, important though that is, but also to make something out of this material – they should aim to develop theories that will allow them to understand, explain and predict from what they observe. But what they make must remain firmly rooted in what they have observed.

Those who have previously handled science, complains Bacon:

…have been either men of experiment or men of dogmas. The men of experiment are like the ant, they only collect and

use; the reasoners resemble spiders, which make cobwebs out of their own substance. But the bee takes a middle course: it gathers its material from the flowers of the garden and of the field, but transforms and digests it by a power of its own. Not unlike this is the true business of philosophy; for it neither relies solely or chiefly on the powers of the mind, nor does it take the matter which it gathers from natural history and mechanical experiments and lay it up in the memory whole, as it finds it, but lays it up in the understanding altered and digested. Therefore from a closer and purer league between these two faculties, the experimental and the rational (such as has never yet been made), much may be hoped.

It is easy to forget that science, as we now understand it, is a comparatively recent development. After language, it may well be our greatest invention. The new approach to understanding the world that Bacon helped develop would, in the space of just 400 years, utterly transform our lives.

We can fail to recognize just how rapid scientific progress has been. In only four centuries we have discovered electricity, anaesthetics and antibiotics, developed computers and satellites, discovered the building blocks of matter and looked close to the edge of the universe; we have travelled to the bottom of the oceans, walked on the Moon, come to understand the basis of reproduction and how life evolved. Without the method Bacon helped develop, none of this would have happened.

Biography

Francis Bacon was born in London, in 1561, into a prominent and well-educated family. The youngest son of Sir Nicholas Bacon, Lord Keeper of the Great Seal, he went on to become one of the leading intellectuals in the courts of Elizabeth I and James I.

Home-tutored to the age of 12, the young Francis then went up to Trinity College, Cambridge, where he stayed with his elder brother Anthony for three years. He travelled to Paris with the English ambassador, Sir Amias Paulet. Bacon's father died in 1579, leaving his 18-year-old son to fend for himself. Bacon studied law, and became a Member of Parliament in 1582. Under James I, he was knighted in 1603, married in 1606, became Solicitor General in 1607 and Attorney General in 1613. He topped off an illustrious career by becoming Lord Chancellor of England in 1618. Unfortunately, just four years later, Bacon was arrested on an unfair charge of corruption. He was found guilty, fined and briefly imprisoned in the Tower of London. After his release, stripped of his titles and banned from public office, Bacon spent the remainder of his days studying and writing.

In 1626, while travelling through London in the snow, Bacon was struck by the thought that snow might be used to preserve meat. He and his companion alighted from their coach and bought a chicken that they proceeded to stuff with snow to see if the cold had a preservative effect. Perhaps as a result of this experiment, Bacon contracted pneumonia and died. But not before first eating the chicken. This incident neatly illustrates the importance that Bacon believes observation and experiment contribute to scientific knowledge.

Major works

Essays

The Advancement of Learning

New Organon (Novum Organum)

Thomas Hobbes

1588–1679

The leviathan state

'…the life of man, solitary, poor, nasty, brutish and short.'

HOBBES ON LIFE IN THE STATE OF NATURE

Hobbes views the universe as a great machine governed by laws. Like many 17th-century thinkers (including John Locke, see page 119), he subscribed to the corpuscular theory – in which the material world is composed of tiny, invisible parts or corpuscles. According to this theory, it is the texture and motion of these that explain the behaviour of the larger-scale physical objects that they make up.

Hobbes extends this explanation of the behaviour of physical objects to societies and the individuals within them. It is the application of this mechanistic understanding of the universe to human beings that leads Hobbes to the political philosophy of *Leviathan*.

The state of nature

Hobbes is one of the founding fathers of modern political philosophy. His fundamental concern is the question of how human beings can live peaceably together. *Leviathan* takes its title from the Old Testament Book of Job, Chapter 41, which describes an enormously powerful and terrifying sea monster. Hobbes argues that the state requires a similarly immense power over individuals if peace and prosperity are to reign.

Hobbes's argument for an all-powerful state begins with the thought that, just as physics is able to predict and explain the behaviour of physical objects by appealing to the law-governed motions of the corpuscles that go to make them up, so the behaviour of a society can similarly be explained in terms of the interactions of, as it were, its human corpuscles. But what are the principles that govern human interaction?

Hobbes identifies one very fundamental principle: human beings have a powerful drive to increase their happiness by satisfying their own desires. Unfortunately, in their natural state, this drive brings individuals into conflict with each other. We often desire the same thing – the same husband or wife, the same food, the same dwelling – and because these things are typically in short supply, competition and conflict ensue. As each human has the power to kill any other to take what they want, or protect what they have, violence, or at least the threat of violence, is never far away.

Worse still, says Hobbes, in the state of nature there can be a powerful incentive to launch a pre-emptive action against those we fear. Unprovoked aggression pays, because it both removes those who might destroy us and makes us appear more fearsome to those who might otherwise be tempted to attack.

And so, in the state of nature, each person lives in perpetual fear of a provoked, or even unprovoked, attack. As a result, the life of man is, as Hobbes put it, 'solitary, poor, nasty, brutish, and short' (*Leviathan*).

The social contract

How might our condition be improved?

Suppose each individual enters into a 'contract' with all the rest to submit to an over-arching sovereign power. Each individual gives up some of their own natural freedom in return for protection against the savagery and chaos of the state of nature that this sovereign state will provide. Such a 'social contract' would both legitimize the power of this state and work to the benefit of all.

However, in order to be effective in keeping chaos at bay, the sovereign state to which individuals hand over some of their freedom must be immensely powerful. If the state is to succeed, it must be able to command the loyal obedience of every citizen. It must be capable of striking fear into the heart of anyone tempted to step out of line.

Belonging to such a powerful state brings huge benefits in addition to safety and security. Since they can be sure that, when they enter into contracts, those contracts will be kept (because the state will ensure that those who fail to honour their agreements are punished), individuals can now begin to trade with one another. The arts and sciences can also start to flourish. Rather than being forced to battle constantly for survival, individuals now have the option of developing their intellectual and artistic skills.

So under a powerful state, life is immeasurably better than it is in the state of nature. Yes, there is a price to pay in terms of loss of individual freedom, but Hobbes believes that this loss of freedom is a price worth paying.

Criticisms of Hobbes's political theory

Social contract theories such as that of Hobbes typically face a number of standard objections. Perhaps the most obvious worry Hobbes's theory raises is that *no such social contract actually exists*. There was never a time when the citizens of this or any other country signed up to such a deal. Nor are new citizens expected to sign such a contract on becoming adults. But if no such agreement was ever brokered – if Hobbes's 'contract' is entirely fictional – then surely so is *the legitimacy of the state.*

Perhaps this worry can be dealt with. As none of us wants to return to the horror of the state of nature, we remain voluntarily within the sovereign state. But then can't we be seen as at least having *implicitly* entered into such a deal, whether or not any such contract is ever explicitly made? Our consent is at least tacitly, if not explicitly, given.

Hobbes is also often accused of having too pessimistic a view of human nature. Some say, 'Doesn't Hobbes take for granted that we are cruel beings? Isn't that his explanation for the barbarism of the state of nature? If we are more warm and compassionate than Hobbes assumes, might not the state of nature turn out to be rather less awful? In fact, might it not turn out to be rather idyllic?'

This criticism of Hobbes is based partly on a misunderstanding. Hobbes doesn't think human beings are *gratuitously* cruel. He says, 'that any man should take pleasure in other men's great harms, without end of his own, I do not conceive it possible.'

The reason the state of nature is barbarous, according to Hobbes, is not that humans enjoy wantonly inflicting pain and death on others – they don't. The reason, rather, is that the situation in which each individual finds him or herself – a situation in which everyone desires what is scarce, and no one is immune to attack – gives each individual a powerful incentive to attack others, not just in order to get what they desire, but to avoid being attacked themselves.

Prisoners' dilemma

Several commentators on Hobbes point out a similarity between his discussion of the situation each of us faces in the state of nature and the situation faced by the two prisoners in the *prisoners' dilemma* – an imaginary case designed to highlight a possible obstacle to co-operation.

The dilemma is this. Suppose you are one of two

suspects caught by the police. There is not enough evidence yet to convict either of you. If you both remain silent, you will both be freed through lack of evidence. However, if you remain silent and your partner confesses and testifies against you, you will receive a 10-year prison sentence and he will be freed as a reward for being honest. Conversely, if you testify against him and he says nothing, he will receive 10 years and you will walk free. If both of you confess, then you will each get a reduced sentence of two years. What should you do?

In this situation, assuming you want to get the shortest sentence you can (and that you have not been able to meet privately and agree a pact to both remain silent), the rational thing to do is confess. That way, you will either walk free (if you testify against your partner and he remains silent), or get just a two-year sentence (if your partner confesses).

But of course, if you both make this rational calculation, and so both confess, the outcome is worse for each of you than if you had both remained silent. You both end up jailed for two years, when you could have both walked free. This dilemma illustrates the point that it is often rational for individuals to choose not to co-operate, even in a situation where co-operation would produce the best outcome for each of them.

Hobbes's state of nature presents individuals with a similar dilemma. In the state of nature, individuals can try to co-operate and enter into contracts with others if they wish. Successful co-operation would certainly be in everyone's interests. But, because there is no mechanism in place to *enforce* these contracts, each individual has a powerful incentive to break any agreement they make. So, if you yourself enter into such contracts, you are actually likely to find yourself worse off than if you refused to co-operate.

Biography

Born 1588, in Malmesbury, Wiltshire, Hobbes was the younger son of a country cleric. He liked to claim that his mother went into labour on hearing of the approaching Spanish Armada, so that, as he puts it, 'fear and I were born twins together'.

A wealthy uncle paid for his schooling and Hobbes did well. After completing his formal education at Oxford, Hobbes was employed by the wealthy and well-connected Cavendish family as a tutor for the young William Cavendish. The tutoring involved Hobbes travelling extensively around Europe with William, and his journeys provided him with an opportunity to meet some of Europe's greatest thinkers, including Descartes (see page 104).

Hobbes's ideas were radical. As a consequence he lived in constant fear of persecution, and not without reason. While in France, he got into trouble for holding anti-Catholic views. When he returned to England, he was suspected of producing atheist writings and was investigated. This led him to burn some of his own work. Yet, despite his radical and, to many, unacceptable views, Hobbes survived, remaining productive into his 80s. He died in Hardwicke, Derbyshire, in 1679.

Major works

The Citizen

On Matter

On Man

Leviathan

René Descartes

1596–1650

The method of doubt

'I think, therefore I am.'

Descartes's *Meditations* attempts to do three key things: to place knowledge upon a secure foundation; to prove that the self is an immaterial substance capable of existing independently of any physical body; and to show that God exists. Below, I describe how Descartes embarked upon the first of these projects.

Doubt as a filter

People regularly claim to 'know' things. Yet our confidence often turns out to be misplaced. Sometimes we happen to be mistaken even about those things that we consider most certain. Beliefs we took to be firmly established are revealed to have been founded on shifting sands. Struck by how much that passes for knowledge seems, on closer inspection, rather dubious, Descartes decided to embark on his grand epistemological project – to rebuild knowledge upon secure, certain foundations.

This project has two distinct stages. The first consists in applying the *method of doubt*. Descartes subjects all his beliefs to the very strongest doubt he can muster. In effect, he applies doubt as a *filter*. Those beliefs that fail to pass through the filter are set aside. Only those that pass safely through – that prove immune even to the severest doubt – are to be retained.

Having filtered his beliefs until he finds those that are indubitable, Descartes then proceeds to the second stage of his project – the systematic rebuilding of knowledge upon those certainties. It is upon the first stage of Descartes's project – the filtering of beliefs by means of the method of doubt – that we concentrate here.

Illusions and dreams

The doubts Descartes applies form three distinct levels, each stronger than the last.

The first level of doubt is generated by the observation that *our senses sometimes deceive us*. A round tower seen in the distance may seem square. A straight stick dipped in water may look bent. Doesn't the fact that our senses sometimes deceive us in these ways throw all beliefs based on our senses into doubt?

Not really. As Descartes himself points out, while our senses sometimes deceive, we can usually tell when they are untrustworthy. For example, I know that, when I see a stick half-immersed in water, how it looks is misleading. I can use my earlier experience of the stick being straight, and of other straight sticks looking bent in water, to correct how this stick looks now.

As yet, we possess no grounds for supposing that our senses are not at least a *fairly* reliable source of true beliefs about the world. So, returning to the analogy of using doubts as a filter: it seems the majority of our beliefs about the world pass safely through this first filter.

Descartes then introduces a second, rather more stringent test. He considers the suggestion that he might at that very moment be dreaming. True, we can sometimes tell when we are dreaming, but not always. It is at least possible that someone might have a dream that is so vivid it is indistinguishable from waking reality. How can Descartes know he is not having such a dream right now? How can you?

The suggestion that you might be dreaming does indeed appear to throw many of the things you believe into doubt. You might think you are sitting by the fire reading this book, when actually you are tucked up in bed. How can you tell that you are not now having such a vivid dream? After all, everything would seem just the same, wouldn't it?

Still, even if you have no way of telling whether you're having such a vivid dream right now, perhaps the doubt generated by the dream hypothesis is still not as serious as it might be. You might reply, 'Even if I am dreaming right now, that doesn't throw into doubt what I have experienced in the past – last week, last month and last year – does it? Even if I can't be sure that what I am experiencing now is a real house, table and book, surely I can still be confident that they do exist. For I have experienced them countless times before.'

To this the reply might be, 'But perhaps your *whole life* has been a dream. Perhaps you have *never* been awake. How can you tell that you have been awake?'

However, even if we acknowledge that the suggestion that your whole life might be a dream makes sense (and maybe it doesn't), perhaps the doubt raised by the dreaming hypothesis is *still* not as destructive as it might be. For, as Descartes also points out, even when you are dreaming, *you are still able to think and reason.* You can still perform mathematical calculations. So even if the dream hypothesis does succeed in throwing into doubt those of your beliefs that are based on the evidence of your senses, it seems it doesn't yet provide you with any grounds for doubting what you believe regarding the truths of reason and mathematics. You still have no grounds for doubting that, say, two plus two equals four.

To throw even this belief into doubt, it seems we will need a still more powerful source of doubt. And so Descartes moves on to the third and final stage in his method of doubt: the *evil demon hypothesis.*

The evil demon hypothesis

Suppose there exists an evil demon, god-like in its power, that is intent on deceiving you. This demon might place all sorts of ideas and experiences into your head. It might cause you to think that you are surrounded by physical objects when in fact nothing exists save just you and this malevolent being.

The evil demon hypothesis immediately throws into doubt

all beliefs based on the evidence of your senses. Perhaps the world you seem to observe around you is, and always has been, an elaborate illusion conjured up by this demon. How can you tell that it is not? After all, everything would seem exactly the same.

However, it is not just your beliefs about the world outside your mind that are thrown into doubt by the evil demon hypothesis. It throws other beliefs into doubt too. Perhaps, whenever you attempt to add two and two, the evil demon makes you conclude that the answer is four when in fact it is five. Again, how can you know that this isn't happening? After all, everything would seem just the same.

The evil demon hypothesis raises a doubt so fierce it looks, at first, as if it will undermine all our beliefs. Will any pass safely through this third and final filter?

The cogito

It seems that at least one will pass the evil demon test. Descartes notes that, even if there is such a demon, this demon cannot deceive him into believing that he, Descartes, exists, when he does not. Descartes here hits upon 'the cogito'. *Cogito, ergo sum*: 'I think, therefore I am.' Even if the demon deceives him, still Descartes continues to think, and if he thinks, then he must exist.

Descartes is not the first philosopher to make the point that in order to doubt, you must at least exist. Augustine (see page 44) offers a similar response to unremitting scepticism in his *City of God*:

> *On none of these points do I fear the arguments of the scep-tics of the Academy who say: what if you are deceived? For if I am deceived, I am. For he who does not exist cannot be deceived. And if I am deceived, by this same token, I am.*

Exactly how Descartes's cogito is supposed to work – indeed, whether it works – remains controversial. One key question we might raise is this: is the cogito intended to be an *inference*?

It certainly looks like an inference. It contains the word *ergo*: 'therefore'. The conclusion that Descartes exists seems to be *in-ferred* from the premise that he thinks:

I think.
Therefore: I exist.

But if the cogito is an inference, and if his hypothetical demon is, as Descartes suggests, able to make Descartes go wrong even in his simplest reasoning, doesn't it follow that his reasoning might well have gone awry here too? Maybe the conclusion doesn't follow. Perhaps the demon is duping him about that as well. In which case, the conclusion is *not* indisputable.

But perhaps this is the wrong way to interpret the cogito. Some philosophers suggest it should be understood not as an inference, but as a performance. By thinking – by attempting to doubt whether he exists – Descartes *demonstrates* he exists. So his attempt at doubting his own existence is necessarily self-defeating. The cogito is not an act of reasoning or inferring. It is an act of *showing*.

However the cogito is supposed to function, Descartes believes it provides him with an indubitable truth. It provides the firm foundation upon which he hopes to rebuild his belief system – rebuilding it in such a way that doubt cannot creep back in.

The doubts Descartes raises are some of the most powerful ever entertained. While Descartes believed he could deal with those doubts and show how knowledge can after all be achieved, few contemporary philosophers are convinced by Descartes's solution. While many reject scepticism, there is still no consensus among philosophers about how exactly, if at all, the sceptic might be defeated.

The bad apple analogy

Descartes intends to apply his doubt to all his beliefs simultaneously – not to subject each belief to doubt in turn. Why is this important? Descartes explains in the seventh of the 'Replies and Objections' included with the second edition of *Meditations on First Philosophy*:

> Suppose [a person] had a basket full of apples and, being worried that some of the apples were rotten, wanted to take out the rotten ones to prevent the rot spreading. How would he proceed? Would he not begin by tipping the whole lot out of the basket? And would not the next step be to cast his eye over each apple in turn, and pick up and put back in the basket only those he saw to be sound, leaving the

others? In just the same way, those who have never philosophized correctly have various opinions in their minds which they have begun to store up since childhood, and which they therefore have reason to believe may in many cases be false. They then attempt to separate the false beliefs from the others, so as to prevent their contaminating the rest and making the whole lot uncertain. Now the best way they can accomplish this is to reject all their beliefs together in one go, as if they were all uncertain and false. They can then go over each belief in turn and readopt only those which they recognize to be true and indubitable.

Descartes seems to suggest that, just as one bad apple will spoil all the others in the barrel, so even one dubious belief undermines the authority of all the rest. But is this true?

If the belief in question is one upon which the credibility of many *others* heavily depends, then any uncertainty concerning the first belief will clearly spread to the others. And if the belief is a foundational belief upon which *all* your other beliefs to some significant extent rest – then they will all be thrown into doubt.

But is it possible to subject *all* your beliefs to doubt in one go? Many philosophers insist that it is not. After all, in order to doubt, we need a language in which to express our doubts. But then, if we throw out even our beliefs about what our words mean, we will end up unable to formulate any doubts at all. So it seems that the attempt simultaneously to doubt absolutely *everything* is necessarily self-defeating.

Biography

René Descartes was born in La Haye, France in 1596. Although he is now best known as a philosopher, in his day he also enjoyed a reputation as a mathematician and, to a lesser extent, a natural scientist.

Often described as the 'father' of modern philosophy, it is true that Descartes marks a turning point. During the medieval period, scholasticism and the philosophy of Aristotle had dominated Western thought. The bulk of intellectual effort was dedicated to clarifying, systematizing and working through the consequences of the ideas found in ancient texts. When Descartes was writing, science was finally beginning to break free from its traditional deference to the wisdom and authority of the ancients. Greater emphasis was placed on observation, experiment and the individual's own power of reason. Descartes attempted single-handedly to provide himself with a secure basis upon which all knowledge might be founded, armed, at the outset, with nothing more than his own faculty of reason.

In 1641 Descartes published his *Meditations on First Philosophy*. Although first published in Latin, the book was unusual in also being quickly translated into the author's native

French – an indication that Descartes wanted his work to be made available to the widest possible audience. The ideas and arguments developed in this book – written in a highly accessible, first-person style – revolutionized philosophical thinking on a number of fronts.

Descartes moved to Stockholm in 1649, taking up an invitation to tutor Queen Christina of Sweden in philosophy. Unfortunately for Descartes, Christina scheduled his lectures at 5 a.m. The combination of the cold and the early hours damaged his health irreparably, and he died in 1650. Because Sweden was a Protestant country, and Descartes a Roman Catholic, he was buried in a cemetery for unbaptized children. His body was later disinterred and the remains taken to Paris.

Major works

Discourse on the Method

Meditations on First Philosophy

Principles of Philosophy

Blaise Pascal

1623–62

The wager

'If you gain, you gain all. If you lose, you lose nothing. Wager then, without hesitation, that He exists.'

According to Pascal, there are no rational grounds to support either belief or disbelief in the Christian faith. Reason cannot settle the matter one way or the other. So should we believe, or not?

Placing a bet

Pascal suggests we approach this question as if it involved placing a bet. We have two options: believe, or fail to believe. What do we stand to win or lose in each case?

If I choose to believe, and there is a God, then the rewards are enormous – I will know eternal happiness. However, what if there is no God? Then obviously I won't receive that heavenly reward. But still, my loss is not so very great, little more than the time I have to spend in worship.

If, on the other hand, I choose not to believe in God, and

God exists, my loss is beyond imagining for I face eternal damnation. Nothing could be worse. And if I choose not to believe in God, and there is no God, then I win, but I don't win very much. Not much more, in fact, than the time that I would have otherwise spent in worship.

We can display these outcomes in a table:

	God exists	God does not exist
Believe in God	Eternal bliss	Small loss of worldly pleasures
Do not believe in God	Eternal damnation	Small gain in worldly pleasures

Now, assuming that we have no more grounds to suppose God does exist than to suppose that he doesn't, surely the rational wager to lay is to believe in God. If I believe, then I will either win big or lose little. If I fail to believe, then I either win small or lose big. Pascal concludes that belief is therefore the more sensible wager. Pascal claims that belief in God is the rational choice even though there are no more grounds for supposing this is true than there are for supposing it is false. His claim sounds paradoxical but, correctly understood, it is not. Consider this analogy. You are diagnosed with a disease that will soon kill you unless you receive treatment. There is only one treatment, and it has a 50 per cent success rate. When the treatment doesn't work, its side effects are rather unpleasant. What should you do?

Clearly, the rational choice, assuming you want to live, is to undergo the treatment, despite the fact that you have no more grounds to suppose that it will work than you have to suppose that it won't. Undergo the treatment and you will either win big or lose little. Fail to undergo the treatment, and you will either lose big or win small (by not having to suffer the unpleasant side effects). If Pascal is correct, the option of believing in God is similarly one it would be irrational to refuse.

Objections to Pascal's argument

Many have found Pascal's argument persuasive, but it does face some well-known objections, including:

1. *We cannot choose what we believe.* Some people will respond, 'But I can't just *choose* to believe that God exists. It may be that, though I can see that belief in God is the rational wager, and so I would very much *like* to believe it, I just can't manage it.'

Pascal acknowledges that we can't usually choose what we believe. Certainly we can't just make ourselves believe something directly, by a sheer act of will. However, he notes that even those who merely start off by going through the motions of religious belief often end up true believers. So if I also make myself go though the motions – if I regularly go to church and pray – I am likely to end up a true believer. This is exactly what Pascal recommends I should do.

2. *Pascal's wager is based on a dubious assumption.* Pascal supposes that the arguments and evidence for and against God's existence are evenly balanced. But are they? Most atheists would deny this. Many say the arguments and the overwhelming evidence support the claim that there is no God. If they are right about that – and the odds of God existing are not 50:50, but more than 99:1 against – then it is not quite so obvious that belief in God is the rational wager.

To illustrate, let's return to the medical example outlined above. If you are told the probability that the treatment will succeed is in fact less than 1 per cent rather than 50 per cent, then it is not so clear the rational choice is to opt for treatment, especially as you know that you will almost certainly experience some nasty side effects as a result. Under these circumstances, you might well calculate that you would be better off rejecting treatment.

3. *Another dubious assumption.* We might question whether Pascal is right to assume all believers will be rewarded with eternal bliss and all disbelievers with eternal damnation. Would God be terribly impressed by someone who believed in him purely on the basis of a self-interested calculation? If he has deliberately arranged the evidence for his existence to be equivocal, would he condemn to eternal damnation someone who then failed to believe in him? Such punishment seems rather harsh, particularly from a God who is supposed to be supremely benevolent. Pascal's estimation of how God, if he exists, will react to our belief or disbelief is certainly open to question.

Biography

Born 1623, in Clermont-Ferrand, France, and educated by his father, Blaise Pascal was a child prodigy who was extraordinarily gifted at mathematics. At the age of 12, he was able to produce a proof that the sum of the internal angles of a triangle is two right angles, and at 18 he built a mechanical calculator for his father. Pascal was also a talented scientist and is credited with inventing, among other things, the syringe. In philosophy, he is best known for his 'wager', which is discussed above.

Pascal became deeply religious after an incident in 1654, during which his carriage almost fell from a bridge. The horses fell but the harness broke and the carriage was left teetering on the edge. Pascal collapsed in shock and 15 days later had a religious experience so profound that it led to his writing extensively on philosophical and religious matters. The most famous of these writings are his unfinished *Pensées*. Pascal died in Paris in 1662.

Major works

Pensées

John Locke

1632–1704

Primary and secondary qualities

'Such qualities, which in truth are nothing in the objects themselves, but powers to produce various sensations in us by their primary qualities, i.e. by the bulk, figure, texture, and motion of their insensible parts, as colours, sounds, tastes, etc., these I call secondary qualities.'

Locke aims to find the limits of human understanding in *An Essay Concerning Human Understanding*. He defends empiricism, arguing that all knowledge, and indeed all concepts, are ultimately derived from experience.

Locke rejects the rationalist doctrine of innate ideas defended, for example, by Descartes (see page 104), insisting instead that the mind at birth is a *tabula rasa* – a blank slate. Locke's *Essay* also sets out and defends one of the clearest and most sophisticated versions of the distinction between primary and secondary qualities. It is on that distinction that we focus here.

What is really out there?

The majority of philosophers interpret Locke as holding a version of the representational theory of perception, whereby we do not perceive the world around us directly. As an empiricist, Locke insists that our access to the world is provided by our five senses: sight, hearing, smell, taste and touch. However, this access is not direct – as if we were looking through an open window. Rather, what each of us is immediately aware of is akin to an inner mental image or representation that, in effect, *stands between* us and the world. Locke calls these inner mental entities that mediate perception *ideas*.

Here is an example. I see you throw me a red apple, which I reach out and catch. According to Locke, as the apple approaches, it produces in my mind a string of ideas, including ideas of red, a round shape increasing in size, and so on. These ideas inform me that the apple is nearing. Reaching out and catching the apple produces further auditory and tactile ideas. When I sniff and bite into the apple, that results in ideas of smell and taste.

If Locke is correct, I never actually get to experience the apple or, indeed, any physical object, *directly*. All perception of the external world is mediated by ideas.

Locke asks – when I perceive the world via these ideas, to what extent is what I perceive independently there? What contribution does my *mind* make to what I experience of the world around me? It is in answering this question that Locke's version of the distinction between primary and secondary qualities comes into play.

Colour as a dispositional quality

According to Locke, colours, smells, tastes and sounds are not, in truth, fully objective qualities of external physical objects. Rather they consist in the *powers* or *dispositions* that those physical objects have in producing certain ideas in us.

In order to understand Locke's thinking, we should begin by looking at some other examples of dispositional qualities. Take, for example, the qualities of being fragile or highly flammable. For something to be highly flammable is just for it to be true that *if* it were exposed to naked flame, then it would burn easily. Similarly, for something to be fragile is just for it to be true that *if* knocked sharply, then it would break.

Notice that, in order for a vase to be fragile, *it need never actually break.* It merely has to be true that it *would* break were it sharply knocked. A dispositional quality consists in the fact that something *would* happen, if the circumstances were right. It need not actually happen.

Locke's view is that colours, tastes and smells are also dispositional qualities. For something to be red is just for it to be true that *if* we were to look at it, then it would then produce in our minds a certain sort of visual experience or idea.

Locke agrees that things are red even when no one is looking at them. A red flower growing in some remote alpine meadow is still red even if no one ever sees it growing there.

And yet, if Locke is correct, the colour of that flower remains essentially *mind-dependent*. It remains the case that for the flower to be red is just for it to be true that if we were to look at it, then we would have a certain idea.

The relativity of colour

To bring out the contribution Locke supposes the mind makes to colour, let's consider some hypothetical beings whose minds are very different to our own. Suppose there are aliens whose nervous systems are put together very differently, so that when they look at the world, it appears to them as a colour negative appears to us. When they look at grass, it produces in them the kind of colour experience that poppies produce in humans, and vice versa.

What colour is grass, from the point of view of these aliens? The answer, from Locke's view, is red. It is not that the aliens mistakenly think that grass is red. No – for the aliens, grass really *is* red. For the aliens, grass has the power to produce in them the idea of red.

In short: Locke's theory of colour makes colour *relative to the minds of perceivers*. For beings with minds like ours, poppies are red, sugar is sweet and garbage smells disgusting. But it's possible that, for beings with different sorts of mind, poppies are green, sugar is sour and garbage smells fragrant. There is no 'objective fact of the matter' as to what colours, tastes and fragrances things *really* possess. All these qualities are, in truth, mind-dependent.

Primary qualities

Locke calls those qualities that consist in the powers or dispositions of objects to produce particular ideas in us *secondary qualities.* He supposes that tastes, smells and colours are all secondary qualities.

But if tastes, smells and colours are mind-dependent qualities, which qualities are primary? Which aren't mind-dependent?

Roundness, according to Locke, is a primary quality. This apple is both red and round. Its redness consists in a power of the apple to produce a certain idea in us. That is not true of its roundness. True, this apple has the power or disposition to produce the idea of roundness in us. When I look at it, it looks round. However, though the object possesses that power, its being round does not *consist* in that power. The apple would still be round even if, for some bizarre reason, it happened consistently to look square.

According to Locke, shape, size, number and position are all examples of primary qualities. They are fully mind-independent qualities of material objects, possessed independently of how those objects might happen to strike us.

Locke's other way of distinguishing primary and secondary qualities

Interestingly, Locke offers a second definition of primary and secondary qualities – a definition that makes use of the notion of *resemblance.* According to Locke, our ideas of primary qualities *resemble* those qualities as they are in an object. But that is not true of our ideas of secondary qualities. There is nothing resembling my idea of red on the surface of this red apple.

Locke embraced the 'corpuscular' theory of matter popular with scientists of the time – a theory in which physical objects were thought to be composed of tiny insensible corpuscles or parts. For Locke, these microscopic particles possess only primary qualities. A physical object such as an apple is ultimately nothing more than a vast collection of corpuscles. It is the microscopic arrangement of these corpuscles that determines how the object will impinge on our sensory organs, and so cause ideas in us.

So according to Locke, when it comes to shape, size, number, motion and the other primary qualities, appearances are not fundamentally misleading. Physical objects really do possess length, breadth, position and number and move around in space, in much the way they seem to. But when it comes to colours, smells, and tastes, *appearances are deceptive*. There is, in truth, nothing like my idea of sweetness in a spoonful of sugar. Ultimately, all there is 'out there' are the tiny corpuscles jiggling about in the void.

Arguing for the distinction

Although the distinction between primary and secondary qualities was not new (the scientists Boyle and Galileo and the philosopher Descartes were among those who had already made it), Locke's version is clearer and more sophisticated. But is the theory correct? Are colours, tastes and smells mind-dependent in the way Locke claims them to be? It's one thing to claim that these qualities are secondary, but it's quite another to show that they are. What arguments might be offered in support of the theory?

Perhaps the most popular argument for colours, tastes and smells being secondary qualities is that scientists make little use of these qualities when formulating scientific laws and offering scientific explanations. Scientists appeal to lengths (such as wavelengths), position (such as the position of an electron landing on a screen) and motion (such as the motion of a particle) in order to explain why things behave in the way they do. Rarely do they appeal to the smell or taste or colour of a thing (certainly not when it comes to the most fundamental explanations). It seems that secondary qualities are ultimately *explanatorily superfluous* – their role in accounting for how things stand in mind-independent reality is redundant. But if taste, smell and colour are redundant in the explanation of how matters stand in reality doesn't that suggest that they aren't, in truth, part of that reality? Doesn't it suggest that they are, after all, mere secondary qualities?

I leave that for you to judge.

Berkeley's attack on Locke's theory

George Berkeley (see page 147), the great idealist philosopher, attacks Locke's distinction between primary and secondary qualities. Berkeley targets, in particular,

Locke's appeal to the notion of *resemblance*.

As we have seen, Locke suggests that while our ideas of primary qualities resemble those qualities as they are in an object, this is not true of our ideas of secondary qualities. There is nothing remotely like our idea of red, or sweet, or pungent in an apple.

According to Berkeley, this use of the notion of resemblance is confused. It does not make sense to suggest that there might be something that resembles an idea, but that exists in a mind-independent reality.

Why does Berkeley suppose the suggestion makes no sense? His objection seems to rest on the thought that an idea is a *subjective* notion in the same way that, say, a sensation, such as a pain, is subjective. And it does seem very peculiar to suggest that there might be something resembling my pain, but existing out there in mind-independent reality. How could there be something *like* a pain, but which no one felt? How could there be something like the feeling of pain, though no one feels it? That does seem to be a suggestion of which we can make little sense.

But then, because ideas are also subjective, so the suggestion that there might be something like an idea, only existing out there in mind-independent reality, would also seem to be a suggestion of which we can make little sense.

Berkeley concludes that, as Locke's distinction between primary and secondary qualities rests on such nonsensical talk about 'resemblance', so the distinction itself collapses.

However, perhaps this is to dismiss Locke's distinction too quickly. As we have seen, Locke also distinguishes between primary and secondary qualities in another way: by maintaining that, unlike primary qualities, secondary qualities consist in *dispositions* to produce certain experiences in us. This other way of drawing a distinction between primary and secondary qualities is not undermined by Berkeley's objection and it remains popular to this day.

Biography

Born 1632, in Wrington, Somerset, John Locke lived through politically and religiously turbulent times. He witnessed the English Civil War of the 1640s, the abolition of the monarchy, the House of Lords and the Anglican Church, and then saw the restoration of all three after Oliver Cromwell's death in 1658. In the early 1680s Locke fled to the Netherlands when suspected of plotting against James II of England, returning only after the Glorious Revolution which forced James to flee to France and be replaced by William of Orange, the Dutch ruler. Locke returned in style – aboard the royal yacht, with William III's wife and co-monarch, Mary II, elder daughter of the deposed James.

Locke's political philosophy has been immensely significant. As a social contract theorist, he defended the right of citizens to revolt against a government that rules without their consent. His thinking influenced the founding fathers of the United States, and their drawing up of the American Declaration of Independence. He is considered to be the first of the British empiricist philosophers. Locke died in Oates, Essex, in 1704.

Major works

An Essay Concerning Human Understanding

Two Treatises of Government

Benedictus de Spinoza

1632–77

Pantheism

'By substance I understand what is in itself and is conceived through itself, that is, that whose concept does not require the concept of another thing, from which it must be formed.'

Spinoza's *Ethics* is not, as the title might suggest, just about ethics. It develops an entire theory concerning the nature of reality. One of the most striking things about the book is its structure, which mirrors that of a geometrical proof – indeed, the full title of the book is *Ethics Demonstrated in a Geometrical Manner*.

A geometrical demonstration

Impressed by Euclid's geometry, which deduces its conclusions from certain explicit assumptions or definitions, Spinoza wanted to provide a similarly transparent and rigorous proof of his own conclusions. Each section of his argument concludes with 'QED' (*quod erat demonstrandum*: 'which was the thing to be proved'), just as if he were providing a geometrical demonstration.

One substance

At the heart of Spinoza's metaphysics lies his conception of the world as a single, unitary substance.

Descartes (see page 104) defines a substance as 'that which requires nothing but itself in order to exist'. According to Descartes, God is, strictly speaking, the only substance, for everything else depends on him. However, once Descartes has set dependence upon God to one side, he then says that there are just two substances – mind and matter – and that each is capable of existing independently of the other (so there can be disembodied minds).

Spinoza rejects Descartes's dualism of substances. He insists that there is only one substance. That substance is the *spatio-temporal world*. Of course, the world appears to us to be composed of many discrete and separable items or substances: houses, tables, humans, ants and so on. But appearances are deceptive. What we consider to be separate things are, in truth, not separate entities or substances in their own right, but, like ripples on a lake, mere temporary undulations in the one great substance.

So the one great substance is the spatio-temporal world. However, surprisingly perhaps, Spinoza claims that this substance *is also God*. Spinoza concurs with Descartes that a genuine substance does not depend on anything else for existence.

Its existence is part of its essence. But of course, this is a definition of God. So the one great substance is both the natural and the divine in a single, indivisible package.

This is obviously an unorthodox conception of God. God is typically thought of as our creator— a *separate* being who brings the world, and ourselves, into existence. What led Spinoza to reject this traditional view?

Spinoza argues that if God is infinite, then the world cannot be something separate from him. There can be nothing that isn't God. If there were, God would not be as great and all encompassing as he might be. He would have limits. But God is boundless. So *everything* must be God.

In Spinoza's view, mind and matter are also really the same thing. They are both God, but God seen, if you like, under different aspects. So Spinoza rejects Descartes's substance dualism of mind and matter. Spinoza is a substance monist (a one-substance theorist).

However, Spinoza does not think mind and matter exhaust God's attributes. Because God is infinite, thinks Spinoza, God must have an infinite number of such attributes. Mind and matter form a vanishingly small fraction of those attributes. We receive only an infinitely narrow glimpse of the totality of God-and-Nature.

Descartes and the interaction problem

One of the advantages Spinoza believed his metaphysics had over that of Descartes is that it does not run into the classic interaction problem that plagues Descartes's substance dualism.

According to Descartes, mind and body are distinct substances. The mind is a substance the essence of which is to think. The body, by contrast is essentially extended: it has depth, breadth and height. But how do these two substances interact?

They certainly do appear to interact. What goes on in my body can have an affect on my conscious mind. Pumping drugs into my body can play havoc with my thought processes and have a profound effect on what I experience. What takes place in my mind can also affect my body. If I make a conscious decision to raise my arm, I can do so.

How does this interaction take place? Descartes suggests that the locus of interaction is the pineal gland – a small gland located in the middle of the brain. However, it remains a mystery precisely how the mind – which Descartes is usually interpreted as supposing to lack spatial location – could causally affect something physical. This 'interaction problem' was well known to Descartes and his contemporaries. Spinoza's solution is simply to abandon the substance dualism that gives rise to it.

If Spinoza is correct, my mind and my body are not distinct substances. They are a single substance that is both mind and body. Mind and body are one substance seen, as it were, under different aspects.

If mind and body are identical, then there is no interaction problem. Suppose that, while visiting a modern building you look out of a window and see two dancers in a courtyard. They are back to back, and yet their enormously complex and seemingly random movements are synchronized perfectly. When one makes a delicate movement with her finger, so does the other. When one makes a sweeping movement with her leg, the other's leg follows precisely. How are the two dancers able to follow each other's movements so perfectly, when they cannot even see each other? Then you realize. There aren't two dancers. There's just one dancing in front of a mirror. Now that you realize that there is only one dancer (of whom you are seeing, as it were, two different 'aspects') the problem of explaining how the dancers causally 'interact' has entirely disappeared.

If Spinoza is correct, then mind and matter are, similarly, just two different aspects of the one great substance. They do not interact, so there is no interaction problem.

That Spinoza's metaphysical system avoids the interaction problem was thought by him to be one of its great advantages over its Cartesian rival.

Spinoza's religious views

Spinoza's religious views are unorthodox. His God is not a

creator God. Nor is he a personal God, with a special affection for human beings. Also, Spinoza does not embrace the traditional religious view that we have immortal souls. If Spinoza is correct that a human being's mind and body are identical – if they are different aspects of a single substance – then the death and destruction of the body must result in the death and destruction of the mind too. We cannot survive as disembodied mental substances in the way Descartes envisaged.

Yet Spinoza does still consider himself religious. He is usually described as a *pantheist* – someone who believes that *God is identical with everything there is.*

Rationalism and empiricism

Spinoza is one of the most important rationalist philosophers (others include Descartes, page 104, and Leibniz, page 137). One of the great historical disputes in philosophy is between the rationalists and the empiricists (such as, for example, Locke, page 119, and Hume, page 158).

Rationalists and empiricists disagree about the origins and grounds of knowledge. According to empiricists, all substantive, non-trivial knowledge of the world outside our minds is ultimately derived from and grounded in sense experience – the experience delivered by our five senses. Rationalists, by contrast, insist that there are at least some substantive truths that can be known independently of experience. Both Descartes and Spinoza, for example, believe that we can establish, without appeal to experience, the existence of God (which is, of course, a very substantive matter indeed).

Note that empiricists needn't deny that we possess some knowledge not based on sense experience. Take, for example, our knowledge that every bachelor is un-married. This is something we can know without observ-ing any bachelors. But of course, if 'bachelor' just means 'unmarried male', this is a very trivial piece of knowledge.

It is *non-trivial* knowledge of the *world outside our minds* that, according to the empiricist, must be based on sense experience.

Biography

Baruch Spinoza, later Benedictus de Spinoza, was born to Jewish parents in Amsterdam in 1632. His parents had fled from Portugal to avoid the Inquisition, which suspected them of having not truly converted to Christianity. Raised amid Amsterdam's close-knit Jewish community, Spinoza soon re-belled against its religious orthodoxy and was excommuni-cated from the synagogue in 1656, at the age of 24. By nature a loner, Spinoza turned down a professorship at the University of Heidelberg to pursue his own independent study. He supported himself by grinding lenses for optical instru-ments and the inhalation of glass dust may have contributed to his death from lung disease at the age of just 45. He died in The Hague in 1677.

Spinoza was a man of considerable integrity, prepared to endure great hardship rather than deny what he believed to be true. Bertrand Russell called him 'the noblest and most lovable of great philosophers'.

Major works

Tractatus Theologico-Politicus

Ethics

Descartes's Principles of Philosophy

Gottfried Wilhelm Leibniz
1646–1716

The indiscernibility of identicals

*'For in nature there are never two beings which are
perfectly alike and in which it is not possible to find
an internal difference, or at least a difference
founded upon an intrinsic quality.'*

Leibniz is one of the greatest German philosophers. He is also
one of the foremost rationalist philosophers of the modern era.
The focus here is on just one of Leibniz's two great metaphysical principles – Leibniz's law – a principle that remains important to philosophers to this day.

The book you hold in your hands right now is identical with
the book you were holding in your hands a few moments ago.
It is *identical* with that earlier book in the sense that it is *one and
the same object.* There is one book not two. Similarly, when two
people look up at the moon from different vantage points on
Earth, they see one and the same object. Again, the number of
objects seen is one, not many.

Leibniz is credited with drawing our attention to an

important principle concerning identical objects, a principle known as the *indiscernibility of identicals*. The principle is this:

If two objects are identical, then they will be indiscernible: they will not differ in their properties.

This principle might well strike you as intuitively plausible. After all, if two things really are one and the same thing, how could one possess a property that the other lacks?

But the principle does face one very obvious sort of counter-example. Perhaps you have accidentally spilt some coffee over the pages of this book during the last five minutes. Five minutes ago its pages were white, now many of them sport a nasty brown stain. In which case, though it is one and the same book you hold in your hands, its properties are different. Identical objects clearly *can* differ in their properties.

But let's not abandon our principle too quickly. One way in which we might salvage it is by restricting it to 'temporally indexed' properties – *the property of possessing such-and-such a feature at such-and-such a time.*

Take, for example, the property of *possessing no brown-stained pages at 10.00 a.m.* Suppose this book gets stained between 10.00 a.m. and 10.05 a.m. While the book has changed, it remains true of it, even at 10.05 a.m., that it had no brown-stained pages at 10.00 a.m. *That* property of the book hasn't changed.

Similarly, if I wear a red jacket on Tuesday but remain jacketless on Wednesday, it is true of me at *both* times that I wear a jacket on Tuesday but no jacket on Wednesday. So, if we restrict Leibniz's principle to such 'temporally indexed' properties, perhaps the principle does still hold.

Numerical and qualitative identity

The word 'identical' is used in different ways. Philosophers, for example, distinguish between numerical and qualitative identity.

Objects are qualitatively identical if they share all the same properties.

Objects are numerically identical if they are one and the same object.

Suppose I have two white wooden balls that share all the same properties – they are the same shape, size, colour, and so on. They are indistinguishable right down to the last atom. These balls are qualitatively identical. But the number of balls is two, not one. So they are not numerically identical.

If I take one of these balls and paint it black, it undergoes a change in its properties. So it is not qualitatively identical with the way it was before, but it is numerically one and the same ball. The later ball is numerically identical with the earlier ball.

When we talk about 'identical twins' we are of course talking about qualitative identity – otherwise they wouldn't be twins (and of course, even 'identical' twins don't share *all* the same properties – they are just physically very similar). When astronomers say that the evening star is identical with the morning star, on the other hand, they don't mean these heavenly objects are qualitatively identical – they mean they are *one and the same* object. Obviously, if we are not clear what sort of 'identity' we are talking about, discussions about what is 'the same' and what is 'not the same' are likely to become very confusing indeed.

The principle of the identity of indiscernibles says, in effect, that numerical identity entails qualitative identity. The principle of the indiscernibility of identicals says, in effect, that qualitative identity entails numerical identity. As this chapter explains, there are some obvious exceptions to both principles.

Applying the principle

Now that we have dealt with one very obvious objection to Leibniz's principle, let's consider how it might be applied. Here's a scientific example to begin.

Imagine I am an astronomer. I believe I have discovered a new planet. But someone else discovered a planet recently, and I want to be sure that my planet is a new, different planet, so that I too get the glory of having made a spectacular astronomical discovery. How might I do this? By applying Leibniz's principle. If identical objects share all the same properties, then

I need only find a property one planet possesses that the other lacks in order to establish that the number of planets discovered is two, not one.

Let's suppose, for example, that the planet discovered by that other astronomer has rings. I can show that my planet is a different planet just by demonstrating that it has no rings. Or I might show that the two planets occupy different regions of space. Or that they are differently coloured. Any one of these discoveries would do to confirm that I am also the discoverer of a new planet.

Philosophers' use of the principle

Philosophers also make regular use of Leibniz's principle. Suppose, for example, that a philosopher wants to show that her mind and her brain are not identical. One way in which she might try to do this is by finding either (i) a property that her mind possesses but her brain lacks, or (ii) a property that her brain possesses but her mind lacks.

Unfortunately, this is not quite as easily done as you might imagine. Some of the most obvious suggestions, such as that my mind is brimming with ideas, whereas my brain is not, or that my brain has a wrinkly surface whereas my mind does not, are simply question-begging. If those scientists who claim my mind is my brain are correct, then my mind does indeed have a wrinkly surface. It is just that I didn't realize until now that it had a wrinkly surface. And perhaps my brain is brimming with ideas. I just wasn't aware of the fact.

Exceptions to the rule

The principle of the indiscernibility of identicals is clearly useful. In fact we make use of it on a day-to-day basis. Whenever you deduce that, say, the man Joe met yesterday is not the man you met yesterday because one had a moustache and the other didn't, you are relying on Leibniz's principle.

It's worth remembering, however, that there are some notorious exceptions to the principle. Take a look at this example:

Superman is someone Lois Lane knows can fly.
Clark Kent is not someone Lois Lane knows can fly.
Therefore: Superman is not Clark Kent.

The two premises of this argument are true. Lois Lane does indeed know something about Superman that she doesn't know about Clark Kent – that the former can fly. So Superman has a property Clark Kent lacks – he is someone Lois Lane believes can fly. So, by Leibniz's principle, the conclusion should follow. Yet it doesn't. Why not?

Unfortunately, we have hit upon one of those properties to which the principle does not apply. The fact that someone *knows* something about one person but not another does not establish that they are not one and the same person. The same is also true of what someone *hopes*, or *desires*, or *believes* and so on about one thing but not another. Generally speaking, the fact that we have different 'psychological attitudes' towards one thing but not another does not reveal that they are not identical.

So, for example, the fact that my father has the property of being someone I trust implicitly, whereas the masked robber that just walked into the bank does not have the property of being someone I trust implicitly, does not establish that my father is not the masked robber. It might yet turn out that, unknown to me, my father is indeed the bank robber – unlikely, perhaps, but certainly not impossible.

The identity of indiscernibles

We have been looking at Leibniz's principle of the *indiscernibility of identicals* – the principle that if things are identical then they share all the same properties. There is a second, similar principle to which Leibniz also subscribed, called the principle of the *identity of indiscernibles*. Leibniz supposed that if things do not differ in their properties, then this must be one and the same thing. The two principles are easily muddled, of course.

This second principle entails that if Clark Kent and Superman share all the same properties, then they are one and the same person.

You might wonder about this principle, though. Surely two things might share all the same properties, yet the number of objects might still be two, not one. Couldn't identical twins be exactly alike in all their properties, for example? Yet they would not be *numerically* identical – there would still be two of them, not one.

Of course, actual identical twins are always a little bit

different. One is always minutely taller than the other, for example. And they obviously differ in their psychological states too. Their memories will be different because they have experienced different things. Still, even if no such non-identical indiscernibles actually exist, is it *impossible* for there to be two individuals exactly alike in every way, as Leibniz maintains?

Consider this hypothetical case. Suppose that, over on the other side of our galaxy, there is a planet exactly like our own. This doppelgänger planet is a molecule-for-molecule duplicate of the one we inhabit. It even contains a perfect doppelgänger of you reading this book.

Of course it is highly unlikely that any such planet exists. But Leibniz's second principle does not just entail that such a planet is unlikely. It is supposed to rule out such pairs of indiscernibles as an *impossibility*. But then the principle seems too strong, doesn't it? For it is not, strictly speaking, *impossible* that such a planet should exist, is it?

One way of dealing with this sort of objection to Leibniz's second principle is to include in those properties that are shared the property of being *in a particular place at a particular time.* You and your doppelgänger on planet X may be molecule-for-molecule duplicates of each other, but you are located on opposite sides of the galaxy. So your properties do differ after all. One of you has the property of being *over here.* The other doesn't.

So perhaps we can salvage this second principle. It does, however, remain controversial. Rather more controversial, in fact, than the indiscernibility of identicals (which, while it has some noted exceptions, such as properties involving psychological attitudes, seems otherwise sound).

These two principles together are often called *Leibniz's law* (though that title is also sometimes given to just the first principle).

Biography

Leibniz was born in Leipzig, Germany, in 1646. Along with Spinoza and Descartes, he is one of the three great 17th-century rationalist philosophers united in the belief that reason alone is able to establish certain substantial truths about reality. He was also a leading logician and mathematician, credited with having invented the integral and differential calculus independently of Isaac Newton.

Sadly, at the time of his death, Leibniz's philosophy was most famous for being the butt of a joke. In *Candide*, Voltaire famously ridicules Leibniz's claim in the *Theodicy* that, as God's creation, this must be the 'the best of all possible worlds'. Voltaire has the ridiculously optimistic tutor Dr Pangloss adamantly insisting, 'All is for the best in the best of all possible worlds', despite the obvious evidence to the contrary. Pangloss is clearly meant to represent Leibniz.

Leibniz's reputation has since been restored and his very considerable achievements recognized. He is now rightly admired, among other things, for his work in developing two important philosophical principles: the principle of sufficient reason (nothing happens, exists or is true without a reason) and Leibniz's law (explained above). He died in Hanover in 1716.

Major works

Monadology

Theodicy

George Berkeley

1685–1753

Berkeley's idealism

'To be is to be perceived.'

Just as younger children sometimes wonder whether the refrigerator light stays on once the door is shut, so the more philosophically minded older child may question whether physical objects continue to exist when they are not observed. George Berkeley's answer to this question is that they do not. According to Berkeley, the physical world exists only while it is being perceived. So what led him to this astonishing conclusion?

Berkeley had two overriding philosophical concerns. The first was to deal with sceptical worries about the material world. How, can we know that such a world exists? The second was to counter what Berkeley saw as the growing tendency of the scientists and philosophers of his day to push God to the periphery in their thinking about the world. Scientists were beginning to adopt an increasingly mechanistic view of how the universe worked, with God required, at best, merely to crank the starting handle on the great world-machine, after which his presence was no longer required. Berkeley wanted to bring God back to centre stage.

Scepticism

Let's begin with the threat of scepticism. According to the *representational theory of perception* embraced by many of the leading thinkers of Berkeley's day, we do not perceive the world directly. Rather, our perception of the world is mediated by certain mental entities called *ideas*.

Suppose, for example, that you look at a tomato on the table in front of you. When you observe the tomato, what you are *immediately* aware of is not the tomato itself, but certain sensory appearances that parade, as it were, before your mind's eye. What you experience directly are shifting ideas of shape, colour and so on, sliding across your internal, subjective cinema screen. The tomato itself lies *behind* these sensory appearances as their cause.

Berkeley's concern about this representational theory of perception (which he associates in particular with the philosopher John Locke, although it is debatable whether Locke endorses it) is the difficulty of knowing whether our senses are a reliable guide to external, physical reality. If we never get to experience that reality *directly*, to check that there is anything out there corresponding to our ideas, what grounds have we for supposing such a reality exists? Rather than *mediating* perception of physical reality, ideas seem to form an impenetrable veil – a barrier beyond which we can never peek – and so threaten to cut us off from knowledge of the world. Philosophers call this *the veil-of-perception problem.*

Berkeley's solution to the veil-of-perception problem is ingenious. Rather than supposing that physical objects lie *behind* our sensory experiences, why not just suppose that they *are* those sensory experiences? When you observe a tomato, the tomato is not the *cause* of your ideas. Rather, it just *is* those ideas. As there is no particular problem explaining your knowledge of your own ideas, so the sceptical problem generated by the representational theory of perception is immediately solved.

If it isn't observed, it isn't there

Of course, while this move might indeed deal with the veil-of-perception problem, it has some very odd consequences. For a start, ideas are mental entities. They are subjective in the same way that, say, pains are subjective. Just as there could not be a pain that no one felt, so there could not be an idea which no one experienced.

It follows then that, if physical objects are just ideas or collections of ideas, they too are mental entities incapable of existing independently of being experienced. Berkeley's idealism has the bizarre-sounding consequence that, if no one is experiencing that tomato, *there is no tomato.* Those portions of the physical that are not observed do not exist. According to Berkeley, for the physical world *to be is to be perceived.*

The rejection of materialism

Berkeley's idealism, which simply identifies physical objects with ideas, involves the rejection of the *materialist* philosophy that says that physical objects are material substances in their own right capable of mind-independent existence. The only genuine substances, according to Berkeley, are mental substances – *minds*. Berkeley does not deny that physical objects exist, but he maintains that they are not anything over and above the ideas entertained by minds. There are no material substances, only mental substances.

The role of God

Berkeley's idealism may deal with a sceptical worry generated by the representative theory of perception, but what of Berkeley's other concern – to bring God back centre stage? How does Berkeley's idealism achieve that?

Actually, Berkeley does not deny that physical objects continue to exist when *we* are not perceiving them – that tomato remains on the table even while none of us observes it; your kitchen continues to exist even after you have turned off the light and gone to bed. Why? *Because God constantly observes everything.* And so, while the materialist philosophers of the day were finding less and less use for God in their thinking about the physical universe, Berkeley gives God a central, universe-sustaining role. The universe is kept in existence, while we do not observe it, by God's constant gaze.

Why the tree continues to be...

The role that Berkeley's Idealism assigns to God is nicely summarized in a limerick penned (at least in part) by Monsignor Ronald Knox:

> *There was a young man who said, 'God*
> *Must think it exceedingly odd*
> *If he finds that this tree*
> *Continues to be*
> *When there's no one about in the Quad.'*

> REPLY

> *Dear Sir:*
> *Your astonishment's odd:*
> *I am always about in the Quad.*
> *And that's why the tree*
> *Will continue to be,*
> *Since observed by*
> *Yours faithfully,*
> *GOD.*

Berkeley's master argument

We have outlined Berkeley's extraordinary theory, but why should we accept it? What grounds do we have for supposing that it is true? In particular, why should we accept that physical objects cannot exist unperceived?

Berkeley offers a number of arguments for this conclusion,

but one in particular stands out. So confident is Berkeley in this particular argument that he is prepared to let everything rest on it. It is, for this reason, often referred to as Berkeley's *master argument*.

Berkeley simply challenges us to try to conceive of a physical object that exists unperceived. Try, for example, to imagine a tree that continues to exist though no one observes it. Can you do this?

No, says Berkeley. You can't. For in imagining the tree, you still imagine yourself perceiving it. You imagine yourself looking at it.

Berkeley concedes that while it might *seem* as if we can entertain the thought that there is a world of unperceived and unconsidered physical objects, it turns out, on closer inspection, that we can't.

But...

Is Berkeley's master argument cogent? An initial worry we might raise is that it appears to take for granted a rather *imagistic* view of thought. It seems that, in Berkeley's view, to think about something is to entertain some sort of *mental image* or other sensory representation of it. When I think of a tree, I conjure up a mental image of a tree, but then I do, after all, imagine myself *looking* at it.

However, is this way of thinking about thinking correct? Not obviously. Clearly, I can conjure up a mental image of a tree.

However, must entertaining the thought that there exists an unperceived tree involve any such an image?

It seems not. Suppose you ask me to visualize a tree. I do so. If you then ask me to describe my visualized tree, I will be able to do so. For in visualizing a tree, I inevitably imagine it having various features that I can then go on to tell you about. For example, my tree may be deciduous or coniferous, rounded or tall, with leaves or without.

If, on the other hand, you ask me simply to suppose there is a tree that exists unperceived, and then ask me to describe it, it may well turn out that I don't have in mind any particular *sort* of tree at all. The tree in question need be neither deciduous nor coniferous, neither short nor tall, neither with leaves nor without.

This rather tells against the assumption that thinking of something involves conjuring up a mental image of it. But, if we can think of something without thinking of ourselves as perceiving it in some way, doesn't Berkeley's argument therefore collapse?

Perhaps not. The reply to this objection may be that, even if you can suppose there exists an unperceived tree, you certainly can't suppose that there exists one that no one *thinks* about. Any tree you think of will inevitably be a tree that *someone* is *thinking* about – namely, you.

In other words, to suppose that you can conceive of a tree no one conceives of involves, as Berkeley himself points out, a contradiction – the tree in question would have to be both conceived and unconceived, both thought of and not thought of – which is an impossibility.

So perhaps Berkeley can at least show that you are unable to entertain the thought that there exists a tree that exists unconsidered by anyone.

And...

Unfortunately, the above argument is also fallacious. We can and should distinguish between *conceiving of* a particular so and so, and *conceiving that there is* a so and so. I can, for example, conceive *that* there was a US president who wore purple underpants without conceiving *of* any particular US president (e.g. Lincoln or Reagan) wearing purple underpants. There need be no particular person *of* whom I am thinking when I suppose *that* there is such a person.

Armed with this distinction, we can now see why Berkeley's argument fails. To suppose we can conceive *of* something of which no one conceives involves a contradiction. But there is no such contradiction involved in supposing we can conceive *that* there is something of which no one conceives. For that is not yet to conceive *of* anything at all.

So Berkeley's conclusion doesn't follow. Berkeley has not shown we can't think *that* there exist things not thought of by any mind.

Illusions and hallucinations

Berkeley's idealism faces a famous difficulty: how to account for hallucinations and other perceptual illusions.

Suppose that, while ill and delirious, I begin to hallucinate pink elephants dancing round my lampshade. Now the way in which we would ordinarily explain this discrepancy between how things look and how things really are is by saying that the elephants exist *only* in my mind. There is nothing corresponding to my experience in external, physical reality.

This explanation, of course, is unavailable to Berkeley precisely because he rejects the suggestion that there is any such external reality. In fact, given that Berkeley simply identifies physical objects with ideas in the mind, and given that I am currently having particularly vivid ideas of pink elephants, it would seem to follow that my pink elephants are real physical objects.

Clearly, this won't do. How, then, does Berkeley distinguish between illusion and reality? How can he allow that my pink elephants are not real physical objects?

He says that not all ideas are of things that are real. Our ideas of real things, suggests Berkeley, are far more *vivid* than those ideas we conjure up with our imaginations. Berkeley also maintains that our ideas of real things are also ideas over which we have no voluntary control being put into our minds by God. The imagination, by contrast, is free to conjure up whatever it likes.

These suggestions do not go quite far enough in accounting

for all perceptual errors, however. After all, nightmares can be very vivid indeed – so vivid we mistake them for reality. And they are terrifying precisely because they are beyond our control.

So how else might the real and the merely illusory differ? Berkeley adds that our ideas of real things have a constancy and regularity to them – indeed, they appear to be governed by laws (such as the laws of gravity). Illusions and hallucinations, on the other hand, fail to fit in with our other experiences in a coherent way. When I hallucinate pink elephants cavorting around my lampshade, these experiences stand out like a sore thumb so far as the texture of the rest of my experience is concerned. Here, suggests Berkeley, lies a further difference between those things that are real and those that are merely illusory.

Here, too, Berkeley's explanation of the difference between illusion and reality seems inadequate. Surely someone might have a vivid but unremarkable dream that fits into the rest of their experience in just the way Berkeley describes. They might dream that they got up in the night for a glass of water, for example, when in reality they remained in bed. Berkeley has a hard time accounting for the possibility of this sort of hallucination.

Few philosophers nowadays are idealists. Still, while almost every contemporary philosopher rejects Berkeley's conclusions, they acknowledge that many of the points Berkeley makes in attempting to justify those conclusions are both insightful and thought provoking.

Biography

Born 1685, in Kilcrin, near Kilkenny, Ireland. Berkeley graduated from Trinity College, Dublin in 1704. Here he became familiar with the works of Descartes and Locke, and three years later he became a fellow of the college. In 1709 he was ordained as a minister in the Anglican Church and in 1734 he was appointed Bishop of Cloyne.

Berkeley is undoubtedly one of Ireland's most important philosophical thinkers and, along with John Locke and David Hume, he is also one of the three great British empiricists.

All the philosophical works for which Berkeley is most famous were written in his 20s. He also wrote on physics, mathematics, economics and medicine. In his day, Berkeley's most often-read works advertised the health benefits of drinking tarwater. In his book *Siris*, published in 1744, he recommended its widely beneficial properties. He died in Oxford in 1753.

Major works

Treatise Concerning the Principles of Human
   Knowledge

Three Dialogues between Hylas and Philonous

David Hume

1711–76

The soul and causation

*'When we … consider the operation of causes,
we are never able … to discover any …
necessary connection.'*

In order to be able to know something, or even believe it, we
must first be able to *think* it. We must at least be able to entertain it as a *hypothesis* – to suppose it *might* be true.

Concepts

For example, take cheese being made from milk. Of course,
that's something most people believe. But notice that, if you
have not yet made up your mind about whether cheese is made
from milk, you need at least to be able to have thoughts about
cheese and milk in order to entertain that it *might* be true. That
requires you to possess the relevant *concepts* – including, here,
the concepts of cheese and of milk.

This point about concepts raises an interesting possibility.
One way to show that a philosophical claim or theory should be

rejected is by showing that it is false. But there is another, more radical possibility. Instead of trying to show that it is false, we might instead try to show that it is empty – that we cannot even entertain the thought it *might* be true. One way of doing this is to show that we do not possess the relevant concepts.

This radical option has been tried against any number of philosophical theories. For example, some have attacked the hypothesis that God exists by trying to show, not that it is false, but that we possess no coherent conception of God. So, the thought, 'God exists', is not so much false as confused or empty.

David Hume is one of the great masters of this technique. Here we examine how Hume applies it both to the claim that we possess immaterial souls and to the claim that there is some sort of causal power at work in the world.

Hume's empiricism

Hume believes he can show that we possess no concept of an immaterial soul. His starting point is his empiricism about concepts.

We can distinguish two fundamental forms of empiricism: about knowledge; and about concepts. An empiricist about knowledge insists that all substantive, non-trivial knowledge of the world around us – the world outside our minds – is ulti- mately founded on sense experience. Our five senses – sight, hearing, touch, taste and smell – provide us with our only win- dow on external reality. Whatever knowledge we possess of the real world comes from observing it, as it were, through this sensory window. Hume is certainly an empiricist about knowledge.

Hume is also an empiricist about concepts. He supposes that *every concept we possess is also ultimately furnished by experience.* To explain precisely how Hume thinks we acquire concepts, it will be helpful if we borrow two of his terms: impressions and ideas. Hume divided the mind's contents into *impressions* – perceptions we have when the world impacts on our senses – and *ideas* – less vivid copies of impressions.

Impressions and ideas

When I observe an apple on the table before me, it produces in my mind certain sensory impressions. I have a sensory impression of its colour: red. I also have an impression of a certain shape. If I lift the apple and bite into it, I acquire still more impressions: smell, taste and texture, as well as the sound of me biting into the apple.

According to Hume, concepts – which are what Hume calls ideas – are acquired by being copied from impressions. Take the simple impression of red that I have when I look at the apple. My mind can produce a copy of this sense impression. This copy can then function as my concept of red. In the same way, I can acquire concepts of shapes, sounds, tastes and smells. By copying impressions, I can gradually build up a large library of concepts.

But this can't be the whole story as far as acquiring concepts is concerned. We know that we are able to conceive of things we have never experienced. We can conceive of all manner of imaginary beasts, from centaurs to unicorns, yet we have never actually observed them. How, then, are we able to conceive of them?

Hume allows us to possess the concept of a unicorn. The key to understanding how Hume supposes we might conceive of a unicorn, despite never having experienced one, lies in his distinction between simple and complex ideas.

Hume's copy principle

Hume distinguishes between two sorts of ideas. There are simple ideas, such as our idea of red. Then there are complex ideas such as our ideas of tables, horses and unicorns. The simple ideas constitute our conceptual building blocks, while the complex ideas are formed by combining simple ideas together.

Take for example the simple (or at least simpler) ideas of cold, hard, round and white. I can combine these to form the idea of a snowball. Or I might combine the simpler ideas of a horse and a horn to form the more complex idea of a unicorn.

Hume's view is that all *simple* ideas must be copies of corresponding sense impressions. Yes, I can have complex ideas of snowballs and unicorns, even though I have never experienced them, so long as I *have* had impressions of the *simple* ideas out of which these more complex ideas are composed.

If Hume is correct and 'red' is a simple idea, then I cannot conceive of 'red' unless I have experienced it. When it comes to simple ideas, the rule is: no impression, then no corresponding idea. This rule is often referred to as Hume's *copy principle*.

There's a great deal of intuitive plausibility to the copy principle. It allows us to conceive of unicorns and centaurs. It also neatly explains why someone who has never experienced colour can never acquire our concept of 'red'.

Of course, someone who can perceive a colour might try to convey to someone who cannot what they mean by 'red' by saying that it is 'like the sound of trumpets' or 'the most angry of colours'. These attempts can't succeed. In order to know what red is – in order properly to grasp the concept – you need to experience it for yourself. Just as Hume's copy principle maintains.

So let's accept that Hume's copy principle does, at first sight, have some intuitive plausibility. How does he go on to apply the principle? First, his attack on the suggestion that we can conceive of the existence of immaterial souls.

No concept of an immaterial soul

Descartes (see page 104) supposes we each possess an immaterial soul. This soul is a *substance*, i.e. something capable of existing on its own, independently of anything else. So your soul might, in principle, become detached from your physical body – indeed, from *any* physical body – and exist on its own as a disembodied self.

Hume believes the hypothesis that we possess such Cartesian souls is not so much false as empty. He applies his copy principle in order to try to demonstrate that we have no conception of such things.

Hume asks from where we might acquire this concept of a 'soul'. Not from our external senses, it seems. Souls are not encountered when we observe the material world around us.

What if we turn our mind's eye inwards? What about introspection? Might we not then experience ourselves as souls?

Hume *does* consider introspection a kind of experience. He also allows that we can acquire concepts from the impressions that introspection generates. So why can't we acquire the idea of an immaterial soul through introspection?

The problem, says Hume, is that there is no such experience of the soul. When I survey my inner, mental landscape, I never catch sight of any soul. There is no further entity that I encounter, beyond a stream of thoughts and experiences. There is only the stream of thoughts and experiences.

But if there is *no* further impression of any such immaterial soul, it seems I can have no conception of such a thing. In which case, Descartes's hypothesis that we possess immaterial souls is not *false*. It's *empty*.

Hume's bundle theory of the self

What then *is* the self, if not an immaterial substance or soul? Here, Hume makes an interesting move.

Berkeley (see page 147), also an empiricist about concepts, argues that we have no conception of any *material* substance underpinning or standing behind our sensory experience. That is because we never experience any such substance. We only ever experience our ideas. So we can have no conception of material substance. The hypothesis that material substances exist is therefore not so much false as empty, according to Berkeley. The only genuine substances are mental substances.

What then are physical objects, if not material substances? Berkeley's reply is ingenious: physical objects just are the experiences we have. They *are* collections of ideas, rather than some sort of mysterious entity standing behind ideas.

Hume mirrors Berkeley's view of material substances with his view of immaterial substances. Hume insists we have no conception of the self as an immaterial substance existing *in addition* to our flow of thoughts and experiences. Rather, the self is just this flow of experiences.

This theory of the self is often referred to as the 'bundle theory'. You *are* not a mysterious immaterial substance in addition to the bundle of thoughts and experiences you are having. You just *are* that bundle.

Causation

Moving on, Hume also applies his copy principle to try to show that we possess no conception of causal power.

Where then does our concept of causation come from? If we accept Hume's empiricism about concepts, it must ultimately be derived from experience. But what experience?

You might wonder whether you acquire the concept of causation from seeing one object causally act upon another. A billiard ball collides with another, causing the second to move.

When you see this, don't you also experience the causation taking place?

No, answers Hume. You observe one ball moving up to another, and the second then moving. You observe that one event *follows* another. There is no further experience of the 'causing'.

You might question that. You don't *just* see one thing happen and then another, you also *see* that one thing *causes* the other!

But *do* you see that? Hume's argument appears to show that you don't. Suppose you could also see the 'causing' taking place. You could then know, on the basis of just this experience of these two billiard balls, that one ball caused the other to move. But you can't actually know, on the basis of that experience, that one caused the other to move. It might just be coincidence that the second ball moved, just as it was coincidence when your phone rang just now, right after the kettle boiled. You are not, as yet, in any position to establish that there is a causal connection.

How might you establish that these events are causally related? In order to know that there's a causal connection, says Hume, you need to observe *many* such pairs of events. You need to see the balls striking each other time after time to rule out the possibility of coincidence.

Yet, if the causal connection were something visible, you could know, on the basis of a single observation, that the movement of one ball did indeed cause the movement of the other. It therefore follows that *you do not directly observe any causal connection.*

The concept of causation

If you don't experience the 'causing', from what experiences is your concept of causation derived? The copy principle says: no impression, no corresponding simple idea.

You may already be able to guess Hume's solution. Berkeley insists that a physical object isn't a mysterious material substance standing behind our experiences, it is *just* a set of experiences. Hume supposes the self isn't a mysterious immaterial substance standing behind our thoughts and experiences, but *just* a bundle of thoughts and experiences. Likewise, Hume also suggests that causation isn't a mysterious hidden power or mechanism *standing behind* those regular happenings that we see in the world. At root, it is *just* those regular happenings. (I am simplifying Hume a little here – but only a little.) Hume analyses causation in terms of what he calls 'constant conjunction' – in terms of one sort of object or event invariably following another. In one of Hume's famous two 'definitions' of cause, to say that one billiard ball causes the other to move is merely to say that whenever one billiard ball rolls against another in this way, the second moves.

A cosmic coincidence?

Hume's theory of causation may not sound very outlandish just yet. However, as stated, it seems to have the consequence that there is nothing in the world that *makes* things turn out regularly. There is nothing that *makes* the second ball move when struck by the first. It's just that, as a matter of fact, it always does.

But isn't this just to admit that such regularities are nothing more than a cosmic fluke? Like someone flipping a coin billions of times and, by sheer coincidence, it always coming up heads? How likely is that? Extraordinarily unlikely! Yet if nothing *forces* the world to be regular, then the existence of such regularities is surely an even more staggering coincidence.

How to interpret Hume on cause?

Is this a conclusion Hume was prepared to accept? Some philosophers believe so. Others are convinced Hume could not really have embraced such an outrageous view. They say he must have acknowledged that there is something-we-know-not-what at work in the world that *makes* things regular. There must be some secret connection – some mysterious power – at work, even if it remains forever beyond our understanding.

The trouble is, given Hume's copy principle, it is difficult to see how he can allow us even to think that there *might* be such a thing out there, let alone consider its existence probable.

Biography

Born 1711, in Edinburgh, David Home (later Hume) was the son of Joseph Home of Ninewells, a small estate in the Scottish Borders, and Katherine Falconer. After Hume's father died in 1713, his mother educated him until he entered university at the unusually early age of 11. Upon graduating, Hume began to question the religious beliefs with which he had been raised and his interests turned increasingly towards philosophy.

After graduating he moved to La Flèche in Anjou, northern France, where Descartes had been educated. There, over the next three years, he worked on his *Treatise of Human Nature*. In 1739, at the age of just 28, Hume published his *Treatise*, one of the great works of Western philosophy. Unfortunately, the book 'fell dead-born from the press'. Disappointed, Hume blamed himself for having rushed its production and publication. He later rewrote and developed the work, republishing it as two separate volumes: the *Enquiry Concerning the Principles of Morals* and the *Enquiry Concerning Human Understanding*.

Many considered Hume's criticisms of religion and the clergy dangerous, and his ideas and reputation came under repeated attack during his lifetime, not least by his most passionate critic, James Beattie. He died in Edinburgh in 1776.

Major works

A Treatise of Human Nature

Enquiry Concerning Human Understanding

Enquiry Concerning the Principles of Morals

Dialogues Concerning Natural Religion

Jean-Jacques Rousseau
1712–78

The general will

'Man is born free, yet everywhere he is in chains.'

When people live independently of any political state they are free. But of course, membership of a state also has its advantages. There is much to be gained from living within an organized society, not least the protection of life and property that membership provides.

The question Rousseau addresses is: can we have both? Can we enjoy all the benefits that a state bestows without sacrificing our freedom? Our basic political problem, says Rousseau:

> …is to find a form of association which will defend and protect with the whole common force the person and goods of each associate, and in which each, while uniting himself with all, may still obey himself alone, and remain as free as before.

Rousseau believes that such an association is indeed possible. He recommends a particular form of democracy.

Individuals can form a state by entering into an agreement or 'social contract' with each other for the sake of their common good (see Hobbes, page 96, for more on this idea of a social contract). But what is the common good?

The general will

It is here that one of Rousseau's central concepts – that of the *general will* – comes into play.

Rousseau contrasts the general will with what he calls the *will of all*. The will of all is the adding up of what each individual thinks is good for him- or herself.

Here's an example. It may be that, within a group of car drivers, each individual driver would like to be able to drive around as fast as their cars will allow – say, at 90 mph. So driving at 90 mph is the *will of all*.

However, if everyone tries to drive that fast, the result will be mayhem. In this case, traffic flows most smoothly, safely and efficiently when a speed limit of 50 mph is imposed. Rousseau would say that under such circumstances, a 50 mph limit is the *general will*. It is not the will of each individual driver. It is not even the will of all. But it is what is in the best interests of society as a whole.

Here is a second example. Suppose individuals would like to pay as little tax as possible. Paying zero tax is what *every* individual would prefer. This is the will of all. However, a zero rate of taxation would be catastrophic for the state as a whole because public services would cease to function. So a zero tax rate, while the will of all, is not the general will. The general will is for whatever rate of tax is best for society as a whole.

Your interests are those of the state

Rousseau argues that within a certain sort of democracy the general will can prevail. If individuals subject themselves to and vote in accordance with the general will, then all the benefits of living in a state can be had. They can be had, suggests Rousseau, *without compromising our freedom.*

You might wonder about that. If I live under such a political regime, my freedom to drive as I please will certainly be curtailed. That's a loss of freedom, isn't it? Similarly, if I prefer to pay zero tax, but am forced to pay a reasonable amount for the sake of the common good, then again, my freedom is curtailed, is it not?

Rousseau thinks not. He argues that, considered as part of the state, *your interests are those of the state.* As a member of the state, *your will is just the general will.* But then if to act freely is only to act in accordance with your will, and your will is the general will, so by forcing you to drive at not more than 50 mph and pay your taxes, the state is *forcing you to be free.*

An elective aristocracy

Rousseau recommends a form of democracy in which the general will can prevail. However, a direct democracy in which everyone votes on every issue is unworkable. Rousseau proposes instead an 'elective aristocracy' in which a leader, or team of leaders, is periodically elected by all, much as they are in many modern democracies.

But why suppose that in such a system, individuals will vote for the general will? Why won't they vote on the basis of narrow self-interest instead, perhaps to the detriment of all?

Suppose, for example, that while some people have cars that can reach 90 mph, others have cars that can't do more than 50 mph. Given this inequality, isn't it inevitable that drivers will vote on the basis of narrow self-interest, with those driving faster cars voting for a higher speed limit?

Similarly, if some are rich and others are poor, while those who would gain from an increase in taxation will vote for it, those who find themselves less well off will no doubt vote against. How does Rousseau imagine that voting won't be heavily skewed in this way by individual self-interest?

Rousseau offers several solutions to these problems, including the following:

1. To the extent that class and inequality in wealth are obstacles to democracy, *they must be abolished.* Differences in wealth and income that would otherwise lead people to vote out of individual self-interest should be removed.

2. We should also raise new citizens so that they identify strongly with the state. Education should aim to strengthen the

social bonds that make us identify with our community. It should also emphasize civic virtue, so that we cherish one another as brothers. We will then vote for the common good, rather than out of individual self-interest.

Rousseau also believes that as religion is a great social adhesive and promoter of virtue, so religion should be obligatory. And he recommends that the state have an official censor to discourage and ridicule anti-social behaviour and encourage conformity.

With these and other mechanisms in place, thinks Rousseau, citizens will no longer vote out of narrow self-interest but in accordance with the general will. And so a happy and harmonious society will result.

Positive and negative liberty

Critics of Rousseau's political philosophy often focus on his idea of freedom. Rousseau believes that our freedom is assured in a democratic state that is run along the lines he suggests.

But of course, Rousseau is working with a very particular concept of freedom. Philosophers often distinguish two kinds of liberty. *Negative liberty* is the freedom to pursue your own desires without external hindrance – no one prevents you from doing what you want or forces you to do something else. *Positive liberty* is when you are able to recognize and lead the kind of life that you ought to live – one that a rational person would choose to live.

Defenders of positive liberty typically argue that negative liberty, alone, is compatible with a kind of slavery. Someone who merely follows their appetites in a wholly unconstrained way is not so much free as enslaved by those appetites (like an ill-disciplined child allowed to spend all day gorging on ice cream and playing games).

This is precisely Rousseau's view, in fact. He recommends we trade our natural, negative liberty for the kind of positive liberty that exists under his proposed state. *True* liberty, thinks Rousseau, is a form of positive liberty – the kind of civil liberty we gain when we allow ourselves to be governed not by our individual wills, but by the *general* will.

Of course, the idea that we can be 'forced to be free' by being forced to do what the state deems right, has, since Rousseau's day, been used to justify the totalitarian activities of some appalling regimes. Clearly, such a state is not what Rousseau has in mind. But critics have argued that, once negative liberty has been sacrificed in this way, any state risks sliding into despotism and tyranny.

Biography

Born 1712, in Geneva, Rousseau's mother died within a week of his birth, leaving the young Rousseau to be raised by his artisan father. When his father was exiled for being involved in a fight with a French officer, Rousseau went to live with relatives. Faced with the prospect of an apprenticeship, he ran away at the age of 16 and escaped to France, where he became secretary to Baronne Françoise-Louise de Warens, who financed the completion of his education. Rousseau was then able to earn a living as a tutor, musician and writer.

In 1750 Rousseau won the prestigious essay prize of the Dijon Academy with his *Discourse on the Sciences and the Arts,* in which he argued that, rather than elevating humanity, science and art had corrupted it.

Rousseau is one of the great political philosophers. He believed that the life of man in the state of nature was not, as Hobbes (see page 96) maintained, brutish and unpleasant. In the *Discourse on Inequality,* Rousseau stresses the superior value of the 'nascent society' we inhabited after the state of nature but before we fully developed a political state. It is, he supposes, the state that enslaves and corrupts us. But, given the *right sort* of state, our freedom can be regained.

Rousseau was unafraid to speak his mind in an age when to do so could be dangerous. His views regularly outraged the powerful. He repeatedly risked prosecution and many of his books were banned. He never fully recovered from a paranoid breakdown that he suffered in the late 1760s. He died in Ermenonville, France, in 1778.

Major works

The Social Contract

Émile

Discourse on the Origin of Inequality

Immanuel Kant

1724–1804

Moral philosophy

*'Two things fill the mind with ever-increasing
wonder and awe … the starry heavens above me
and the moral law within me.'*

According to some philosophers, such as Hume, morality is ultimately rooted in our *sentiments*. Reason has little, if anything, to do with right and wrong. Kant, by contrast, says that how we feel is morally irrelevant – what matters is that we do our moral duty, which *reason alone* can establish. It is the particular way in which Kant believes morality is rooted in reason that we explore here.

Intention

According to Kant, what matters about an action, so far as its moral worth is concerned, is the *intention* with which it is performed. The outcome is irrelevant.

That has some plausibility. Suppose that I believe my moral duty is to help those less fortunate than myself. I buy food and distribute it to the poor. Unfortunately, through no fault of my own, the food I distribute is contaminated, and several malnourished children die. I feel pretty awful about this. But am I morally to blame? Intuitively not. My *intention* was good. So my action was not blameworthy, even though the consequences of my action turned out to be tragic.

Here's another illustration. Suppose I mean to kill a rich uncle by pushing him under a bus. My intention is terrible. However, in a bizarre twist of fate, I misjudge the deed and merely knock him sideways, which blocks the path of a runaway pram that was about to run under the bus. So, as a result of my action, a child's life is saved. Was my action morally worthy? Of course not. Again, it is not the *consequences* of what I did that matter, morally speaking. It is my *intention* that matters. My *intention* was to benefit from committing a murder. So what I did remains very wrong indeed.

Kant concurs with these common sense judgements. He insists that what really matters, morally speaking, is the *intention* with which an action is performed. The consequences are always irrelevant.

But what is the right intention? To do our moral duty, says Kant. But how can we determine what that is? It is here that reason enters the picture.

The maxim

According to Kant, whenever we perform an action, we are guided by one or more principles. He calls these principles *maxims.* A greedy person might act on the maxim, 'Always act to maximize your wealth', while a hedonist might be guided by the maxim, 'Always act to increase your happiness'. In each case, the maxim gives our *reason* for acting.

Kant believes that, as rational agents, we have certain moral duties, duties forced on us by reason alone. These duties are *categorical* rather than hypothetical. They apply independently of whatever consequences might follow from the action.

What does Kant mean when he says that moral duties are categorical?

The categorical imperative

Let's begin with hypothetical imperatives. A *hypothetical* imperative tells you what to do if you want to achieve a certain goal. It says:

If you want to achieve P, do A.

For example, you might act on the maxims, 'If you want to avoid going to prison, don't murder anyone', or, 'If you want people to trust you, don't lie.'

Whether or not we should act on such hypothetical imperatives depends on what we desire. If I really don't care whether I end up in prison or whether people trust me, these maxims don't give me any reason not to murder or lie.

A *categorical* imperative, by contrast, does not say, 'If you want to achieve P, do A.' It simply says, 'Do A.' According to

Kant, genuinely *moral* principles have this categorical character. Our moral duty is: don't steal, *period*. It's not: don't steal *if you don't want to get caught.*

So genuinely *moral* imperatives tell us what we should do *irrespective of what outcome or consequences we might desire.*

The test of universalizability

According to Kant, we can establish what our moral duty is by testing our maxims against one basic categorical imperative:

> *Act only according to maxims which you can will also to be universal laws.*

In other words, for an action to be moral, the underlying principle on which you act must be *universalizable*: it must be a maxim that everyone can adopt.

Let's look at a specific example. Take the maxim, 'Always steal when you can't afford what you want.' This maxim fails Kant's test of universalizability. If everyone just took whatever they wanted but could not afford, the very idea of ownership would quickly break down. We could no longer describe anyone as owning anything any more. But if no one owns anything, then the possibility of stealing no longer exists. So it is not possible for everyone to act on this maxim.

Here's another example: 'Always lie.' If everyone lied all the time, there would be no point in lying, because no one would believe what you said. Lying only works if people are generally fairly honest. So, again, the maxim, 'Always lie', fails the test of universalizability.

By contrast, 'Always tell the truth' passes the test. This is a maxim on which we *can* all act.

There is great plausibility to the test of universalizability. Surely any genuinely moral principle won't just apply to one particular person or group of people. It will apply to *everyone equally*.

Means and ends

This brings us to Kant's second key moral principle:

> *Act in such a way that you always treat humanity, whether in yourself or in another, never simply as a means, but always at the same time as an end.*

It is of course morally acceptable to treat many things purely as means to an end. There's nothing morally wrong with my using a hammer to bang in a nail. However, according to Kant, there is something wrong with using a *human being* purely as a means to an end. Why?

In Kant's view, human beings are unique in that only they are both rational and free. It is this that makes them moral beings. A robot is not free, because everything it does is determined physically. If a robot is programmed in such a way that it ends up killing someone, the robot can't be held morally responsible. Being a mere robot, it couldn't do otherwise. Because it has no freedom, it can't be held morally accountable for what it does.

Human beings, by contrast, are free. Being rational, they also know what their moral duty is. That is precisely why they are genuinely moral agents, and why they can be held morally responsible for what they do.

According to Kant, being rational and free moral agents, *human beings deserve a special sort of respect.* Of course, Kant isn't suggesting we never use others as means to an end. You would certainly use a plumber to fix your central heating and a doctor to treat your sick child. Kant doesn't object to 'using' people in this way. But he does believe it wrong to use someone *purely* as a means to an end.

To illustrate Kant's view, suppose your son is very ill and will soon die if he is not treated immediately. However, his treatment will have to be paid for, and you have no money. You know you won't have any money in the near future either. You might now do either of the following:

1. Go to the doctor and *lie*, saying that you will pay for the treatment and drugs next week (even though you know you still won't be able to pay then).

2. Go to the doctor and be honest; explain your situation to her, hoping she will be generous and treat your child for free.

Which course of action is morally acceptable, according to

Kant? True, both involve 'using' the doctor to get what you need. But Kant would consider only the first option to be morally wrong. This is because only the first option involves using the doctor *purely* as a means to an end.

By following the first course of action and tricking the doctor, you use her entirely instrumentally – you treat her as a mere thing, as a tool to get what you want, much as you might use a screwdriver or hammer. By being honest and explaining your situation, on the other hand, you respect the doctor as a free and rational agent. You allow her to make a free decision about whether or not to help you. So you do not violate Kant's principle.

Three criticisms of Kant's moral theory

To sum up: Kant's view is that *reason alone can determine what is morally right and wrong*. By relying on nothing more than our own rationality, we can establish two key moral principles – the principle of universalizability and the principle concerning means and ends. These principles in turn allow us to figure out which maxims it is our moral duty to follow. The principles allow us to determine that it is always wrong to steal and lie, for example, irrespective of the consequences.

Now we turn to three of the best-known criticisms of Kant's moral theory:

1. *Allows no exceptions to moral rules.* One of the most striking features of Kant's moral philosophy is that there are *no*

exceptions to the moral rules we should follow, including the rules about not lying and stealing. But is this plausible? Surely there are at least *some* exceptions to the rule 'Do not lie.' Suppose that a maniac breaks into your house bent on killing your children and demands to know where they are hidden. Surely it wouldn't be wrong to lie under such circumstances. After all, the consequences of not lying are obviously going to be horrific.

Kant considers exactly this sort of case, yet is adamant that you should still not lie. True, you may believe that the consequences of not lying will be horrible. But remember, says Kant, the *consequences* of an action are morally irrelevant. All that matters is that you do your moral duty. And your moral duty is not to lie.

This is a pretty unpalatable consequence of Kant's moral philosophy. Isn't it obvious that there are circumstances in which it would be morally acceptable to lie? Isn't it also obvious that, at least in some circumstances, the consequences of an action *can* be morally very relevant indeed?

2. *Conflicting duties.* A second difficulty with Kant's theory concerns *conflicting* moral duties. For example, it may be that you have a moral duty not to lie, but also a moral duty not to allow an innocent person to be murdered. In certain circumstances you will not be able to fulfil both duties. In the case of the maniac breaking in and demanding to know where your children are hidden, you may have no choice but to fulfil one duty at the expense of the other. Unfortunately, Kant does not tell us how to resolve such conflicts. That is a major omission.

3. *Irrelevance of feeling.* A third worry raised about Kant's moral philosophy is that it downplays feeling and emotion rather *too* much. Perhaps morality is not *entirely* rooted in our sentiments, as some philosophers have suggested. But that is not to say, as Kant does, that the feelings and emotions we experience are entirely morally irrelevant.

Kant is clear that, if we act solely out of, say, a feeling of compassion, *we are not acting morally.* But is this true? Suppose a hospital patient has two visitors. Each visitor arrives every day, bringing flowers, fruit and gifts. Each does their best to lift the patient's spirits.

One of the visitors, Sally, visits out of sympathy for the patient. She can imagine how the poor patient must feel. Her heart goes out to him. She wants to relieve his suffering and make him happier – these feelings motivate her behaviour.

The other visitor, Sue, has a rather different motive. She is a strangely cold fish. She visits, not because she feels for the patient and wants to reduce his suffering – she doesn't – but simply because she thinks it is her moral duty to do so. She believes reason dictates that she should behave in this way – so that is what she does.

Which of the two visitors' behaviour is of greater moral

worth, would you say? Most of us would consider Sally's behaviour morally rather more admirable. Certainly, it is not *less* admirable, is it?

Yet Kant would insist that *Sally is acting wholly amorally*. Her behaviour has no moral worth at all:

> *There are many persons ... so sympathetically constituted that without any motive of vanity or selfishness they find an inner satisfaction in spreading joy, and rejoice in the contentment of others, which they have made possible. But I say, however dutiful and amiable it may be, that kind of action has no true moral worth.*

In Kant's view, only Sue does the right thing for the right reason. Again, this is counter-intuitive, to say the least. Morality may not be *wholly* a matter of emotion. However, isn't the suggestion that morality has *nothing* to do with emotion equally implausible?

Biography

Born into poverty in 1724, in Königsberg, East Prussia (now Kaliningrad, Russia), Kant studied, tutored and finally became Professor of Logic and Metaphysics at the University of Königsberg. He taught geography, anthropology, physics and philosophy. The vivacity and originality of Kant's philosophy was not reflected in his daily life – he never wandered more than 80 km from his hometown and his routine was unremittingly like clockwork. It is said that people even set their watches by him.

Some of Kant's most important work lies in metaphysics and epistemology. Kant rejects Hume's empiricist claim (see page 158) that all concepts are derived from experience, such as our concept of causation having to be drawn from sense experience. Kant maintains that the concept of causation is logically prior to and involved in the ordering of experience, so rendering it capable of being thought about or understood in the first place. In Kant's view, thinking of the world as structured in terms of space, time, causation and substance is a necessary condition of our acquiring any experiential knowledge of it. However, while Kant thought that these concepts unavoidably structured our experience, as a result allowing us to have empirical knowledge of the *phenomenal* world (the world-as-experienced), he maintained that we could draw no conclusions concerning what the world-as-it-is *in itself* (what Kant calls the *noumenal* world) is like. Kant died in Königsberg in 1804.

Major works

Critique of Pure Reason

Critique of Practical Reason

Prolegomena to Any Future Metaphysics

Jeremy Bentham

1748–1832

Utilitarianism

*'…the greatest happiness of the greatest number is
the foundation of morals and legislation.'*

Bentham is best known as one of the founding fathers of an
ethical system called *utilitarianism*. Utilitarianism is one form
of a broader theory called *consequentialism*, which says that the
extent to which an action is morally right or wrong is determined by its *consequences alone.* Nothing else matters.

Supposing we agree that it is just the consequences of an action that matter, morally speaking, what consequences should
we aim to achieve? The answer, according to utilitarianism, is
happiness. Bentham argues we should act in order to *maximize
pleasure and minimize pain*:

> Nature has placed mankind under the governance of two
> sovereign masters, pain and pleasure. It is for them alone to
> point out what we ought to do…

Of course, utilitarianism is not the selfish view that it is just your own happiness that matters. Everyone's happiness is to count equally. Our aim, according to Bentham, should be to promote *the greatest happiness of the greatest number.* As Bentham himself put it, 'the greatest happiness of the greatest number is the foundation of morals and legislation.'

How might Bentham's theory be applied in practice? Take for example, the moral dilemma: should you steal food if that is the only way you can feed your family? A simple utilitarian approach to this question would be to calculate, as best we can, what the consequences of stealing or not stealing are likely to be. If you steal to feed your family, that will make you and them happier, at least in the short term. But the theft will result in the unhappiness of the shopkeeper from whom you steal. His unhappiness must be included in the calculation too.

Bentham developed a *felicific calculus* for this purpose – something akin to a formula for determining what the morally right course of action is in any given circumstance. He believes that it is not which particular pleasures and pains we suffer that matter, but their *intensity* and *duration.* A long and intense pleasure counts for more than one that is short and feeble.

The felicific calculus

According to Bentham, the hedonistic value of an action – the sum total of pleasure it brings about – is calculated by taking into account:

- how *intensely* the pleasure/pain is felt
- how *long* that pleasure/pain lasts
- how *certainly* the pleasure/pain is to follow the action
- how *quickly* the pleasure/pain will follow
- how *likely* the pleasure/pain is to be followed by experiences of the same kind
- how *likely* the pleasure/pain is to be followed by experiences of the opposite kind
- how *many* people experience it

The utilitarian radical

Utilitarianism possesses a number of radical features. What people found particularly shocking about utilitarianism in Bentham's day was the way in which it gives God no role at all in determining what is right and wrong. Many believed, as many still do today, that morality is ultimately about following God's laws: about conforming to a system of rules handed down from on high. Many suppose that those who follow God's commands can then look forward to happiness in the next world. The utilitarian rejects this traditional religious view of morality. For the utilitarian, all that matters, morally speaking, is enhancing happiness in *this* world. For many religious people, such a view is shocking and beyond the pale.

Utilitarianism led Bentham and many of his fellow utilitarians towards *legal and social reform*. Many of the laws, customs and institutions of Bentham's time were clearly a cause of great misery to many people. Utilitarianism suggests not just that it is desirable to alleviate such suffering where we can, but that it is actually a *moral requirement*. Bentham felt this moral obligation acutely, and acted upon it.

Animal rights

Bentham was one of the earliest thinkers to suggest that animals have rights too. If what matters, morally speaking, is pleasure and pain, then, because animals also experience pleasure and pain, so they too are deserving of moral consideration.

Many philosophers had previously deemed animals to be of little if any moral significance because, it was supposed, they lack the faculty of reason. Both Descartes (see page 104) and Kant (see page 177), take this view, for example. But Bentham disagrees. It is the ability to suffer, not the ability to reason, that matters:

The question is not, Can they reason?, nor Can they talk? but, Can they suffer?

After all, if reason were the criterion distinguishing those due moral consideration from those who are not, then we would have to exclude babies and the seriously mentally impaired from moral consideration. Yet babies and the mentally impaired surely are deserving of very great moral consideration. So why not animals?

Bentham believed, 'the day may come when the rest of the animal creation may acquire those rights which never could have been witholden from them but by the hand of tyranny.'

More recently, the philosopher Peter Singer (see page 361) has developed this utilitarian stance towards animals in a very sophisticated way.

The pleasure machine

Utilitarianism has been criticized in a variety of ways. Here we will look at just one classic criticism (for two more, see John Stuart Mill, page 205).

Utilitarianism insists that happiness is what we ought to aim for. But is happiness what we do, or should, value most?

The following thought-experiment has been used to test the suggestion that happiness alone is what ultimately matters. Suppose a new machine is built – the pleasure machine. This device can replicate perfectly any experience you like. Do you want to know what it is like to climb Mount Everest, to converse with Aristotle, or to enjoy a romantic evening with a supermodel? The pleasure machine can show you. Just strap on the helmet, and a vast supercomputer will stimulate your brain in order to induce any experience you desire.

Many of us would relish the opportunity of trying out the pleasure machine for a day or two. But what if you were given the option of permanently immersing yourself in its virtual world? Your experiences would be carefully managed by the machine so that you enjoyed the most intense pleasures possible for the rest of your life. Would you take up the offer of being *permanently* attached to the machine?

Surely, most of us would refuse. We value pleasure, but not

above everything. We don't just want to live a life filled with pleasure. We want other things too. We want *real* achievements. We want to forge *real* relationships. To live out your life in an endlessly pleasurable computer-generated world would surely amount to a life sadly wasted (though it might appeal to some). Most of us want to live lives that are authentic. Even if we knew the machine could convince us that what we were experiencing was real, so that we would *think* we were living lives that are authentic, that still wouldn't be enough to convince us to plug ourselves into the pleasure machine forever.

In fact, wouldn't there be something *immoral* about trapping some unwitting subject inside such a virtual world in order to maximize their happiness?

But if that is true, then isn't Bentham wrong to suppose that maximizing happiness is ultimately *all* that matters, morally speaking? We can agree that happiness is important without conceding that it is the *only* thing of importance.

Biography

Born in 1748, in Spitalfields, London, Jeremy Bentham was brought up in a wealthy family and educated at Westminster School and Queen's College, Oxford. Although Bentham trained as a lawyer, he never went on to practise, devoting himself instead to writing on moral and political philosophy. Oddly, Bentham attempted to publish little during his life – most of his work appeared posthumously.

He was a great advocate of legal and social reform and was

considered very radical for his day owing to his criticism of many legal and political institutions. He was also particularly critical of the determination to adhere to the traditions of the legal system propounded by Sir William Blackstone, the most famous legal mind of his generation. The leaders of the French Revolution made him an honorary citizen in 1792 in recognition of his advanced theories on reform. Bentham's design for a panopticon – a type of prison in which all prisoners could be viewed by guards at all times, without the prisoners knowing whether they were observed or not – was to greatly influence prison design.

Something of an eccentric, Bentham requested that his body be preserved and displayed in a glass-fronted cabinet at University College London. The body is, on occasion, taken to meetings of the College Council, where he is recorded as attending but not voting. He died in London in 1832.

Major works

Introduction to the Principles of Morals and Legislation

Georg Hegel

1770–1831

The philosophy of history

'The history of the world is none other than the progress of the consciousness of freedom.'

Hegel is a philosopher of history. Few other philosophers have had much interest in developing such a philosophy, so why does Hegel consider it important?

Generally, philosophers are particularly focused on ideas and concepts. Plato (see page 27), for example, believes the task of the philosopher is to try to arrive at knowledge of ideas. But he thinks of ideas as timeless and changeless entities – the forms – residing on some mysterious and separate plane of existence.

Hegel, by contrast, insists that our particular ideas and ways of thinking are far from inevitable. They are very much historically conditioned and constituted – a product of their time. If this is correct it becomes clearer why a historical understanding of why we have these particular ideas might provide valuable philosophical insights.

The rise of individual consciousness

Hegel's key idea is that history is never static, but always moving forward in a particular direction. This constant change is driven by an engine – the 'dialectical process'.

In order to understand how the dialectic works, let's look at a specific example of the process in action. In Kant's day, reason and desire tended to be viewed as being in conflict. Kant (see page 102), for example, sees us as being eternally torn between our animal and rational natures.

Hegel argues that this conflict, which Kant views as an essential feature of humanity, is actually far from inevitable. In ancient Greece, reason and desire were more harmonious – Greek citizens were not conscious of any conflict between the two. So what or who, according to Hegel, was responsible for bringing about a change?

Hegel's answer is Socrates. Socrates began to ask probing questions of his fellow Athenians. He encouraged them to question and reflect. As a result, they began to recognize that they, *as individuals,* could make judgements about right and wrong, independently of the Athenian state. He also began to make them see that the accepted collective wisdom about right and wrong was untenable. As a result of Socrates's questioning, they began to develop an *individual conscience* – a conscience that had, until that point, been absent.

Previously, the Athenians had felt so closely bound to their state that the possibility of making an individual judgement simply did not occur to them. Now they began to see themselves as individuals with a duty to make independent judgements. This development of individual conscience resulted in the unravelling of the Greek state by undermining the naive harmony on which it had formerly depended.

The seeds of rational individualism sown by Socrates finally blossomed, according to Hegel, during the Protestant Reformation and the Enlightenment. The stress was on building a rational society, the reasonableness of which could be recognized by everyone.

Hegel considers this emphasis on reason important. But in revolutionary France, reason was misunderstood as something wholly abstract, to be imposed on reality, resulting in the Reign of Terror. Hegel argues that the revolutionaries overlooked that reason cannot simply be forced on a society without any thought to its character or the way individuals have been formed within it. Armed with this insight, we are now in a position to create a more rational and harmonious society in which we can all be genuinely free.

The unfolding dialectic

The historical transformation outlined above exhibits Hegel's dialectical engine of history at work. According to Hegel, history is essentially cyclical – at each stage internal contradictions and conflicts are resolved to produce a new, higher form of society.

In the example above, we begin with a harmonious Greek society, but one that is inherently unstable, containing the seeds of its own destruction in the form of Socrates's probing questions. However, within the society to which these new ideas give birth, there is also instability, producing yet more conflict: the bloody tyranny of 'reason' that was to emerge in the French Revolution. Resolution of this conflict comes through a synthesis of harmony and individual conscience.

Hegel believes that this kind of dialectical unfolding at the level of ideas is the engine that fundamentally drives all social, economic and political change.

Geist

What is it that Hegel supposes undergoes this dialectical process? His answer is *Geist*, which is perhaps best translated as 'mind' or 'spirit'. *Geist* is the ultimate reality. It is not the mind of an individual – such as your particular human mind, or mine. Nor is it the sum of such individual minds. Rather, it is a sort of overarching mind of which everything that exists is a manifestation.

Where are we going?

So, reality consists in the cycle of change in *Geist*. But where is the process headed? Towards greater freedom and greater knowledge, says Hegel. History involves the overcoming of various one-sided conceptions of who we are as we move towards greater – and, ultimately, total – freedom. Finally, *Geist* arrives at what Hegel calls *absolute knowledge* – the knowledge that

Geist is reality and that history is the unfolding of its own inherent rationality.

Hegel, not immodestly, believes that his own philosophy thus represents the ultimate culmination of history.

Biography

Georg Hegel was born in Stuttgart, Württemberg (now in Germany) in 1770. Although Hegel originally had ambitions to become a cleric and entered a seminary, he chose an academic career, studying philosophy, and eventually became the foremost German philosopher of his day. He has acquired a reputation for being a 'difficult' thinker. His work forms a unified whole that can make it hard for the lay person to access, with a writing style that can at times be both opaque and somewhat pretentious. Yet some of Hegel's key ideas are fairly simple to grasp, in essence. They have also proved extraordinarily influential, particularly as adapted by Karl Marx. Hegel died in Berlin, Prussia (now Germany), in 1831.

Major works

Phenomenology of Spirit
Philosophy of Right
Science of Logic

Arthur Schopenhauer

1788–1860

The world as will

'My body is the only object of which I know not merely from one side, that of representation, but also the other, that is called will.'

Schopenhauer's great work *The World as Will and Representation* was published in 1818, when he was 30. In it Schopenhauer argues that the underlying nature of reality is horrific. Perhaps the easiest route into Schopenhauer's philosophy is to begin with Kant, whose philosophy Schopenhauer develops.

Kant (see page 177) makes a distinction between the world as we experience it and the world as it actually is in itself. The former, he calls the *phenomenal world* and the latter the *noumenal world*.

Here's an analogy. Suppose a fisherman repeatedly casts his net into the sea and discovers that all the fish he has caught are more than five centimetres wide. The man concludes that the sea must contain few, if any, fish less than five centimetres wide. Is he justified in drawing that conclusion? No, not if his net has

ARTHUR SCHOPENHAUER

a five-centimetre mesh. The fact that his fish are all more than five centimetres wide is explained, not by any fact about the sea, but by the character of his net. In Kant's view, when we think about and experience the world, we do so through our mental and sensory faculties. Drawing an analogy, we might say that these faculties constitute the 'net' that we cast into the world. These faculties are not wholly passive. Just like the fisherman's net, they impose an order on what we 'capture', *structuring the phenomenal world in terms of time, space and causality.*

The noumenal world is the 'sea' into which we cast our 'net'. It is the world as it is in itself, as it exists independently of our minds. According to Kant, the noumenal world is unknowable. We can know that it exists. But we cannot know anything positive about it.

Schopenhauer accepts Kant's basic division of the world into the phenomenal and noumenal. However, unlike Kant, Schopenhauer is less sceptical about our ability to know anything positive of the world as it is in itself. Schopenhauer thinks that we possess at least some clues to the underlying nature of reality.

No noumenal 'things'

Schopenhauer takes Kant's basic metaphysical framework, but he thinks through its consequences in an interesting way.

He notes that we can only conceive of concrete particular things – such as *this* cup or *that* dog – in so far as we think of them as located in time or space or both (for more on particulars, see Aristotle, page 38). But time and space are merely part of our 'net'. Once time and space are removed, so too is any possibility of there being such particulars. As, according to Kant, the noumenal world is a world without time or space, it seems to follow, therefore, that *it is a world lacking particular things.*

So, Kant is wrong to think of the noumenal as things as they are in themselves. There can be no 'things' in the noumenal world. The noumenal is without parts – it is an undifferentiated 'something'.

Nor, adds Schopenhauer, should we think of this undifferentiated something as the *cause* of the world as we experience it. For of course, if Kant is correct, causation is a concept that applies only *within* the phenomenal world.

It might be more accurate to say that, for Schopenhauer, the noumenal world is not the remote cause of our experiences, but the 'inside' of the world as it appears to us. He believes the world has an inner core or nature that is hidden from our senses.

The world as will

What is this core like? Schopenhauer thinks our own bodies provide a clue. I can observe my body from the outside, such as when I look at my outstretched hand. But I am also aware of my body from the inside. I am aware of moving it, for example. Here I have access to an object other than via my five senses. This subjective awareness of my own body gives me a glimpse of reality *unmediated by these sensory faculties.*

What, according to Schopenhauer, does this glimpse reveal? That the world as it is in itself is the *world as will.* When we experience the movement of our bodies from the inside, as it were, we experience them as willed. And this, thinks Schopenhauer, is *true of the world in general.* The world has two aspects: an outer aspect, revealed to our senses, and an inner aspect, the world as will. So, for Schopenhauer, at its deepest level the world is a sort of vast, undifferentiated cosmic will – a kind of ceaseless striving for life and existence. When Schopenhauer says that the world is will, he does not mean that this underlying willing and striving is conscious and intentional. It is more a kind of blind, undirected energy.

According to Schopenhauer, the phenomenal world we see around us is a manifestation of this underlying reality. Even an inanimate rock is a manifestation of will. Schopenhauer does not view this underlying reality as something positive. The world as will is horrific. When we look around us, we see appalling suffering and torment caused by the ceaseless striving of man and, of course, nature.

How much of Schopenhauer's philosophy is true? He is certainly working close to the very limits of the knowable. Kant would of course insist that Schopenhauer has wandered beyond them.

Biography

Born 1788, in Danzig (now Gdansk, Poland), into a wealthy

merchant family, Schopenhauer was educated for a life of business, not academia, but he had no interest in the world of commerce, and insisted on going to university, using independent means to support a life of study.

In 1820, Schopenhauer began teaching philosophy at Berlin University. He deliberately scheduled a series of his own lectures to coincide with those of Hegel (see page 195), of whom Schopenhauer was fiercely critical. When only five students turned up, Schopenhauer left the university, never to teach again. In 1831 a cholera epidemic broke out in Berlin and Schopenhauer fled, settling permanently in Frankfurt in 1833, where he subsequently worked and lived alone. Schopenhauer is one of the first major Western philosophers to be openly atheist. He is also unusual in being clearly influenced by Eastern philosophers, including the Buddha (see page 1). He died in 1860, in Frankfurt-on-Main.

Major works

The World as Will and Representation

On the Fourfold Root of the Principle of Sufficient
Reason

John Stuart Mill

1806–73

Utilitarianism

'It is better to be a human being dissatisfied than a pig satisfied; better to be Socrates dissatisfied than a fool satisfied. And if the fool, or the pig, is of a different opinion, it is because they only know their own side of the question.'

Mill, like Bentham, embraces the moral philosophy known as *utilitarianism*, which asserts that all that matters, morally speaking, are the *consequences* of our actions – the degree to which they increase or decrease *happiness*. The obvious contrast with Mill, here, is Kant, who insists that the consequences of our actions are morally irrelevant (see page 103).

The attractions of utilitarianism

In many respects utilitarianism is an attractive theory. One of its advantages is that it dispenses with the need to introduce any sort of supernatural being or dimension to the universe in order to accommodate morality (which immediately introduces such difficult questions as: Does this supernatural dimension even exist, and, if it does, how are we to gain knowledge of it?). According to the utilitarian, in order to evaluate the extent to which something is morally right or wrong, we need not focus on anything other than what takes place in the *natural* world.

Another attractive feature of utilitarianism is that it is *impartial* – it says that everyone's happiness counts equally. It doesn't matter who, or indeed, what you are. I say 'what', because many utilitarians agree that the pleasure and pain experienced by animals should be taken into account as well – see also Bentham (page 188) and Singer (page 361).

Mill on higher and lower pleasures

Mill's version of utilitarianism differs from Bentham's in at least two important respects. The first is that, unlike Bentham, Mill makes a distinction between higher and lower pleasures.

Bentham distinguishes between pleasures in terms of their *quantity* – their duration and strength – but he makes no distinction when it comes to their *quality*. According to Bentham, when it comes to calculating the right course of action, the satisfaction one person gains from eating caviar, listening to Mozart and reading Proust should not count any more or less than the pleasure another derives from eating chocolate, listening to pop music and reading trashy magazines. All that matters is the duration and intensity of the pleasures produced. Mill, on the other hand, believes that the more cerebral pleasures – those of thought, feeling and imagination – should be given greater weight than those of the body and senses.

Some might criticize this appeal to higher and lower pleasures on the grounds that it is unjustifiably elitist. After all, many people – probably the majority – prefer the 'lower' pleasures to the 'higher'. Why should we consider their judgement, about which pleasures are best, any less reliable? Surely, a critic might insist, the pleasure that the aesthete gets from watching Shakespeare is really no 'better' than the pleasure a teenager derives from watching cartoons. Those who suppose otherwise are, in truth, simply snobs.

Mill on competent judges

Mill is ready for this objection, however. He points out that yes, many people prefer the lower pleasures to the higher. But these people are not *competent judges*, since they have not usually been given the chance to acquire a taste for the higher pleasures. Only those who have properly experienced both sorts of pleasure are in a position to judge which one is the better. And the fact is, says Mill, that *those who have experienced both tend to prefer the higher.*

But is this true? It is true that those who have been given the opportunity to enjoy both sorts of pleasure typically *say* they prefer the higher. But perhaps this is just because they want to convince others, and perhaps themselves, that their tastes are rather more sophisticated than those of the common rabble. Certainly, when they think no one is looking a significant number of these competent judges turn out to be as eager to overindulge their taste for the 'lower' pleasures as everyone else.

And certainly, most of us find abhorrent the suggestion that, faced with having to choose between saving the life of two people, the right life to save, other things being equal, is that of the person with more 'sophisticated' tastes. Yet that seems to be a consequence of Mill's theory.

Some basic criticisms of utilitarianism

Utilitarianism, as formulated here, faces a number of well-known objections and counter-examples. Two classic examples are explained below.

What these two illustrated cases bring out, it's suggested, is that the right course of action is not always to maximize happiness. Indeed, it's claimed that what such cases demonstrate is that human beings have certain fundamental rights, including a right to life and a right to justice, and that these rights ought not to be trampled upon, whatever the consequences.

Two classic counter-examples

Transplant case Suppose you're the doctor in charge of six patients. The first has a minor medical condition that is easily cured. The others have failing organs and will soon die without transplants. No replacement organs are available. But then you discover that the first patient could provide perfect donor organs for the

208

others. So you can kill the first patient and save the rest. Or you can cure the first and watch the rest die. Which is the right course of action, morally speaking?

A simple utilitarian calculation suggests that you should kill one patient to save the rest. After all, this action would result in five happy patients and only one set of grieving relatives rather than one happy patient and five sets of grieving relatives. Yet the killing of one patient to save the rest strikes most of us as very wrong indeed.

Frame the innocent case Suppose a black person kills a white person in an area torn by racial strife. As a result there are daily riots and escalating levels of violence leading to increasing levels of unhappiness. As a visitor to the area, you know you could secure the arrest of an innocent black person for the original crime simply by testifying against him. The riots would immediately cease and further bloodshed would be avoided – a much happier outcome. A utilitarian calculation suggests that morally the right thing to do is to frame an innocent black person. But surely that would be very wrong indeed, whatever the consequences might be for happiness overall?

Act and rule utilitarianism

Some utilitarians attempt to deal with these kinds of case by distinguishing between act and rule utilitarianism:

Act utilitarianism. Each *action* should be judged solely on its ability to produce the greatest happiness.

Rule utilitarianism. We should follow those *rules* that will produce the greatest happiness.

A rule utilitarian might say that 'Do not kill the innocent' and 'Do not punish the innocent' are rules that increase happiness *overall*. So we should always follow these rules, even on those rare occasions (such as the transplant case) when following them does reduce happiness.

So there are versions of utilitarianism that can deal with this type of counter-example.

Mill's version of rule utilitarianism

This brings us to the second way in which Mill's version of utilitarianism differs from that of Bentham. Bentham is an *act* utilitarian. He believes the rightness or wrongness of a course of action should be calculated individually. Mill, on the other hand, supposes that we should be *rule* utilitarians *except where we face a dilemma generated by two rules.* So, for example, Mill might say that 'Do not steal' and 'Do not allow people to starve' are rules that will generally produce greater happiness.

So they are the rules that we should generally follow. Indeed, they are the rules that we should follow even in those cases where, as a matter of fact, happiness is not increased.

However, there are a few cases where these rules give

conflicting verdicts. If I can feed a starving person only by stealing food for them, I must break one or other of these two rules. I must either allow someone to starve, or I must steal.

Under these special circumstances, says Mill, when the rules do not determine the right course of action, I must revert to *act* utilitarianism and judge the case solely on the basis of what will produce the happiest outcome in this *particular* situation.

Jim and the Indians

One of the most interesting objections against utilitarianism is raised by the following thought-experiment devised by the philosopher Bernard Williams.

> Suppose Jim finds himself in the square of a small South American town. Before him are 20 captive Indians in front of a few armed men in uniform. The captain explains to Jim that the Indians are protesters about to be killed as an example to others. As Jim is an honoured visitor from another land, the captain offers Jim the privilege of killing one of the Indians himself. If Jim accepts, then as a special mark of the occasion, the other 19 Indians will be freed. If Jim refuses, then all 20 will be shot. Jim knows there is no possibility of him rescuing the Indians. And the other villagers are begging him to accept the offer. What should Jim do?

A utilitarian calculation suggests that the right course of action is for Jim to accept the offer and save 19 lives by taking one. This will produce the happiest outcome.

But Williams suggests that, while accepting the offer and shooting an Indian might be the happiest outcome, it is far from obvious that it is *automatically* the right course of action for Jim to take.

Williams insists that there is also an issue of *personal integrity* at stake here. To suppose that, if Jim feels he ought to refuse the offer, despite the consequences, would simply be squeamishness on his part, is to overlook something important. Williams suggests that such feelings are intrinsic to our sense of ourselves as moral beings. For Jim to disregard all such feelings entirely and act simply on the basis of a cold calculation as to what would result in the greatest happiness of the greatest number would be for Jim to lose any sense of his own moral identity and integrity. It is certainly not *obvious*, suggests Williams, that Jim should simply cast his moral integrity aside in this way, as the utilitarian recommends.

Biography

Born 1806, in London, Mill's father, James, was a radical Scottish thinker who moved to London and worked to promote the utilitarian philosophy of Jeremy Bentham. James educated his eldest son John in accordance with the psychological and educational principles developed by Bentham. Whether or not as a result of this, John developed prodigiously. He was taught the Greek alphabet at the age of three, and had read most of the classic Greek and Latin texts in the original language by the time he was 14. Like his father, John also rose through the ranks of the East India Company to become its chief administrator.

At the age of 21, Mill experienced a bout of intense depression. He believed that this was due to the suppression of feelings that he had experienced during childhood under the cold, disciplined tutelage of his father. Mill found comfort in the poetry of William Wordsworth, but after about a year, the cloud lifted and his capacity for emotion returned.

In 1851, Mill married Harriet Taylor. They had been close friends for 21 years, and married two years after the death of her first husband. Taylor was a brilliant thinker in her own right and an important influence on Mill, as he himself emphasized. Unfortunately, Harriet died just seven years later.

Mill became an independent Member of Parliament in 1865, though only for a single term. A prominent political figure of his day, his influence was significant. Mill was the first person in Parliament to call for women to be given the right to vote.

Although now best known for his work on liberty and utilitarianism, Mill also worked in logic, the philosophy of science, metaphysics and epistemology. He died in Avignon, France, in 1873.

Major works
Principles of Political Economy
System of Logic
On Liberty
Utilitarianism

Søren Kierkegaard

1813–55

Abraham: the knight of faith

'Faith is the highest passion in a human being.
Many in every generation may not come that far,
but none comes further.'

Kierkegaard's book *Fear and Trembling* is a fascinating, and to my mind rather disturbing, account of what Kierkegaard considered to be authentic Christian faith, as opposed to the diluted 'Sunday Christianity' that he thought most of his contemporaries professed.

Kierkegaard pointed out that most people who describe themselves as Christians are born into their faith, and that their involvement extends little beyond attending church on a Sunday. He thought that Danish Christians were churned out by the Danish state church 'with the greatest possible uniformity of a factory product', and this, according to him, is not true faith.

Nor is the *true* Christian one who rationally recognizes the truth of religious claims, in the way that many Christian philosophers, including Aquinas (see page 65), have thought possible. Faith is certainly not a sort of second-rate form of belief for those not sufficiently clever and well educated to recognize the proofs of God's existence (as Averroës supposed, see page 62). True faith is not inferior to, but is higher than, reason.

An authentic Christian faith, thinks Kierkegaard, involves making a deeply passionate and personal commitment to accept divine authority above all else. It involves making a fearful, life-transforming leap beyond what is reasonable and rational to accept what is profoundly paradoxical. It is a leap that must be made, not once, but repeatedly.

Abraham and Isaac

In *Fear and Trembling,* Kierkegaard writes under the pseudonym Johannes de Silentio (John of Silence) about God's commandment to Abraham to sacrifice his own son. God says, 'Take your son, your only son Isaac, whom you love, and go to the land of Moriah, and offer him there as a burnt offering upon one of the mountains I shall tell you of.' Abraham obeys. An angel appears only at the very last moment – when the knife is in Abraham's hand – to revoke God's instruction.

Kant thought Abraham wrong to follow the instruction of a voice in his head that commanded him to do something profoundly immoral – to kill an innocent child. Kierkegaard, on the other hand, considers Abraham's faith a rare example of authentic Judeo-Christian faith. The true Christian is one who realizes that our duty is ultimately not to the moral law, but to a higher authority still – God himself, who is, after all, the source of the moral law.

Kierkegaard contrasts Abraham, whom he considers a true 'knight of faith', with the tragic hero or 'knight of infinite resignation': someone who recognizes that a sacrifice must be made on the basis of principle. A general who, standing on principle, sends an entire regiment to certain death, knowing his own son is among the soldiers, makes such a sacrifice.

Abraham's sacrifice is different. Unlike our tragic hero, the general, who simply expects his son to die, Abraham has faith in something higher than the moral law; Abraham has faith that his son will be restored to him by God. Being a true Christian involves placing your trust in something higher than the moral principles that govern society. There is a sense, then, in which it makes you an outsider – someone who stands apart from conventional, rule-based morality, who looks to something greater.

Criticism of Kierkegaard

Assuming Kierkegaard is sincere (remember, he writes as Johannes de Silentio, and some have questioned whether de Silentio's views are really Kierkegaard's), a critic might suggest that Kierkegaard is, in effect, giving people licence to slaughter the innocent in the name of whatever they believe their God wants. Kierkegaard anticipates this criticism, pointing out that

Abraham also acts out of love for his son. He is not motivated by hatred. That is a crucial difference between Abraham and, say, a hate-filled terrorist. But of course, it seems Kierkegaard must, then, still admire the faith of the crank that smothers his own children because he trusts the 'voice of God' in his head. For Kierkegaard, the only difference between the admirable Abraham and this religious crank is that, in the story, God does indeed save Abraham's child while the crank's children die. But of course, precisely because Abraham's faith is supposedly beyond reason, Abraham was no more *justified* in trusting in such a happy outcome than is the crank.

It seems, then, that either Kierkegaard must also admire the faith of our crank, or else he must say that the reason Abraham's faith is admirable while the crank's is not is that Abraham happened to *get lucky*.

But that, surely, hardly makes Abraham worthy of our admiration.

Biography

Born 1813, in Copenhagen, Denmark, Søren Kierkegaard was born into a prosperous family, the youngest of seven children. Deeply religious, Kierkegaard's father was convinced that, because of his own sins, none of his children would live beyond 33, the age at which Christ died – and only Søren and his brother Peter did. He also encouraged the young Kierkegaard to become a pastor.

His university career began tentatively, but after his father's death in 1838, he achieved a *Magister Artium* (the equivalent of a PhD). Supported financially by a large inheritance, Kierkegaard began a career as an independent thinker and writer. He travelled little, other than a few trips to Germany and Sweden, and spent his entire life in the city of Copenhagen.

Like his father, Kierkegaard was consumed by inner torment – by feelings of guilt and dread. He considered himself a permanent outsider. Two events in particular contributed further to his misery. The first was the breaking of his betrothal to Regine Olsen, who was 10 years his junior, which he did both to save Regine from his own brooding and miserable nature, and also as an act of sacrifice, so that he could pursue his own work with greater intensity.

Kierkegaard also became involved in a spat with the satirical paper *The Corsair,* which was in the habit of ridiculing the great and the good of Danish society. *The Corsair* published a piece of which Kierkegaard disapproved, and he attacked the paper, adding that he too would like to be abused: 'May I ask to be abused – the personal injury of being immortalized by *The Corsair* is just too much.' The paper duly obliged by making fun of Kierkegaard's personal appearance and habits, and he found himself a laughing stock. He died in Copenhagen in 1855.

Major works

Karl Marx
1818–83

The philosophy of history

'Philosophers have only interpreted *the world in
different ways; the point is to change it.'*
INSCRIBED ON MARX'S TOMB IN HIGHGATE CEMETERY

Like Hegel, Marx believed that there is a kind of logic to history
– a way that it is determined to unfold. Marx also takes from
Hegel the idea that the fundamental engine of change driving
history forward is the dialectic. He also agrees that this historical process is headed in a particular direction, towards greater
freedom and, ultimately, a society free of conflict.

The fundamental difference between Hegel (see page 195)
and Marx is that while Hegel thought that the process was ultimately unfolding at the level of mind and ideas, Marx thought
it was fundamentally one of material change. Hegel is a *dialectic idealist* – he believes all change is ultimately change to what
he calls *Geist* – roughly translated as 'mind' or 'spirit' – while,
as Marx puts it, his philosophy turns Hegel's dialectic 'right side
up'. He dispenses with Hegel's mysterious *Geist*. Marx insists

that it is our material situation – in particular, the way in which production takes place – that shapes what is going on at the level of ideas, including political and religious thought.

According to Marx, if you want to understand why we *think* the way we do, you need to understand the dialectical process as unfolding *materially*.

Forces and relations of production

In Marx's view, society passes through great epochs that are characterized by their particular economic structures. We are currently living in a capitalist society. Before the capitalist society, there was feudal society, and the capitalist system will eventually be replaced by a communist society. Each of these economic systems is shaped by the dominant productive forces of the day.

People are essentially productive. They produce things – knives and forks, food, shelter, art, and so on. The character of each epoch is shaped by the particular *forces of production* dominant at the time. These forces of production consist of human labour and the means through which production takes place, such as a mill powered manually or by steam. Different productive forces give rise to different *relations of production* – different economic structures having different property relations. As Marx wrote:

The hand-mill gives you a society with the feudal lord; the steam-mill, a society with the industrial capitalist.

As technology advances and the forces of production continue to develop, so they eventually outstrip and become cramped by the relations of production. Ultimately, the strain becomes too much and the system ruptures, giving birth to a new system better suited to the advancing forces of production. And so the cycle continues.

Alienation

Marx's view is that under the capitalist system, the productive output of the vast majority – the proletariat – is harnessed to a market system over which they have no control and under which they must labour ceaselessly to survive. The proletariat do not own the fruits of their own labour; that is owned by the capitalist class – the bourgeoisie. So the proletariat are trapped in an endless cycle of meaningless activity. They are 'alienated' both from each other and from what they produce. Of course, the market pretends to be free, but it is, in truth, an inhuman mechanism that enslaves the majority of us. Marx wants to free the working classes from this enslaved and alienated existence. He wants to change their miserable situation, not just describe and explain it.

Communist society

According to Marx, true freedom requires the development of a society in which man is genuinely self-determined and able to engage in forms of production through which he can properly express his humanity. The forces of production have now developed to the extent where this has become a genuine possibility. Man can now finally free himself, by overthrowing the capitalist economic system that currently enslaves him, and by building a new communist society.

Although Marx did not describe a communist society in detail, he is clear that within it the mechanism that currently traps people in this alienated existence – private property – is gone. Within a communist regime, you are no longer forced to produce what others demand of you. You can produce what you genuinely *want* to produce.

Marx on religion

Marx famously says that religion is 'the sigh of the oppressed creature, the heart of a heartless world, just as it is the spiritless situation. It is the opium of the people.' He thought religion a delusion that the oppressed and alienated proletariat indulged in to avoid being confronted by the reality of their situation, namely their miserable enslavement. Religion holds out the false promise of living a meaningful and fulfilled life now, to be followed by eternal bliss later. In so doing, it helps keep the proletariat compliant. The only way the proletariat can escape from their condition is for them to recognize the reality of their situation – that they are enslaved – and break free. Rather than dream of a better life in an imaginary next world, they should seek to change this one.

Biography

Born 1818, in Trier, Germany, Marx's jewish parents converted to Christianity when his father, a lawyer, found he could not practise owing to Prussia's anti-Semitic laws. Marx studied at the universities of Bonn and Berlin, where he discovered philosophy. Shunned by the establishment for his radical views, he turned to journalism instead of becoming an academic.

After the Prussian government shut down the liberal paper for which he wrote, Marx moved to Paris where he met Friedrich Engels, with whom he collaborated for the rest of his life. It was Engels who directed Marx's attention towards economics. Further political persecution forced Marx eventually to move to London, where he spent the rest of his life with his family. Marx earned very little from journalism, and three of his six children died from the effects of poverty. During the 1850s and 60s Marx, in failing health, would spend 10 hours a day writing in the Reading Room of the British Museum. It is here that he wrote his seminal work, *Das Kapital*. He died in London in 1883.

Major works

Communist Manifesto (with Engels)

Das Kapital

Charles Sanders Peirce

1839–1914

Consensus, truth and reality

'The opinion which is fated to be ultimately agreed to by all who investigate is what we mean by truth.'

Peirce, like William James (see page 231), is not always consistent in his remarks about truth and reality. Presented here is the 'consensus theory' of truth that Peirce does, in several places, appear to advance.

The consensus theory of truth

What do we actually mean by truth and reality? These questions lie close to the heart of philosophy. Peirce offers some very surprising answers.

Suppose several scientists are investigating the speed of light. They use different methods and experiments but though their ideas and beliefs may diverge when they begin, they will gradually make their way towards the same answer. The more research they do, the closer to a consensus they come, until finally, agreement is reached.

Peirce defines truth in the following way: *what those who investigate a matter will all eventually agree on.*

The opinion which is fated to be ultimately agreed to by all who investigate is what we mean by truth and the object represented by this opinion is the real.

Note that what Peirce is offering here is not just an optimistic *claim* about truth – that the truth happens to be what we all eventually agree on. He is offering a *definition* of truth – of what 'truth' *means*. To say that something is true *is just* to say that it is what we will all eventually agree on.

A counter-example?
The suggestion that truth is, fundamentally, whatever we agree it to be might seem open to a very obvious sort of counter-example. Suppose I manage to convince both myself and others that the Earth is ruled by lizard-people from outer space. If the truth is whatever we end up finally agreeing it to be, then it is true that the Earth is ruled by lizard-people from outer space. But of course, this is ridiculous – we can't just make a claim true by collectively agreeing to it, can we?

The role of scientific inquiry
In fact, Peirce's view entails that if only we *could* all finally agree that the world was ruled by alien lizards, then it would, indeed, be true. However, Peirce also thinks that the only way we will

ever achieve consensus is by engaging in scientific inquiry. Why?

He believes that we will only agree if we collectively appeal to something independent of us. When we observe the external world, that world imposes the same kind of experiences on all of us, and so, in the end, it *forces us to agree*. If we do not appeal to scientific method and objective reality, no agreement will be reached.

But...

Hasn't Peirce now helped himself to a very different theory about truth – isn't he saying, in effect, that beliefs are true if they correspond with how things stand in *objective reality* – the reality that forces us to agree about it over the long term? He's not defining 'truth' in terms of agreement or consensus after all, but in terms of correspondence with how things stand in this mind-independent reality.

The social theory of reality

Actually, this would be to misunderstand Peirce. Yes, he does want to say that there are 'real' things and an 'objective' external reality, but it turns out to be 'objective' only in the sense that Peirce supposed it to be independent of what any *individual* might take it to be. If *I* think the world is ruled by lizard people but no one else does, I am mistaken. For the 'objective' fact is that the world is not ruled by lizard-people from outer space. But, for Peirce, if *everyone* were agreed that the world is ruled by alien lizards, *then it would be true.* Indeed, it would become an 'objective fact.' He offers a 'social theory' of truth and reality, in which truth and reality are whatever the community ultimately agrees on. As Peirce puts it:

My social theory of reality, namely, that the real is the idea in which the community settles down.

A concern about Peirce's theory of truth and reality

One tension in Peirce's thinking is that, once he has acknowledged that objective reality is essentially social – it is whatever we finally agree it to be – it is no longer clear how it can force us to agree about it. How can it *force* us to agree, if it's not there to force us *until* we agree?

Biography

Born 1839, in Cambridge, Mass., Peirce was the son of Benjamin Peirce, professor of astronomy and mathematics at Harvard University. At the age of 12, Charles read a standard logic textbook by the 19th-century philosopher and theologian, Richard Whately, and immediately developed a fascination with logic and reasoning. He studied at both Harvard and the Lawrence Scientific School.

During his lifetime, Peirce was best known as a scientist. He was employed by the United States Coastal Survey between 1859 and 1891. His work on geodesy and gravimetrics at the Survey gained him international recognition, and he was elected a member of the National Academy of Sciences in 1876. In 1879 Peirce became a lecturer in logic at Johns Hopkins University.

His first wife left him in 1875, after which he lived openly with his mistress until they could marry following his divorce in 1883. When his employer discovered that Peirce had lived and travelled openly with a woman who was not his wife, he was fired. He left the Coastal Survey after an investigation into financial irregularities (of which Peirce himself was exonerated).

Towards the end of his life, Peirce lived in abject poverty on a farm he had bought with his inheritance. He was disorganized, lived beyond his means, and repeatedly found himself in considerable financial difficulties. His great friend William James (see page 132) helped bring Peirce's philosophical work to a wider audience. James also helped Peirce with his financial affairs and arranged for him to give some lectures at Harvard. Peirce died in Milford, Penn. in 1914.

Major works

Studies in Logic (ed.)
Collected Papers

William James

1842–1910

Pragmatism

*'…not only as a matter of fact do we find our
passional nature influencing us in our opinions,
but that there are some options between opinions
in which this influence must be regarded both
as an inevitable and as a lawful determinant
of our choice.'*

Many people who believe in God acknowledge that their belief
lacks a strong basis. They believe anyway, despite insufficient
evidence. They have faith.

However, not everyone is impressed by this sort of faith. The
19th-century mathematician and philosopher W. K. Clifford
argues, 'It is wrong, always, everywhere and for anyone to believe anything upon insufficient evidence.' Clifford means it is
morally wrong to believe on insufficient evidence. As he supposes belief in God is based on insufficient evidence, he considers religious belief to be immoral.

James rejects Clifford's view. He insists that it can be

legitimate to believe even when the evidence is inconclusive. In *The Will to Believe,* James argues that this is precisely the situation regarding belief in God. He uses the following analogy to help make the case.

The mountaineer example

Suppose you are climbing a mountain. To return home safely you must leap a wide chasm, but your chance of making it is not particularly strong. In order to succeed, you must feel confident. Hesitate and all may be lost. So, despite the fact you are not entirely justified in believing that you will make it safely across, it is nevertheless sensible for you to believe it, particularly as belief will make it more likely that you will succeed.

James concludes that Clifford is mistaken. It is *sometimes* sensible to allow what James calls our *passional nature* – interests, hopes, desires and fears – to influence our beliefs, even though there is insufficient evidence to warrant that belief.

Live, forced and momentous

When is it legitimate to allow our passional natures to rule our beliefs in this way? James posits that the following three conditions must be satisfied:

1. We must be faced with a choice between options that are *live.* A live option is one that is a genuine possibility – one that we can at least take seriously. Believing in Zeus or in Santa Claus are not live options for most contemporary adults. On the other

hand, believing in God or in the existence of life on other planets are genuine possibilities.

2. The choice must be *forced*. A forced choice is one where you *have no option* but to make a choice. For example, I cannot help but choose between having a pizza today or not having one. Though I might defer the choice for a few hours, ultimately, I have no option but to make a decision, but the choice between travelling to Africa or India is *not* one I have to make.

3. The choice must be *momentous* – one that will have a major impact on your life, such as the choice to have children or of an ex-alcoholic to have a drink.

All three conditions are met in the mountaineering example. The choice is between *live* options. It is also forced: you must either believe or fail to believe. And the consequences are momentous. To leap without belief may be fatal. For James, there is nothing wrong with letting your passional nature lead you to belief under these circumstances.

According to James, we face a similar choice when it comes to religious belief. The choice between believing and not believing is forced. It is also momentous: depending on your choice, your life will, no doubt, be very different. And, in the case of Christianity, both choices are *live* for many of us. So, under these circumstances, says James, it is legitimate to allow our passional natures to lead us to belief.

An objection to James's defence of religious belief

I think we should concede that there are circumstances in which allowing our passional natures to determine what we believe is the right thing to do. However, it can be debated whether this is the case when it comes to many religious beliefs.

Consider a rather different religious belief – that the entire universe was created about six thousand years ago. Many Westerners hold this belief, but (though few of them would accept this), there is little evidence to support their belief and overwhelming evidence against it. Is it, nevertheless, legitimate for them to hold it?

It seems the three conditions James says are necessary, if we are to allow our passional natures to determine belief, are satisfied. The choice between believing and not believing in a six-thousand-year-old universe is *forced*. It is also, for many, *momentous*. Given the option is also *live*, is it, then, acceptable for people to believe it?

Surely not. Given the weight of evidence, these people really shouldn't believe what they do. Indeed, isn't there something rather irresponsible about anyone who would allow their beliefs to be shaped in this way, given the evidence available to them?

James would probably agree. He says (our emphasis):

the freedom to believe can only cover living options which the intellect of the individual cannot by itself resolve.

That the universe is more than a few thousand years old is, presumably, something most of us are now able to figure out intellectually, at least beyond reasonable doubt.

Notice that the moral carries over to belief in God. If the evidence for and against the existence of God is more or less evenly balanced, then perhaps it is acceptable for us to allow our 'passional natures' to lead us to religious belief. But, if, as most atheists maintain, the evidence is actually stacked heavily against belief in God, then James's 'will to believe' does not extend to belief in God.

Biography

Born 1842, in New York City, William James was the son of Henry James, Sr., a well-connected eccentric whose circle of acquaintances included Mark Twain, H. G. Wells, Sigmund Freud and Gertrude Stein. The family was gifted – William's younger brother was Henry James, the novelist. William James was both psychologist and philosopher and, along with Charles Sanders Peirce (see page 226) and John Dewey, was one of the pioneers of the philosophical movement known as pragmatism. He died in Chocorua, New Hampshire in 1910.

Major works

The Will to Believe

Pragmatism

The Varieties of Religious Experience

Friedrich Nietzsche

1844-1900

The genealogy of morality

'In heaven, all the interesting people are missing.'

Genealogy – the tracing of ancestral roots – has become a popular pastime over the last few years. There are websites and magazines designed to help people trace their long-lost ancestors. Sometimes what we uncover as we reconstruct our family tree can provide insights into why we are the way we are.

This is most apparent in our *genetic* predispositions – to colour-blindness, or certain diseases, for example. The discovery that Bert's recent ancestors were balding Swedish immigrants may well explain his receding blond hairline.

Modern moral concepts

In *On the Genealogy of Morals*, Nietzsche also engages in a genealogical investigation. The difference is that the family tree he plans to excavate is that of contemporary Christian morality. Nietzsche attempts to trace the ancestry of modern-day moral *concepts*. Our current practices of describing things as

236

being morally 'good' and 'bad' have a long history, one that Nietzsche intends to expose.

Why might uncovering the origins of our modern moral concepts be philosophically illuminating? Many see morality as transcendent and immutable – indeed, as handed down by God. By showing how morality has evolved over time, Nietzsche begins to undermine this view of morality as absolute and God-given. By revealing their origins, he wants us to recognize that our current moral concepts are far from inevitable. We can develop a new morality. Indeed, Nietzsche thinks we *should* develop a new morality.

Nietzsche does not deny that morality can play a useful role. He acknowledges that a shared morality can help forge a sense of community and check those natural drives that might otherwise tear society apart. So he is not *against morality, per se.* It is the *particular* morality we have inherited that is the focus of his attacks.

By revealing the ancestry of our moral concepts, Nietzsche believes he can show that morality is natural, not supernatural, in origin. It is shaped by our worldly circumstances, by the situations in which we find ourselves. Circumstances change, however, and as a result, a morality can begin to inhibit life rather than enhance it. It can become suffocating. Where that is the case, morality needs to change too.

Nietzsche argues that this is true of contemporary morality. The time has come to move on – to replace our stultifying Christian morality with a more positive, life-affirming alternative.

The ancient roots of Christian morality

Nietzsche's account of how Christian morality appeared is essentially psychological. In ancient Rome, at the time when Christian morality first began to emerge, the Christians were slaves. Their aristocratic masters had a non-moral conception of good and bad. They saw themselves as strong, powerful, courageous, and more physically able and favoured than the common herd. These attributes were admired and therefore deemed good, while the absence of such properties was deemed bad. So weakness and meekness were both deemed bad.

The Christian slaves were powerless. They hated and resented their masters. It was out of this resentment that Christian morality grew. The feeling of hostility that the slaves felt towards their masters was not something upon which they could *physically* act. They were consumed with hatred and desired revenge, but they were impotent. How could they achieve superiority over their masters? By developing a new moral code.

The Christians began to develop an alternative, *moral* way of describing things as 'good' and 'bad' that, in effect, reversed their masters' use of those terms. The bold, self-interested acquisitiveness of their masters was now deemed bad. By contrast, those who were weak, meek and pitiable were considered good. They supposed God valued and rewarded what they called good, and that he despised and would punish what they deemed bad.

It is here that Nietzsche finds the roots of current Christian morality. The real motive behind the Christian elevation of compassion, altruism and pity to the noblest of virtues lay in the feelings of hatred and *resentment* (Nietzsche uses the French word *ressentiment*) that the slaves felt towards their masters. They wished to assert their superiority over their masters. They could not do this physically, so they did it spiritually.

Revenge

The slaves' final act of revenge was to get the masters to judge themselves and others from this new perspective.

According to Nietzsche, human beings have a natural drive to impose their will and power on others. We derive pleasure from controlling, and even instilling pain and suffering in others (the child who pulls the wings off an insect for fun illustrates Nietzsche's point). When this outward drive is frustrated, it manifests itself in other ways. It can be turned *inwards* in an unhealthy, self-destructive way.

Once the masters began to embrace the same moral code as the slaves, their own 'will to power' could no longer be exerted outwardly in the same spontaneous way. The masters could no longer impose their will on the slaves with carefree abandon. And so they began to turn their power inwards, to control and punish *themselves*. They began to develop a Christian conscience, to torment themselves with guilt.

The slaves' revenge was complete. They were now the 'superior' group, while their masters became increasingly consumed with controlling and punishing not the slaves, but themselves.

Of course, for this final act of revenge to be successful, the slaves had to *appear* to be acting from only the purest and highest motives. According to Nietzsche, they fooled their masters, and in fact *even fooled themselves*, about their real motivation, which was not selfless, sincere compassion, but bitter hatred and seething resentment.

Asceticism

Nietzsche's belief that our natural 'will to power', when frustrated, tends to be turned inwards in an unhealthy, self-destructive way is also used by him to explain the traditional Christian fondness for asceticism.

Unlike their masters, the slaves could not exert power outwardly. So they directed their 'will to power' inwards. Because they could not enjoy imposing their will upon and torturing others, they imposed their will upon and tortured themselves.

The Christian practices of self-denial and self-flagellation are manifestations of this inwardly turned 'will to power'. This self-destructive, self-denying tendency became, under Christianity, an ideal – something to which we were all encouraged to aspire.

Modern Christian morality

According to Nietzsche, the slave morality had a useful function for the Christian slaves. It helped them deal with their own situation – in particular, with their own powerlessness and feelings of resentment and hatred. It was a great help to them. But of course *we* are no longer slaves. The morality that we have inherited is no longer a help, but a hindrance. It is our bitter inheritance. We find ourselves saddled with a morality born of hatred and resentment, a morality that, rather than enhancing our lives, cripples them.

Nietzsche wants to help us recognize that there is nothing inevitable about our current morality. Once we understand why we have the values we do, we can set about changing them, so that they become life enhancing once more. We can, through an immense act of will, free ourselves from the stultifying, masochistic prison of Christian morality, and embrace a new set of values that will allow us to flourish in a psychologically healthier, more positive way. We can become what Nietzsche calls *Übermensch* (sometimes translated as 'superman').

This isn't to say Nietzsche recommends we entirely abandon all those values that Christianity upholds. The Nietzschean superman need not be an utterly selfish individual concerned only with imposing his own will on others. Nietzsche does not reject compassion, for example. He recommends only that if we are compassionate, we are compassionate for the *right reasons*. Within a Christian context, compassion is driven by feelings of hatred and resentment and applied in an unhealthy way. But that is not to say that compassion *must* be motivated in this way.

Is Nietzsche correct?

Is Nietzsche correct about Christian morality? Some Christians would agree that some, perhaps a great deal, of what passes for Christian morality is, in truth, motivated as much by the drive for personal power and control as it is by selfless devotion to others.

But is Christian morality *entirely* motivated in that way? So Nietzsche claims. And of course, that is much more difficult to establish.

Notice that Nietzsche is offering a psychological theory about what really motivated, and continues to motivate, Christians, whether they realize it or not. And as a *psychological theory* it surely stands in need of evidence. Yet there is surprisingly little hard evidence to be found in Nietzsche's writing. Many would say that he presents us with little more than a vast amount of *speculation*.

Perhaps the most we can say in Nietzsche's favour is that he has produced a fairly plausible account of what motivated, and what continues to motivate, Christian morality psychologically.

The extent to which Nietzsche's account is actually correct is rather more difficult for us to assess.

Biography

Born 1844, in Röcken bei Lützen, Germany, Nietzsche had originally intended to be a pastor. Yet he ultimately came to criticize and reject Christian morality, which he saw as life denying. He was an accomplished scholar, beginning his career as a philologist before turning to philosophy. He was appointed to the chair of classics at the University of Basel at the age of 24.

Plagued by ill-health throughout his life, Nietzsche eventually went mad. The incident widely thought to have tipped him into insanity was his witnessing a horse being viciously whipped in a Turin street. Nietzsche supposedly threw his arms about the horse's neck to protect it and then collapsed (though whether this story is true is debatable – it's suspiciously similar to an incident in Dostoyevsky's *Crime and Punishment*).

Nietzsche is often linked with Nazism and anti-Semitism, though with little justification. So why does he regularly stand accused of both?

After his final descent into insanity, his sister Elisabeth took control of his life upon the death of their mother, renting a house in Weimar to house the Nietzsche Archive and moving into it both Nietzsche and the collected manuscripts of his work. Robed in white and now mute, Nietzsche himself became an exhibit in the archive Elisabeth created. Elisabeth was certainly anti-Semitic. Before she took over Nietzsche's life, she had started an anti-Semitic Aryan colony in Paraguay, which she and her husband dubbed 'New Germany'. She also forged links with both Mussolini and Hitler. The common misconception that Nietzsche was a proto-Nazi is largely due to Elisabeth's unfortunate influence on his legacy. She was certainly unscrupulous, forging letters from Nietzsche to herself and misrepresenting his views to make them support her own.

Nietzsche's writing style is idiosyncratic – much of it is chaotic in appearance, comprising many aphorisms piled up in a seemingly random fashion. There are angry rants and diatribes together with plenty of insults directed against both individuals and nations – 'Socrates ... was ugly', or, 'How much beer there is in German intelligence!' This can make for engaging reading but it also tends to disguise just how brilliant, insightful and, above all, how *careful* a thinker Nietzsche really was.

The focus here is upon Nietzsche's attack on Christian values. *On the Genealogy of Morals* (1887) is one of his most important works. It is also one of the most accessible, being much more conventional in style. In the *Genealogy,* Nietzsche attempts to undermine Christian morality by tracing it back to its ancient, psychological roots. Nietzsche died in Weimar in 1900.

Major works

The Birth of Tragedy

Beyond Good and Evil

On The Genealogy of Morals

Thus Spoke Zarathustra

Gottlob Frege

1848-1925

Identity claims

*'The reference of "evening star" and "morning star"
are the same, but not their senses.'*

Suppose you know a man called Chris at work – a rugged,
clean-cut chap always in a business suit. Then, while on an office night out, you watch the stage act of a female impersonator
called Lisa. Later, one of your colleagues points out something
surprising: *Chris is Lisa*. Chris and Lisa are one and the same
person: office gent by day, femme fatale by night.

You now know the truth of an identity claim:

Chris is Lisa.

In an identity claim, the word 'is' indicates that what might have
appeared to be *two* distinct entities are in fact *one and the same*
thing. Philosophers sometimes call this the *'is' of identity*, contrasting it with the *'is' of predication*, where 'is' is used to

indicate that an entity possesses a certain property, as in this example:

Chris is tall.

Here, the claim is not that Chris is *identical* with tall, which makes no sense. Rather it's claimed that Chris possesses the property of tallness.

Identity claims are of interest to both scientists and philosophers. Scientists have discovered that certain *objects* are identical – for example, that the evening star and the morning star are one and the same heavenly body. They have also established that certain *properties* are identical (for example, heat is molecular motion). And, of course, both philosophers and scientists argue over the question of whether mind and brain are identical.

Frege's puzzle

One of the classic puzzles about identity claims concerns their *informativeness*. When you discovered that Chris is Lisa, you learned something new – something you didn't know before. That Chris is Lisa came as a surprise. Similarly, when scientists discovered that the evening star and the morning star are one and the same object (i.e. the planet that we now know as Venus) it constituted a major astronomical breakthrough. They now possessed valuable information that they did not have before.

The problem is that it is extremely difficult to see how these claims *could* be informative, given a natural way of under-standing how proper names function.

So, what is this natural way of understanding how names function? It is that the linguistic function of a name within a sentence is simply *to refer*. Take the name 'Chris', for example. It's tempting to suppose that the purpose of this name within a sentence, such as:

Chris is tall,

is just to pick out a certain person. The sentence will be true if, and only if, the person to whom the name refers *is* tall.

However, if referring is *all* that names do, linguistically speaking – if that is *all* they contribute to the sentence – then you can begin to see why we might now face something of a puzzle. Frege himself considers the sentence:

Hesperus is Phosphorus.

'Hesperus' is an ancient name for the evening star and 'Phos-phorus' an ancient name for the morning star. That Hesperus is Phosphorus was a major discovery. By contrast, the sentence:

Hesperus is Hesperus,

does not provide us with any new information. It is trivial and uninformative. But if names do nothing more than refer, then, because 'Hesperus' and 'Phosphorus' refer to the same object, so *it should be possible to switch one name for the other in a sentence without changing the piece of information communicated by that sentence.*

The problem is, if we substitute 'Phosphorus' for the second occurrence of 'Hesperus' in that last sentence, we turn an *uninformative* sentence into an *informative* one.

How can this be? If it is only the reference of a name that is relevant (so far as the information captured and communicated by sentences in which it appears is concerned), then 'Hesperus is Phosphorus' should be no more informative than 'Hesperus is Hesperus'. The latter is not informative at all. Yet 'Hesperus is Phosphorus' *is* informative. There is the puzzle.

Frege's theory of sense and reference

Philosophers have, over time, developed a number of different solutions to this puzzle. There is still no consensus as to which, if any, of these solutions is correct. Frege himself presented the most famous, and probably still the most popular, solution. It is called the *theory of sense and reference.*

Frege's theory involves giving up on the thought that referring is the *sole* linguistic function of a proper name. Names refer, says Frege, but they also have a second important linguistic feature, a feature Frege calls *sense* (or *Sinn* in German).

Suppose one evening you observe Hesperus, the evening star, and then the next morning you see Phosphorus, the morning star. You have in fact observed the same star twice over, since it presents itself in two quite different ways, changing its position in the sky according to the time of day.

The sense of a name is the particular mode of presentation associated with that name. The senses of the names 'Hesperus' and 'Phosphorus' differ, because the modes of presentation associated with them differ. While 'Hesperus' and 'Phosphorus' may share the same reference, they differ in sense.

The declarative sentences in which these names appear have truth-values – they are either true or false. These sentences can also be used to communicate pieces of information. Frege says that the feature of the name relevant to the truth of the sentence in which it appears is its reference, whereas the feature of the name relevant to the information communicated is the sense. And so, to return to our earlier example, take the sentence:

Hesperus is Hesperus,

and substitute 'Phosphorus' for one occurrence of 'Hesperus', like so:

Hesperus is Phosphorus.

This won't affect the truth of the sentence, given that the two names *refer* to the same object. But, because the *senses* of the names differ, *we do change the piece of information communicated.* Problem solved! By supposing that names don't *just* refer

– by introducing a *second* linguistically important feature: *sense*
– Frege solves the puzzle.

But do names have sense?

Frege's solution is neat. But is it correct? Do names have sense? Many contemporary philosophers of language accept Frege's theory, but many do not. Here is just one of the worries raised about the theory.

Frege claims that sense is objective. But in what way? Well, we all associate different ideas with names, of course. What I believe about, say, Elvis Presley, may differ from what you believe about him. Perhaps all I know about Elvis is that he sang 'Hound Dog' and appeared in several films, whereas you are ignorant of these facts but do know that he sang 'Are you Lonesome Tonight?' and his home was called 'Graceland'. Clearly, we associate different ideas with the name. However, according to Frege, while such 'ideas' may vary from person to person, *the sense cannot*.

Why does Frege insist that the sense cannot vary? He was interested in pinning down how declarative sentences are able to communicate pieces of information from one person to another. Clearly, they can do this. When I tell you, 'Elvis married Priscilla', I provide you with exactly the same piece of information that someone else provides you with when they say, 'Elvis married Priscilla'. But if it is the sense of the name that is relevant so far as the information that is communicated is concerned, then it follows that sense cannot vary from person to person. If the sense that I associate with 'Elvis' is different from that which you associate with 'Elvis' then we *would* communicate different pieces of information using that sentence. As we don't communicate different pieces of information, the sense cannot vary.

Now you can see the problem. Frege insists that the sense of a name must not vary from person to person. Yet he also says that the sense is a mode of presentation. It is difficult to see how modes of presentation won't vary from person to person – particularly when the beliefs people associate with the bearer of the name are entirely different.

Perhaps Frege's notion of sense can still be defended. However, if it can't – if we are going to have to abandon the notion of sense – then of course we will have to come up with some other solution to Frege's puzzle.

Biography

Born 1848, in Wismar, Mecklenburg-Schwerin (now in Germany), Gottlob Frege may well be the greatest logician that ever lived. He invented modern quantificational logic, and made groundbreaking developments in the philosophy of mathematics and language. He had an important influence on other philosophers of logic and language, such as Bertrand Russell (see page 258) and Ludwig Wittgenstein (see page

276). Yet, during his lifetime, his work was not widely known and it was Russell who helped bring Frege's work to the attention of a much wider audience. He died in Bad Kleinen (now the Mecklenburg-Vorpommern province of Germany) in 1929.

Major works
Conceptual Notation
The Foundations of Arithmetic
On Sense and Reference

Edmund Husserl

1859–1938

Phenomenology

'...*the whole world, when one is in the phenomeno-*
logical attitude, is not accepted as actuality, but only
as actuality-phenomenon.'

Husserl's philosophical focus is on the conscious subject. He
wants to investigate consciousness. But how should such an investigation proceed? Conscious awareness, Husserl notes, is always directed towards an object. You are never merely
conscious, you are always conscious *of* something: a book, a
tree or a headache, for example.

Husserl's radical approach to the study of consciousness is to
try to investigate it by *studying the objects of conscious awareness.*
He calls this discipline *phenomenology*.

Intentionality

Before outlining Husserl's phenomenological approach, we
should begin by clarifying what philosophers mean by
intentionality.

I am currently sitting in a café typing on my laptop. As I look around me, I *perceive* various physical objects: this laptop, that chair, and a man sitting across the room. I have also been thinking about various things, including my future travel plans and about God. These and other mental states are directed towards objects.

The philosopher Brentano calls this aspect of mental states *intentionality*. Their intentionality is their directedness or, if you like, their 'aboutness'.

An interesting feature of intentional states is that they can be directed towards things that do not exist. Perhaps there is no God. In which case I have been thinking about something that doesn't exist. Brentano calls those things to which our mental states are directed *intentional objects*. So God is, at the very least, an intentional object, whether or not he actually exists. Similarly, the dagger that Macbeth hallucinates in the air before him is an intentional object, despite not being real.

Intentionality involves some rather surprising powers. Notice, for example, that I am able instantaneously to direct my thoughts to objects that are enormous distances away, such as distant stars and galaxies. These objects are so far away it would take light years to reach them, yet when I think about them, my thoughts reach them *instantly*. Thought, it seems, *can travel faster than light*. But how is that possible?

The method of bracketing

Let's now return to the matter at hand: Husserl's philosophical project of investigating consciousness by investigating its objects.

Suppose I look at the cup on the table in front of me. I observe the cup. Or at least I think I do. Of course a sceptic will insist that, for all I know, there may be no cup there. It might be a hallucination, or I might be dreaming, or perhaps I am the victim of Descartes's evil demon (see page 107).

Still, even if I can't be sure that there really is a cup before me, I can at least be sure that the cup exists *as an intentional object*. The cup, as an object of my awareness, is simply a given. And so I can *bracket* such thorny philosophical questions as whether there *really is* a cup present and focus my attention solely on the intentional object. I can directly study what Husserl calls the *content* of my conscious awareness without having to make any dubious philosophical assumptions about whether such a cup really exists.

Indeed, considered purely as an intentional object, the cup seems to be something to which I have infallible access. Yes, I might be mistaken about there actually being a cup of coffee before me. But I can't be mistaken about the fact that it is what I *take* to be there.

This access to the objects of his own consciousness, infallibly given, provides Husserl with the data from which he hopes to develop his new science of phenomenology. By revealing and systematically classifying the basic structures of consciousness through the method of *epoché* or 'bracketing', Husserl believes he can build up a rich and scientifically valuable taxonomy of conscious states and the many different ways in which they are directed towards objects.

So, in the same way that subatomic physicists classify and study particles, or biologists classify and study living things, Husserl intends to classify and study the objects of consciousness.

Indeed, Husserl believes that by developing such a classification system he can ultimately map out the conditions under which any conscious subject might encounter anything at all.

For a criticism of Husserl's approach to phenomenology, see page 290 in the chapter on Heidegger.

Biography

Born 1859, in Prossnitz, Moravia, then part of Austria, now known as Prostejov in the Czech Republic, Edmund Husserl is the founder of the philosophical movement known as phenomenology. His work influenced many others including Martin Heidegger (see page 288) and Jean-Paul Sartre (see page 315).

Born a Jew, Husserl converted to Christianity in 1887. A lifelong academic, he taught at the universities of Halle, Göttingen and Freiburg. After his retirement in 1928, Husserl continued to use the library at Freiburg until banned because of his Jewish origins. The rector of the university at that time was Husserl's former pupil, Martin Heidegger. Under the Nazis, Husserl was the victim of anti-Semitic attacks. His works were also banned. Having attended lectures given by Franz

Brentano, an influential figure in philosophy and psychology, in 1883 he completed his doctorate at Vienna. In 1939, shortly after his death, the Husserl Archives were founded. The Franciscan father, H. L. Van Breda, managed to take his manuscripts, extensive library and correspondence, under threat in Nazi Germany, to safety in Leuven, Belgium. The manuscripts comprised approximately 40,000 pages. Husserl died in Freiburg in 1938.

Major works
Logical Investigations

Ideas Pertaining to a Pure Phenomenology and to a Phenomenological Philosophy

Bertrand Russell

1872–1970

Names and descriptions

'If a man is offered a fact that goes against his instincts, he will scrutinize it closely, and unless the evidence is overwhelming, he will refuse to believe it. If, on the other hand, he is offered something that affords a reason for acting in accordance to his instincts, he will accept it even on the slightest evidence. The origin of myths is explained in this way.'

Our focus is on Russell's *theory of descriptions,* and his view on how ordinary proper names function. Russell considered his theory of descriptions to be one of his most important contributions to philosophy.

A puzzle about existence

Let's begin by sketching out an ancient and infernal puzzle: how do proper names – such as John, Paris or Jupiter – function? What role do they play in those sentences within which they appear? An obvious suggestion would be that they *refer*. Take the sentence:

John is tall.

We use 'John' to refer to a particular individual. We then assert something about this individual – namely, he is tall. The claim is true if the individual to whom we refer is tall, and false if he isn't. Another apparent use of a referring expression is:

The tallest building is in Kuala Lumpur.

Here, it's tempting to suppose we use the description 'the tallest building' to refer to a particular building. We then claim that the building in question is in Kuala Lumpur. Our claim is true if, and only if, the building referred to is in Kuala Lumpur.

This is a natural way of understanding how both names and descriptions function, but it famously generates the baffling *puzzle of empty reference,* with which philosophers continue to grapple:

If names and descriptions are referring expressions, how can we succeed in using them to say something true, when they do not in fact succeed in referring to anything?

To illustrate, look at these examples:

The golden mountain does not exist, *and* Pegasus does
not exist.

Both sentences are true. However, if the job of a name or description within each sentence is to refer, *how can they be true?*
In each case there is nothing for the name or description to refer
to. But then the name or description cannot do its linguistic
job. With no reference, surely the sentence might as well contain
a gap where the name or description appears, like so:

...does not exist,

which is obviously *not* a sentence, let alone a true one.

An attractive feature of Russell's theory of descriptions is its
success in explaining how the sentence, 'The golden mountain
does not exist', can be true (it solves a number of other puzzles
too, which we won't explore here).

Russell's analysis of descriptions

According to Russell, when we use a description, 'the F', in a
sentence like so:

The F is G,

we are actually making three distinct claims. We are, in effect,
claiming:

- At least one thing is F;
- At most one thing is F; and
- Whatever is F is G.

To illustrate, suppose I say, 'The queen of Denmark is in Brazil.' According to Russell, I make three distinct claims. First, I claim there *is* a queen of Denmark. I assert that *at least one thing* is queen of Denmark. However, I don't *just* claim that there exists a queen of Denmark – use of 'the' indicates that whoever is queen of Denmark is uniquely queen of Denmark. So, I am also claiming that, *at most, one thing* is queen of Denmark. Finally, I claim that whoever is queen of Denmark is in Brazil.

Russell here offers us an *analysis* of a sentence containing a description. The surface appearance of the sentence suggests it is used to make a single claim. According to Russell, appearances are deceptive – the surface appearance disguises the sentence's true 'logical form'. We are actually dealing with a conjunction of three distinct claims. A little analysis reveals this hidden logical structure.

An interesting feature of Russell's analysis of sentences containing descriptions is that it entails *descriptions are not referring expressions*. To see why, let's take a brief look at another sort of expression – the *quantifier*. Consider this expression:

…is happy.

Obviously this is not a sentence. However, we can turn it into a declarative sentence by inserting a referring expression into the gap. So, if I refer to a particular person as John, I can slot 'John' into the space, thus:

John is happy.

This sentence will be true if and only if the individual I refer to is happy.

Another kind of expression could also be slotted in to produce a declarative sentence. Consider these *quantifiers*:

Someone	Something
Everyone	Everything
No one	Nothing

Instead of referring to a specific individual, they talk about *quantities*. The sentence:

Someone is happy,

for example, says that the number of individuals who are happy is *at least one*.

No one is happy,

on the other hand, says that the number of individuals who are happy is zero.

It's worth emphasizing that quantifiers are *not* referring expressions. To say, 'No one is happy' is obviously not to refer to anyone at all. Nor do I refer to anyone using, 'Someone is happy'. For the latter to be true, it doesn't matter *which* individual is happy, so long as someone is. There is an obvious contrast here with, 'John is happy'. If 'John' refers to a specific individual, then what I say will be true only if *that individual* – the one referred to – is happy. Whether anyone else happens to be happy is irrelevant.

Russell's solution

You may have noticed that Russell's analysis of 'The F is G' involves quantifiers ('at least one thing' and 'at most one thing' are obviously quantifiers). For the three claims to be true, all that is required is that something be uniquely F, and that whatever is F also be G. It doesn't matter what is uniquely F and also G, so long as *something* is. In other words, no reference is made to any specific individual. So according to Russell, descriptions such as 'the queen of Denmark' and 'the tallest building' are not, after all, referring expressions. The surface appearance of language deceived us into supposing that they were.

Now let's return to the puzzle of explaining how 'The golden mountain does not exist' can be true. How do we apply Russell's theory here?

Well, that sentence is just the negation of:

The golden mountain exists,

which, according to Russell, says:

1. At least one thing is a golden mountain; and

2. At most one thing is a golden mountain.

(Note that we do not add, 'Whatever is a golden mountain exists', as (1) and (2) together already assert that there exists exactly one such mountain.)

Russell's analysis of 'The golden mountain does *not* exist', therefore, is:

It is *not* the case that:

1. At least one thing is a golden mountain; and

2. At most one thing is a golden mountain.

Because (1) is false (there are no golden mountains), so the original sentence comes out as true. Our puzzle was to explain how, 'The golden mountain does not exist' could be true. Russell's theory allows us to solve that puzzle.

Russell on meaning

Russell's theory of descriptions allows him to solve a

second puzzle generated by a further assumption concerning sentences such as, 'The golden mountain does not exist'.

The meaning of a referring expression is just the thing to which it refers.

For example, if 'John' refers to a person, then that person is the meaning of 'John'. Russell accepts this, supposing that, for referring expressions, meaning equals reference.

Of course, if this simple theory of meaning is correct, and if the description 'the golden mountain' is indeed a referring expression, then not only is it puzzling how the sentence,

The golden mountain does not exist,

can be true, it is equally puzzling how it can succeed in saying something meaningful – for it contains a meaningless expression.

By applying his theory of descriptions, Russell shows how the sentence could still be meaningful even if there are no golden mountains. Russell retains the theory that meaning equals reference, but abandons the theory that descriptions are referring expressions.

However, the theory that meaning is reference is

dubious. Many contemporary philosophers of language reject it. One of the most important critics of the theory is Ludwig Wittgenstein (see page 276), who suggests that, rather than thinking of meaning as reference, it is usually more helpful to think of meaning as *use*.

Clearly, a name or description might still have a *use* even if it lacks any reference ('Santa Claus', for example, has a clear use, despite the fact that we don't use it to refer to anyone). Notice that, if meaning equals use, then we don't need Russell's theory of descriptions to explain how, 'The golden mountain does not exist' can be meaningful (though perhaps we still need it to explain how the sentence can be true).

Ordinary proper names

A puzzle remains. We have explained how, 'The golden mountain does not exist' can be true, but we have not yet explained how, 'Pegasus does not exist' can be true. 'Pegasus' is not a definite description, but a proper name. So Russell's theory cannot directly be applied. How does Russell solve the puzzle here?

As commonly interpreted (not every philosopher interprets Russell in this way), Russell solves this puzzle by suggesting that ordinary proper names are, in effect, *definite descriptions in disguise*. Suppose that 'Pegasus' is synonymous with the description, 'the winged horse'. Then the sentence, 'Pegasus does not exist', has the same meaning as, 'The winged horse does not exist.' So we *can* now apply Russell's theory of descriptions.

Of course, the suggestion that ordinary proper names are not referring expressions is counter-intuitive. In fact, while Russell's theory of descriptions is still widely accepted, many contemporary philosophers of language believe Russell was wrong to claim that proper names are synonymous with definite descriptions. The chapter on Saul Kripke (see page 356) says more on this.

If proper names are not synonymous with definite descriptions, then we cannot apply Russell's theory of descriptions to explain how, 'Pegasus does not exist' can be true. That puzzle remains.

Biography

Born 1872, in Trelleck, Wales, UK. Russell's father was a viscount, his grandfather prime minister and his godfather the renowned liberal philosopher John Stuart Mill (see page 205). He was privately tutored and won a mathematics scholarship to Trinity College, Cambridge.

Russell's main focus is in the philosophy of mathematics, the theory of knowledge and the philosophy of language. He was a courageous freethinker with strong, if shifting, political convictions. Russell sought election to Parliament as an independent on behalf of the women's suffrage movement and was a pacifist during the First World War. Prosecuted and fined for writing in defence of a conscientious objector, he was also imprisoned for six months for supposedly libelling the British Government and the US army.

Russell later became founding president of the Campaign for Nuclear Disarmament and, arrested at a demonstration, he was imprisoned again, aged 89.

Russell died 1970, in Penrhyndeudraeth.

Major works

Principia Mathematica (with A.N. Whitehead)

The Problems of Philosophy

The Philosophy of Logical Atomism

George Edward Moore

1873–1958

Proof of an external world

'I can prove now … that I have two hands.'

In his paper 'Proof of an external world', Moore tackles the problem of establishing that 'external objects' exist, an external object being something not dependent on our experience for its existence. Sceptics about the external world argue that we cannot know anything about the world outside the mind.

Descartes (see page 104), for example, though not a sceptic, considers the sceptical hypothesis that, for all he knows, his experiences of the external world might be placed in his mind by an immensely powerful demon intent on deceiving him. Perhaps tables and chairs, mountains and valleys, and even his physical body, are illusions conjured up by this malevolent being. But then how can Descartes know that any of these external objects really exist?

Moore believes he can, in fact, provide a 'rigorous proof' that such an external world exists. In particular, he believes he can prove that he has two hands. But how?

By holding up my two hands, and saying, as I make a certain gesture with the right hand, 'Here is one hand', and adding, as I make a certain gesture with the left, 'and here is another'.

Moore points out that outside of a philosophical context, this would be considered a perfectly acceptable proof of the conclusion that he has two hands. In effect, Moore presents us with an argument:

Here is one hand.
And here is another.
Therefore: I have two hands.

The logic of this short argument is certainly valid. The conclusion really does follow from the two premises – and the premises, Moore insists, are both things he *knows*. He says about his first premise – here is one hand – that it would 'be absurd to suggest I did not know it, but only believed it'.

What is perhaps true is that *outside of philosophy* we would think it absurd to suppose Moore doesn't know he is holding up a hand. That he does know this is the 'common sense' view. Indeed, Moore may be right that the 'common sense' view is that this little argument constitutes a perfectly rigorous 'proof' of the existence of his two hands.

The trouble, of course, is that this little argument is hardly likely to satisfy a philosophical sceptic. Certainly, from the point of view of the sceptic, Moore's argument looks hopelessly question-begging. Moore attempts to prove the existence of an external world. But his proof seems merely to *presuppose* that there is one. Perhaps Moore's mind is in the grip of Descartes's evil demon. Perhaps, when Moore thinks he waves a hand about in front of his face, he really does no such thing. All that happens is that the demon notices Moore's intention to wave his hand about, and so places in Moore's mind the illusion that that is what is going on. If that is what happens, everything would seem exactly the same to Moore. But then how can he know that there is a hand there?

Moore's refutation of idealism

Even if we set to one side such sceptical worries, there remains a further problem with Moore's proof. Perhaps Moore has succeeded in establishing that he does indeed have two hands. But how can he know that his hands are what he calls 'external objects' – that is to say, *mind-independent* objects?

An idealist like Berkeley (see page 147) is unlikely to be persuaded that Moore has presented us with a proof of the existence of a mind-independent reality. According to Berkeley, we can know that physical objects, including our hands, exist. But physical objects are, in truth, nothing more than ideas existing in our minds. As ideas are mind-dependent, so are physical objects.

We can now see Moore's difficulty. Perhaps Moore can know that this is a hand he is waving about, but how can what he is currently experiencing settle whether or not his hand is an 'external object' – something that exists mind-independently? It seems it cannot. In which case, it seems that not only is Moore's 'proof' question-begging against a sceptic, it is equally question-begging against an idealist such as George Berkeley.

A baffling proof

So Moore's proof of an external world is somewhat baffling. It appears hopelessly question-begging. Yet Moore does, perhaps, have a point when he claims that his argument would ordinarily be considered a rigorous proof. 'Common sense' deems it to be cogent. But then 'common sense' has been wrong about many things in the past, including that the Earth is flat. Perhaps it is wrong in this case too. In fact, isn't that precisely what the sceptic has shown?

The challenge of scepticism

Scepticism concerning the external world is extraordinarily difficult to defeat. If the sceptic can be defeated, it seems it will be in some other way.

Wittgenstein on Moore's proof of an external world

Interestingly, Ludwig Wittgenstein (see page 276) accuses both the sceptic and Moore of making the same basic mistake. According to Wittgenstein, they both assume that, when I say, 'Here is a hand' while waving my hand in front of my face under normal circumstances, I am making a claim, a claim that according to Moore I do know to be true, but according to the sceptic I don't.

According to Wittgenstein, philosophical problems are generated by our failure to attend properly to how expressions are used – in particular we overlook *differences* in their use. In Wittgenstein's view, both Moore and the sceptic assume, mistakenly, that the sentence, 'Here is a hand' is used, under *these* circumstances, to make a *claim*. But it isn't. It is used to *define* what the word 'hand' means. It is an example of an *ostensive definition* – where we define a term by pointing to or otherwise indicating an *example* of something.

True, the sentence 'Here is a hand' *can* be used to make a claim. For example, if I am on an archaeological dig, rummaging among some small bones, I may suddenly say, 'Here is a hand'. Here is a claim, and because I make a claim, it makes sense to ask how I know it is true, to doubt it, and so on. And of course, I might well be able to supply good grounds for supposing my claim is true by, for example, pointing out features of the bones and the way they are arranged.

But of course this is not what Moore is doing. He is saying, 'Here is a hand' while waving his hand about in broad daylight. This is what I do if, say, I want to explain to a class of Italian students what the English word 'hand' means. When we give such a definition, it does not make sense to then ask, 'How do you know that?' Someone who attempts to raise such doubts has simply misunderstood how the sentence is being used. Consider, for example, another definition: 'Vixens are female foxes.' Someone who asks, 'But how do you know all the vixens are female?' simply demonstrates that they have misunderstood how this sentence is used. They think it is being used to make a claim, when in fact it is used to *define* 'vixen'.

In Wittgenstein's view, both Moore *and* the sceptic make the same fundamental error: the mistake of supposing that 'Here is a hand' is used, under *these* circumstances, to make a claim. As soon as Moore concedes that he is indeed making a claim, the sceptic can then point out that the claim cannot be justified, and so will conclude that Moore doesn't know that the claim is true. The trick, so far as avoiding that sceptical conclusion is concerned, is to refuse to concede that any claim is made.

Biography

Born 1873, in London, England. G. E. Moore (as he preferred to be known due to his dislike of his first names, George Edward) grew up in south London. Along with the logician Frege and two of his colleagues at Trinity College, Cambridge – Bertrand Russell and Ludwig Wittgenstein – Moore is one of the founders of modern 'analytic' philosophy. As an undergraduate, Moore was persuaded by the young Russell and J. M. E. McTaggart, a young philosophy fellow at Trinity, to pursue philosophy as well as classics. Moore flourished as a philosopher, gaining a first class degree in the subject, and then winning a prize fellowship.

Moore initially embraced the idealist philosophy of McTaggart, but soon came to reject it. He became a professor of philosophy at Trinity and editor of the philosophy journal *Mind*. In Cambridge, he was friends with some of those who later formed the Bloomsbury Group, including Lytton Strachey, Leonard Woolf and Maynard Keynes.

Moore is perhaps best known for his ethical theory and his 'common sense' approach to philosophical questions. His 'proof of an external world', discussed here, provides a slightly baffling example of this 'common sense' approach in action.

Moore died 1958, in Cambridge.

Major works

Principia Ethica
Philosophical Studies
Some Main Problems of Philosophy
Philosophical Papers

Ludwig Wittgenstein
1889–1951

Private language argument

'Imagine someone saying: "But I know how tall I am!" and laying his hand on top of his head to prove it.'

One of the aims of Wittgenstein's *Philosophical Investigations* is to show that one widely held view of what minds are like is fundamentally confused. The 'private language argument' of the *Philosophical Investigations* is one of the arguments that Wittgenstein uses to support this view. I introduce it at the end of this chapter. But first let's begin by sketching out the view that Wittgenstein rejects.

The private mind

How do sensation terms like 'pain' function? How do they acquire their meaning?

When we first start to think about these questions, most of us find ourselves quickly drawn to a certain sort of picture. To be in pain, we suppose, is to be in a certain mental state – a state from which other people are *necessarily* excluded. It is as if our mental life takes place behind *an impenetrable barrier.*

I don't mean a mere physical barrier, such as my skull. My brain is physically hidden behind my skull, and so others can't normally observe it. But my brain is not necessarily hidden from others. The barrier around it can, in principle, be breached. I could have a brain scan or my head could be penetrated via fibre-optic probes, enabling others to look inside.

My mind, on the other hand, is not merely physically hidden. Unlike any mere physical barrier, the barrier around my mind is something that it is *in principle* impossible for others to breach.

Others can observe my outward behaviour, of course. They can observe that, when I drop that very heavy rock on my foot, I hop about and cry out in pain. They might also find out what is going on physically inside my head when I am in pain. But that still would not give them access to my pain as *I* experience it. They can't, as it were, enter my mind, to find out how the experience is *for me*, from the point of view of the *subject*.

So it seems the inner, subjective quality of the pain I feel is necessarily hidden from others in a way that the physical activity in my brain is not.

Unlike my brain, my pain is *essentially* private.

'Pain' as a label for something private

If the picture of the mind sketched out above is correct, how do sensation terms like 'pain' function? The answer seems obvious. I use 'pain' as the name of something that confronts me within this private, inner realm. I can define 'pain' by saying, 'By "pain", I mean *this*' and focusing my attention on the unpleasant sensation with which I'm currently inwardly presented.

But if that is how I use the word 'pain', then not only is my pain essentially private, *so too is the meaning of 'pain'*.

Wittgenstein: the meaning of 'pain' is wholly public

This view of the mind, in which sensation and other psychological terms function as labels that are applied inwardly to private phenomena, may sound plausible, at least to begin with. Different versions of it crop up in the thinking of many philosophers down through the centuries. But if Wittgenstein is correct, this picture of the mind as an essentially private realm is fundamentally muddled. There is no such realm. It is a philosophical illusion.

So how does he think that sensation terms like 'pain' function, if not as the names of private phenomena?

He believes their meaning can only be captured by referring to what is *publicly* available – to what can be seen and heard by others.

Is Wittgenstein a behaviourist?

This might make Wittgenstein sound as if he thinks pain is just publicly observable behaviour. But that is not Wittgenstein's view. Nor is he a logical behaviourist who insists that all talk about pain can be reduced to talk about complex behavioural dispositions (this is the view of Gilbert Ryle; see page 293 for an explanation of *logical behaviourism*). Wittgenstein's position is subtler than that of the behaviourist. Certainly, he would deny that we can *reduce* the meaning of psychological talk to that of non-psychological talk. But he does have at least this much in common with the behaviourist: *he thinks that the meaning of 'pain' can be fully explained solely in terms of what is publicly available, including, of course, our behaviour.*

Is Wittgenstein denying the obvious?

To many, this will sound strange. It's tempting to ask, 'Isn't Wittgenstein denying the obvious? Isn't it perfectly obvious that these private, inner phenomena *do* exist? I am experiencing a pain right now. Surely nothing could be more certain than the fact that *this* exists?'

Not according to Wittgenstein. The private 'something' is an illusion.

This is not to deny that you're in pain. Nor is it to suggest that it's not excruciating. Wittgenstein merely wants to remove the philosophical picture of pain that hypnotizes you into believing there is something *essentially private* about pain, and about our mental life more generally.

Two views about how 'pain' functions

We can bring out the difference between Wittgenstein's view of how 'pain' functions and the picture he rejects by asking, 'Could people who can't feel pain (they do exist) know what the word "pain" means?'

Notice that, if 'pain' really was the name of something private and inner, then people who don't feel pain can't know what 'pain' means. They can know what people who say they are in pain say and, of course, do. They know I turn a funny colour and yell when I hit my thumb with a hammer. But they don't know what pain itself – the inner, private sensation – is like, as they've never felt it themselves.

In Wittgenstein's view, by contrast, someone who has never experienced pain can still know exactly what the word 'pain' means. If he's right, the meaning of 'pain' is explained solely by pointing out what is publicly available – to what we say and do. Because there is nothing 'private' about the meaning of 'pain', no part of its meaning need be unknown to those who can't feel it.

Wittgenstein's private language argument

Let's now turn to the private language argument. The aim of this argument is to show that, not only does 'pain' not function in the private way we're tempted to suppose, but that *no term could function in that way*. Even if there were such private, inner sensations, *we could not introduce meaningful signs for them*. But why not? Why couldn't I do the following?

I have a certain private inner sensation. I inwardly focus my attention on this sensation, and say to myself, 'By "S" I mean *this* – what I am experiencing right now.' In this way, I introduce a name the meaning of which is itself essentially private. No one can peek inside my mind and discover what I mean by 'S'. Why can't I introduce a meaningful term in this manner?

Wittgenstein insists such a definition can't work. I might be under the illusion that, having engaged in this inner act, I have now given 'S' a meaning. But its meaning is just that – an illusion.

Let's look at a crucial passage from *Philospohical Investigations*. Suppose that, in order to introduce 'S':

> *...I speak, or write the sign down, and at the same time I concentrate my attention on the sensation – and so, as it were, point to it inwardly. – But what is this ceremony for? For that is all it seems to be! A definition surely serves to establish the meaning of a sign. – Well, that is done precisely by the concentration of my attention; for in this way I impress on myself the connexion between the sign and the sensation. – But 'I impress it on myself' can only mean: this process brings it about that I remember the connexion right in future. But in the present case I have no criterion of correctness. One would like to say: whatever is going to seem right to me is right. And that only means that here we can't talk about 'rightness'.*

The argument presented in this passage is notoriously difficult to decipher. Some philosophers are convinced that Wittgenstein here establishes that we can't introduce meaningful signs in this manner. In which case it would seem to follow that '*pain*' *can't function in this way either*. However, other philosophers remain unconvinced. Let's take a closer look at the argument.

No criterion of correctness

Wittgenstein insists that after I define 'S' by focusing my attention on my private sensation, I possess no 'criterion of correctness' by which I might check whether I apply the term correctly in future.

This does seem to be true. If, later on, I have another sensation that I think is S again, there's nothing available against which I might check whether my memory of how to apply 'S' is correct.

There is an obvious contrast here with public terms. If I am unsure about whether I have remembered, say, how to apply the term 'puce' correctly, I can always go and consult a colour chart. At the very least, I can go and ask others who are more knowledgeable than me about how such terms are applied. But in the case of 'S', no such independent check is available. All I know is that this *seems* to me like S again. But *is* it S again? There's no way of checking.

The final step

At the end of the quoted passage, Wittgenstein moves from the observation that I possess no criterion of correctness to the conclusion that 'we can't talk about rightness'. The idea here seems to be that, because I can't check whether I apply 'S' correctly, there is no such thing as the 'right' or 'correct' way to apply it. But if there is no such thing as the 'right' way to apply 'S', then surely 'S' has no meaning. And so, while I might *think* I have introduced a meaningful sign, 'S' turns out to be meaningless.

Many philosophers consider this final step in the argument dubious, to say the least. Why does it follow that if I can't check whether I apply 'S' correctly that there is no such thing as 'correct'? Even if I can't check whether I apply 'S' correctly, perhaps I *do* apply it correctly, all the same.

Is Wittgenstein's argument cogent? I will leave that for you to decide.

The beetle in the box

Later in the *Philosophical Investigations*, Wittgenstein offers an argument designed to show that, whether or not I have succeeded in giving 'S' a meaning, the word 'pain' certainly does not function in the way 'S' is intended to.

Here is what Wittgenstein says:

Suppose everyone had a box with something in it: we'll call it a 'beetle'. No one can look into anyone else's box, and everyone says he knows what a beetle is by looking at his beetle. – Here it would be

*quite possible for everyone to have something dif-
ferent in his box. One might even imagine such a
thing constantly changing. – But suppose the word
'beetle' had a use in these people's language? – If so
it would not be used as the name of a thing. The
thing in the box has no place in the language-game
at all; not even as a something: for the box might
even be empty. – No, one can 'divide through' by the
thing in the box; it cancels out, whatever it is.*

The moral is that, even if we concede, for the sake of argument, that the mind is a sort of private inner space
populated by private mental phenomena – like a box that
no one else could peek inside – the words of our public
language (such as 'beetle' and 'pain') can't name anything in the box. So far as the public meaning of these
words is concerned the 'thing in the box' is irrelevant.

There is some plausibility to this point. 'After all,' you
may ask, 'how can there be more to the meaning of our
shared, public language than we are capable of teaching
to and learning from each other? And if there can't, then
the "thing in the box" – the secret thing that we can't be
shown by anyone else – can't be part of the public meaning of either "beetle" or "pain", can it?'

Again, I leave it for you to judge whether this argument
is cogent.

Biography

Born 1889, in Vienna, Austria. Ludwig Wittgenstein was born into a wealthy Jewish family, the youngest of eight children. His parents were highly cultured and well connected, and musicians such as Mahler and Brahms visited their home. Ludwig's own brother Paul became a renowned concert pianist – and remained so even after losing his right arm during the First World War. Unfortunately, depression ran in the family – three of Ludwig's brothers committed suicide.

Wittgenstein was educated at home until 1903, when he became a pupil of the technical school in Linz. His attendance at the school overlapped with that of Adolf Hitler, and it's been suggested that Hitler's anti-Semitism was fed by his dislike of the young Ludwig.

In 1906 Wittgenstein began studying mechanical engineering, ending up at the Victoria University of Manchester in 1908. His work in engineering led him on to the study of mathematics and its foundations. This in turn led Wittgenstein to start up a correspondence with the renowned German philosopher of mathematics and language Frege (see page 245), who recommended that Wittgenstein go and study under Bertrand Russell (see page 258) at Cambridge. When Wittgenstein turned up at Cambridge unannounced and presented Russell with some of his work, Russell was impressed, and Wittgenstein became his pupil. Russell later wrote that Wittgenstein 'is the ablest person I have come across since Moore' (for Moore, see page 269).

In 1913 Wittgenstein retreated to a house in a remote corner of Norway where he began his first great published work, the *Tractatus Logico-Philosophicus*. When the First World War broke out Wittgenstein fought for the Austro-Hungarian army and was captured by the Italians, becoming a prisoner of war until 1919. He kept the manuscript of the *Tractatus* in his rucksack throughout the war, completing it during captivity. The book, which appeared in 1921, is the only major work published in his lifetime.

After the war, Wittgenstein began to lead a very different life to the one he had previously enjoyed. He gave his fortune to his siblings and lived frugally. This marked change in lifestyle may have been a result of his wartime experiences.

After publishing his masterpiece, Wittgenstein turned away from philosophy for a time. He worked as a schoolteacher and a gardener, and designed and built a house for one of his sisters. But then Wittgenstein became increasingly interested in philosophy once again. His views changed, and he began to think that the *Tractatus* was not, after all, his last word. Wittgenstein gradually developed a different view, questioning and rejecting some of the central claims of his earlier philosophy.

In his second great work, *Philosophical Investigations*, published posthumously in 1951, Wittgenstein claims that philosophical problems are a result of linguistic confusions generated by our failure to attend to how language is used. While the *Tractatus* presents all language and representation as having a single function – to picture facts – Wittgenstein's later philosophy emphasizes the radically different ways in which language and other forms of representation are used. Our failure to recognize this diversity is, says Wittgenstein, a major source of philosophical confusion.

Wittgenstein died in Cambridge in 1951.

Major works

Tractatus Logico-Philosophicus
Philosophical Investigations

Martin Heidegger

1889–1976

Heidegger's hammer

'Making itself intelligible is suicide for philosophy.'

Heidegger's fundamental concern is with what he calls 'the question of being'. It is a question he thinks the Western philosophical tradition has largely forgotten since the time of the Greeks. The kind of 'being' Heidegger is interested in is *that which is peculiar to human beings.*

Here, I briefly contrast Heidegger's view of the human situation with that of Descartes (see page 104).

According to Heidegger, the fundamental mode of human consciousness (which he calls *Dasein* – literally meaning *being there*) is not, as Descartes supposed, a kind of detached, separate existence, but something always firmly located in the world.

Since Descartes's time philosophers have tended to view the human condition as essentially one of a *subject* in a world of *objects*. What essentially marks us out as subjects is conscious awareness – we have conscious experiences and engage in conscious reflection.

Once we begin to view ourselves in this way, as subjects divided from a world of objects, certain classic philosophical problems arise. Not the least of these is the problem of explaining how we might acquire *knowledge* of the world. Descartes's inner world of consciousness threatens to become a prison, cutting us off from the external world of *objects* and making knowledge of it impossible. For all I know, I might be hallucinating, or asleep in bed dreaming, or the victim of an elaborate illusion conjured up by an evil spirit.

By focusing on reflective consciousness, Descartes detaches us from the world – making us disembodied observers of it. He then faces the problem of explaining how we might know about, or even interact with, the world.

Heidegger's hammer

Heidegger, on the other hand, engages in an analysis of the notion of the kind of being that is specific to human beings. He believes that this analysis reveals that the human condition is *not, as Descartes supposes, fundamentally one of detached conscious reflection of the world.* It is one of actually *being in the world.*

One of Heidegger's favourite illustrations of this point is of a man using a hammer. If the man is competent with the tool, he will typically use it, not with conscious deliberation, but unthinkingly. If he is consciously aware of or thinking about anything at all, it may be something entirely unrelated. He might, for example, be involved in deep philosophical debate with a colleague while he hammers in the nails. The act of hammering is engaged in without any conscious reflection at all.

Heidegger does not deny that we *can* attend consciously and deliberately to what we are doing. I can, if I wish, focus my conscious attention on my hammering. But that is not how we normally use a hammer. Conscious, reflective engagement typically arises only when something *goes wrong*.

If my hammer cracks and is at risk of falling to bits, then I am likely to hammer with greater care, acutely aware of every movement that I make. Similarly, if my car's steering is faulty, I will move the steering wheel with great deliberation. And if the pavement is broken and uneven, I may well give it my full attention as I walk along in order not to trip. But if Heidegger is correct, this sort of reflective, conscious engagement with the world is not, as Descartes supposes, our primary way of encountering it.

From Descartes's view of the human situation, which divides us from the world, the fundamental philosophical puzzles are epistemological. How can we *know* anything of the world? But the world is not a place we are separated from, as if by some sort of screen. So then it is not something we need to *infer* the existence of, as Descartes supposes. It is, if you like, the place where we start.

Heidegger's criticism of Husserl

Like Husserl, Heidegger is a phenomenologist – he also offers a descriptive philosophy of experience. However,

Heidegger's version of phenomenology differs markedly from that of Husserl.

Husserl believed that in studying consciousness and conscious experience we can, in effect, 'bracket' the objective world – set aside questions about whether what is experienced is objectively real – and focus purely on the content of the conscious experience itself.

Heidegger rejects Husserl's approach to the study of consciousness. Like Husserl, Heidegger believes that consciousness is essentially 'intentional' – it is *about*, or, if you like, *directed towards* objects. We are never just conscious, we are always conscious *of* something. But what generates this intentionality, according to Heidegger, *is precisely our activity in the world*. It is through our engagement with the world that meaning and intentionality are created.

Accordingly, for Heidegger, conscious experience is itself *essentially rooted in the world*. We cannot, as Husserl attempts to do, bracket the world and study consciousness in isolation.

Biography

Born 1889, in Messkirch, Baden, Germany. Born into a Roman Catholic family, Heidegger's education was supported by the Church. His plans to become a Jesuit priest were dashed by illness and he became an academic instead. He studied under Husserl (see page 253) at the University of Freiburg for several years, eventually becoming rector of the university in 1933, shortly after the Nazis came to power.

Heidegger joined the Nazi Party in May 1933. His inaugural address as rector culminated with three exclamations of 'Heil Hitler'. But, although the university was increasingly sympathetic to National Socialism while under Heidegger's stewardship, he appears to have distanced himself from the party quickly and resigned his post just a year later. He was at one point investigated by the Gestapo.

After the war, Heidegger's earlier Nazi associations led to his being banned from teaching until 1951. He died in 1976, in Messkirch

Major works

Being and Time

Gilbert Ryle

1900-76

Behaviourism

'Overt intelligent performances are not clues to the workings of minds; they are those workings.'

Suppose you are showing some guests around your home. 'Here is the bathroom', you say, 'And here are the bedrooms'. But as you complete the tour, one guest asks a strange question. 'This is all lovely – the bedrooms are delightful, the kitchen cosy – but where is your *home*?'

Your guest has just committed what Ryle terms a *category mistake* – they suppose a *home* belongs to the same category of thing as the various rooms that go to make it up. The supposition is that your home is some further place that exists in addition to those rooms, whereas in fact those rooms comprise your home.

A category mistake involves attributing a property to something in one category that can actually only be attributed to something in another.

In the above example, your guest makes the mistake of

thinking that your home has the property of being one of the rooms within your house, when in fact it is the house itself.

Another example of a category mistake would be, on being told, 'Ted gave Mary an insolent stare', to search Mary for the stare. Here, the mistake is to suppose that an insolent stare is some sort of material object, like a marble or a banana, that could be handed to someone physically. Insolent stares are of course an entirely different category of thing altogether.

Descartes's alleged category mistake

Ryle considers category mistakes to be a major source of philosophical confusion. Indeed, he supposes that Descartes (see page 64), in effect, commits just such a mistake.

Descartes believes the mind to be an immaterial substance – a thing capable of existing independently of any material substance, such as your material body. But this, claims Ryle, is an error.

When we observe others, we witness their public behaviour. Human beings possess an extraordinarily rich range of behavioural capacities and dispositions. Noting these behavioural dispositions, we may still be inclined to ask, but what about *their mind*? The mind, Descartes supposes, is a further 'something' that exists *in addition to* these behavioural capacities and dispositions. Something existing behind the scenes, as it were.

In Ryle's view, this hidden 'something' is an illusion – it is, in his words, a 'ghost in the machine'. If you are looking for 'the mind', *look no further than our complex repertoire of behavioural dispositions.* That, ultimately, is what minds are.

Descartes treats 'the mind' as the name of a substance – of something capable of independent existence. But this raises all sorts of puzzles. The mind then begins to seem a very peculiar and elusive sort of substance. Where is it exactly? And what is it like?

The solution, according to Ryle, is to realize that the philosophical hunt for 'the mind' is a bit like the hunt for Ted's insolent stare. In both cases, we make the mistake of supposing we are dealing with some sort of substance.

The philosophical theory of mind in which 'minds' are reduced to such complex behavioural dispositions is known as 'behaviourism'.

Ryle's behaviourism

The kind of *philosophical* behaviourism to which Ryle subscribes (or at least, in places, certainly seems to subscribe) should not be confused with the *methodological* behaviourism of psychologists like J. B. Watson and B. F. Skinner, who insisted that a properly scientific approach to the study of mind should restrict itself to what is publicly observable – to behaviour. This type of behaviourism recommends a way of *studying* the mind. It involves no commitment at all in defining what the mind actually *is*.

Philosophical behaviourism, by contrast, is a theory about what it is to have a mind. It insists that psychological talk about minds, pains and so on can be entirely translated into non-psychological talk about behavioural dispositions. To say that someone is in pain is just to say that they are disposed to say 'ouch!'

I don't mean that the philosophical behaviourist thinks that the mind is *just* behaviour. That would clearly be too crude. A great deal of mental activity can take place even when a person is standing perfectly still. There is mental activity, but no outwardly observable behaviour.

The philosophical behaviourist offers a more sophisticated analysis of the mental. Pain, claims the behaviourist, is a *dispositional* property. To be in pain is to be disposed to behave in certain ways (for example, to cry out). And you may be disposed to behave in those ways even if you do not actually do so.

Compare the property of being soluble. It too is a dispositional property. For a sugar cube to be soluble is merely for it to be true that *if* the cube is placed in water, then (other things being equal) it will dissolve. That is all that there is to the concept of solubility.

Similarly, in a behaviourist's view, we can exhaustively characterize what it is for someone to be in pain just by talking about how they are disposed to behave. That is not to say that they will behave in these ways. Just as a sugar cube will dissolve only if placed in water, so someone in pain will behave in the relevant ways only if the conditions are right.

Two classic puzzles solved

One of the most attractive features of behaviourism is the way in which it immediately solves two classic philosophical puzzles concerning the mind.

1. *The problem of other minds.* The first puzzle is the problem of other minds. If your mind is hidden, if it is something behind your outward behaviour, then how can I know you have one? For all I know, you might be a mindless shell. Yes, your outward behaviour is like mine, but what grounds do I have for supposing that this outward behaviour is accompanied by a hidden mind in the case of anyone other than myself?

Behaviourism solves this puzzle by supposing that the mind just is a highly complex set of behavioural dispositions. Behavioural dispositions are something that we can establish merely by observing how something does in fact behave. Just as I can know a sugar cube is soluble by studying how it behaves in water, so I can establish that you have a mind by observing how you behave in a range of different circumstances.

2. *The mind–body problem.* The other classic philosophical puzzle that behaviourism neatly solves is that of explaining how mind and body are related. If we suppose that Descartes is right and your mind is an immaterial substance, how this immaterial entity and your physical body *connect* is a mystery. How do they *interact*? When I decide to raise my arm, how does my mind make my arm obey? Isn't an immaterial substance far too

philosophically flimsy a thing to be able to get any real purchase on something as substantive as the several kilos of flesh and bone that comprise my arm?

Again, philosophical behaviourism provides a solution to this puzzle. If all that is required for something to possess a mind is to possess various complex behavioural dispositions, then even a material substance – a living organism, for example – can possess a mind. Rather than placing minds outside the material realm, logical behaviourism allows us to locate them firmly within it.

Today, most philosophers reject philosophical behaviourism because of a number of well-known objections and counter-examples. One classic objection is set out below.

A classic objection to behaviourism

As we have seen, philosophical behaviourism has two very important advantages – it provides neat solutions to two time-honoured problems concerning the mind. Yet few contemporary philosophers are behaviourists. Behaviourism faces a number of famous objections, one of which is outlined below.

Zombie attack If philosophical behaviourism is correct, claims about mental states can be analysed into claims about behaviour – whether actual behaviour or behavioural dispositions. To describe someone as having a mind is just to describe them as possessing a whole range of complex behavioural dispositions.

However, is that really all there is to having a mind? What about the subjective, felt quality of conscious experiences, for example? Can that really be reduced to behavioural dispositions?

Arguably not. It seems conceivable, for example, that *zombies* might exist. I don't mean the kind of zombies you see in movies – the sort that drool and stumble about. I am talking about *philosophical* zombies. A philosophical zombie is someone who (unlike a movie zombie) is outwardly *exactly* like you or me, but who lacks any conscious experiences at all. When a philosophical zombie bites into a lemon, they *behave* outwardly like you or me. They spit out the pips, grimace. But this outward show of behaviour is not accompanied by any of the rich conscious experience we have. When we bite into a lemon, we experience an acidic, bitter taste that makes us recoil a little. The zombie recoils too. But not because it has any such experience. It merely behaves *as if* it does.

Take a moment to think about it – does the suggestion that such zombies could exist at least *make sense*? I am not saying it is likely they exist, of course. But is it *in principle* possible that they might, perhaps on some other planet? Or might *robot* zombies exist, i.e. mechanical wonders that merely perfectly *simulate* conscious minds?

Most of us are inclined to answer 'yes' to these questions. The possibility of zombies does indeed appear to make sense. There doesn't seem to be any *conceptual* problem with the thought that there might be beings that are outwardly just like us, but lacking any inner conscious life.

The trouble is, if logical behaviourism were true, there *should* be a conceptual problem with the suggestion that zombies might exist. Compare solubility. That's a dispositional property. To say something is soluble is just to say it will dissolve when placed in water, other things being equal. Given the meaning of 'soluble', a sugar cube that is soluble but doesn't dissolve when placed in water simply doesn't make sense. Such a cube really is *inconceivable*. In fact it involves a logical contradiction: the cube would have to dissolve in water and not dissolve in water.

However, if having a mind is similarly a dispositional property, neither should it make sense to suppose that there might be beings that have all the same outward dispositions as us, but that lack conscious minds. Such philosophical zombies should also involve a contradiction. The fact that zombies are conceivable and involve no such contradiction seems straightforwardly to refute logical behaviourism.

Defending behaviourism Perhaps there are moves that might be made to defend some form of behaviourism. Here is one suggestion.

The behaviourist might say, 'The only reason you are inclined to think that zombies are conceivable is because you have already subscribed to the confused, Cartesian conception of the mind in which conscious minds are things that exist in addition to our behavioural dispositions. That's why you think you can imagine a being that is physically just like you, but lacks a mind. The fact that your philosophical intuitions support the view that zombies are conceivable is merely a symptom of your philosophical confusion.'

Whether or not this response is adequate to deal with the zombie counter-example to logical behaviourism is for you to consider.

Biography

Born 1900, in Brighton, Sussex, England. Gilbert Ryle was educated at Brighton College. He gained first class honours at Queen's College, Oxford, and became a lecturer at Christ Church in 1924. His career remained centred in Oxford where he was Waynflete Professor of Metaphysical Philosophy for a quarter of a century. He was a member of the 'ordinary language school' of philosophy that supposed that philosophical problems could be solved, or dissolved, by paying scrupulously close attention to the subtleties of ordinary language and its use. Ryle worked for British intelligence during the Second World War, after which he received his chair at Oxford.

He edited the influential and prestigious journal of philosophy, *Mind*, from 1948 to 1971, inheriting the post from G. E. Moore (see page 269). He died in Whitby, Yorkshire in 1976.

Major works

The Concept of Mind
Collected Papers
Dilemmas
Categories

Karl Popper

1902–94

Falsificationism

'In so far as a statement speaks about reality, it must be falsifiable: insofar as it is not falsifiable, it does not speak about reality.'

How does science progress? An obvious suggestion is that it progresses through theories being *confirmed*. Suppose that Mary, a scientist, is considering the hypothesis that all swans are white. She can confirm her hypothesis by observing many swans. Each white swan she observes further confirms her hypothesis. Surely, if she observes enough white swans (and no non-white ones), it eventually becomes *reasonable* for her to believe all swans are white.

Hume's problem of induction

Hume (see page 92) raises a famous problem concerning inductive reason. He claims that the only reason we suppose that the premises of an inductive argument give us good grounds for thinking the conclusion is true is that we make an assumption. The assumption is that *nature is uniform.* We assume that there are certain basic regularities and patterns that hold throughout every corner of the universe – at all times and all places – including those portions of the universe that we have not yet observed.

Suppose that we did not make that assumption. Then we certainly wouldn't conclude that all swans are white given the fact that the first thousand we observed were white. For all we know, these thousand white swans might just be a local regularity – a regularity that will come to an end with the very next swan we observe.

The challenge that Hume sets us is this. We are surely only justified in concluding that all swans are white if we can justify this background assumption that nature is uniform. How might the assumption be justified?

There are but two options. We might:

(i) justify it independently of observation;

or

(ii) justify it by appeal to observation.

It seems that we cannot do (i). How can we possibly know that nature is uniform without observing it? So that leaves (ii). But of course we cannot *directly* observe all of nature – we cannot establish by direct observation that the universe is uniform throughout. In particular, we cannot directly observe the future.

It seems that the only option left, so far as justifying the assumption that nature is uniform is concerned, is to note that nature is uniform *locally*, and then *infer* that nature is uniform *generally*. But of course, this would itself be a piece of *inductive reasoning*. We would then be using inductive reasoning to *justify itself*. But then our justification of inductive reasoning would be circular. Circular justification is no justification at all. Just as you can't justify trusting a second-hand car salesman by pointing out that he himself claims to be reliable, so you can't justify the claim that induction is reliable by relying on an induction.

So, it seems that we are only justified in reasoning inductively if we can justify the assumption that nature is uniform. However, this assumption cannot be justified. Therefore, we are *not justified* in reasoning inductively. The conclusion is not that inductive reasoning is not *very justified,* or not *as justified* as we would like it to be, but rather *not justified at all*.

Certainly, the fact that every swan Mary has ever observed has been white does not *logically* entail that they are all white (there is no logical contradiction involved in supposing the next one won't be white).

As we have seen, the philosopher David Hume has

constructed an ingenious argument that appears to demonstrate that, no matter how many white swans Mary observes, she will never possess the *slightest* grounds for supposing that all swans are white.

If Hume is correct, this is bad news for science. Scientific theories and hypotheses depend for their confirmation upon inductive reasoning. If inductive reasoning is wholly irrational, as Hume maintains, then so too are all our scientific theories and hypotheses.

True, we would ordinarily consider mad someone who thought that, instead of the sun appearing over the horizon tomorrow morning, a million-mile-wide luminous panda will appear instead. But if Hume is correct, this 'mad' expectation is actually no more irrational than the expectation that the sun will appear instead. If Hume is right, the predictions of madmen are no less reasonable than those of our greatest scientists.

Falsification

Popper's response to Hume's problem is ingenious. Popper suggests that, rather than science progressing by theories being confirmed (i.e. through inductive reasoning), it progresses instead by theories being *falsified*.

Here is an example of falsification at work. Mary believes all swans are white. But then, on a visit to New Zealand, she observes a black swan. Her observation that a black swan exists *falsifies* the theory that all swans are white. She now knows that her original belief was false.

Popper argues that science similarly progresses by theories being falsified. Scientists construct theories about the world. They then *test* their theories. Deductively, they derive certain observable conclusions from their theories and then check to see if those conclusions are true. The theories that remain unfalsified are retained, while those that are falsified are discarded and replaced by new theories that are in turn tested, and so on.

So, if Popper is correct, *science is not dependent upon inductive reasoning at all.* It progresses instead through theories being falsified. In which case, Hume's problem of induction is neatly sidestepped.

Inductive and deductive reasoning

In philosophy, an *argument* is made up of one or more premises and a conclusion. The premises are supposed rationally to support the conclusion.

In a *deductive* argument, the premises are supposed logically to entail the conclusion, as in this example:

I am a man.
All men are 10 feet tall.
Therefore: I am 10 feet tall.

This argument is indeed deductively *valid*, i.e. *if* the premises are true (and, of course, here the second premise isn't), then the conclusion will be true too.

In an *inductive* argument, by contrast, the premises

are merely supposed to provide the conclusion with rational support. We suppose that, if the premises are true, then the conclusion is *likely* to be true – though there is no logical guarantee that if the premises are true then the conclusion is too, as there is in a valid deductive argument.

Here's an example of an inductive argument:

Swan 1 is white.
Swan 2 is white.
[...]
Swan 1,000 is white.
Therefore: all swans are white.

This argument has a thousand premises, though I have only listed three. We suppose that the truth of all the premises makes it reasonable to suppose that the conclusion is true.

Notice that scientific theories make claims about what has not yet been observed. However, claims about what has been observed up to now never *deductively* entail claims about what has not yet been observed. Therefore, scientists have to rely on *inductive* reasoning to justify their theories.

The more falsifiable, the better

We have seen that, according to Popper, science progresses

through theories being falsified. But he does not suppose that all theories yet to be falsified are equally good. Some are better than others. Popper suggests that what makes one unfalsified theory preferable to another is the fact that it can be *more easily falsified*.

One way in which a theory might be more easily falsified is if it is *wider ranging*. Consider these two theories:

All Dobermann dogs have four legs.

All dogs have four legs.

The second theory is obviously wider ranging. It predicts everything the first predicts, and a great deal more, which makes it more easily falsified.

Another way in which one theory can be more easily falsifiable than another is if its predictions are more *precise*. Suppose I tell you: 'All large dogs are happy'. This is a pretty vague claim. What, exactly, does 'large' mean, here? And what counts as 'happy'? These are vague terms picking out properties that are not easily quantifiable or measurable. For that reason, there's always room for me to sidestep an apparent falsification. You might try to falsify my theory by pointing to your collie Rover and saying, 'Rover's pretty big, and he growls all the time'. But then I might reply, 'Ah, but Rover is not exactly what I meant by large – I meant *really* large', or, 'I wouldn't say Rover isn't *happy*, exactly – he's just aggressive.'

Clearly, a theory that makes unambiguous predictions about precisely quantifiable and measurable phenomena will be that much more easily falsified. The claim that every dog weighs exactly two kilograms can easily be falsified with the aid of scales.

Popper on Freud and Marx

According to Popper, any genuinely scientific hypothesis will be falsifiable. That is to say, there will be some possible observation that would falsify it. In Popper's view, a properly scientific statement makes a positive claim about how things stand in the world, and so runs the risk of being false. The world may turn out not to be as the theory claims. Unfalsifiable statements fail to make any such claim. They are consistent with however the world might be. But then they lack any genuine empirical content.

The following is an obvious example of an unfalsifiable claim:

Either I weigh 76 kg or I do not weigh 76 kg.

This claim is unfalsifiable. Whatever we might observe is consistent with its truth. So it is not properly scientific.

Popper suggests a way of distinguishing between those theories that are genuinely scientific and those that are mere pseudo-science. Genuinely scientific theories are falsifiable. Theories that claim to be scientific but are unfalsifiable are pseudo-science. According to

Popper, Marx's theory of history (see page 126) and Freud's theory of the unconscious both fail this test of falsifiability. Popper argues that whatever evidence we might try to bring against Marx's or Freud's respective theories, there always turns out to be a way in which the theories can accommodate it (just like the predictions of some astrologers). In Popper's view, the theories of Marx and Freud are not bad scientific theories. Rather, they are *not scientific theories at all.*

Avoiding falsification

However, there is one question that Popper still needs to deal with. Surely, with a little ingenuity, any theory can be protected from falsification?

Take Aristotle's theory that every heavenly body is perfectly spherical. When Galileo developed a telescope that revealed mountains and valleys on the Moon, that appeared to falsify Aristotle's theory completely. But not everyone accepted that conclusion. One ingenious thinker suggested that there is in fact an invisible substance that fills in the valleys of the moon up to the tops of its mountains, a substance Galileo's telescope failed to reveal. So the Moon is perfectly spherical, and Aristotle's theory is not falsified.

But if every theory can be protected from being falsified by means of such moves – and of course it can – then *no theory need ever be considered falsified.* Isn't this a problem for Popper's theory?

Ad hoc moves

Popper anticipates this objection, and adds a refinement to his theory to deal with it. In Popper's view, it was not legitimate to defend Aristotle's theory by appealing to an invisible substance. He agrees that *sometimes* it is possible to defend a theory legitimately by adding to or developing it. But such moves are legitimate only when they introduce *new, independently testable* consequences.

Here's an example. Newton's theory of universal gravitation predicts that the planets will move in elliptical orbits around the sun unless they are acted upon by some other body. When Uranus turned out to have a wobbly, non-elliptical orbit, was that taken to falsify Newton's theory? No. Scientists defended Newton's theory by saying there must be some as yet undetected object acting upon Uranus.

Was this argument legitimate? Yes, according to Popper. For it led to *new tests* – scientists could now check to see if there was an object near Uranus and in looking for it they discovered a new planet: Neptune.

The attempt to defend Aristotle's theory by positing an invisible substance filling up the valleys of the moon, by contrast, was illegitimate. For it led to *no new tests*. There was no way that anyone could, at the time, check whether such an invisible substance existed. Popper calls such untestable modifications or additions to theories *ad hoc*. Popper's view is that theories can sometimes legitimately be protected from being falsified.

We might defend the theory by adding to or modifying it in some way. But we should not make *ad hoc* moves.

A concern about falsificationism

One of the most commonly raised concerns about Popper's falsificationism is that it requires that we simply accept Hume's conclusion that no scientific theory is ever confirmed – not even to a small degree. Consider these two predictions: (i) *Tomorrow morning the sun will appear over the horizon;* and (ii) *Tomorrow morning a million-mile-wide luminous panda will appear over the horizon.*

Which hypothesis is more reasonable? Popper, in effect, accepts Hume's conclusion that they are equally reasonable.

But of course we all believe that the first prediction is much more reasonable. True, there is Hume's problem of induction to solve. But Popper doesn't solve it. He merely sidesteps it by, in effect, abandoning the claim that one prediction is more reasonable than the other.

Clearly, if there were some *other* way of dealing with the problem of induction – a way that allowed us to say what seems obviously true: that the first prediction is more reasonable than the second – then that would surely be preferable.

Biography

Born 1902, in Vienna, Austria. Karl Popper is best known as a philosopher of science and for his criticisms of utopian political philosophies. Popper took a doctorate in philosophy in

Vienna in 1928, and was friendly with some members of the famous Vienna Circle of philosophers, including Moritz Schlick. Popper shared the Vienna Circle's interest in the question of how to distinguish science from non-science, but was critical of their positivism.

In 1937 the rise of Nazism led Popper to leave Austria for New Zealand, where he taught at the University of Canterbury. In 1946 he took up a readership at the London School of Economics, becoming a professor in 1949. He remained at the LSE for the rest of his career. He was knighted in 1965, became a Fellow of the Royal Society in 1976 and received the Insignia of a Companion of Honour in 1982. Popper died in Croydon in 1994.

Major works

The Logic of Scientific Discovery
The Open Society and its Enemies
Conjectures and Refutations

Jean-Paul Sartre

1905–80

Freedom and 'bad faith'

'Man is condemned to be free.'

According to Sartre, human beings are free. This freedom can be an enormous burden and responsibility, which we do not always wish to acknowledge. So we deceive ourselves, pretending that, like mere physical objects, we are wholly predetermined to be what we are and to behave the way we do. When we deceive ourselves like this, we are guilty of 'bad faith'.

An illustration of bad faith

Sartre asks us to imagine that a woman has met a man in a bar. The man flirts and the woman enjoys the attention. But she deceives herself. Rather than confront the fact that she is clearly being pursued sexually, a fact she would find uncomfortable, she convinces herself that the man's interest is entirely platonic so that she can enjoy his company without having to acknowledge his desire.

But then the man takes her hand. This clearly signals more

than a mere friendly gesture. But the woman doesn't pull her hand away. That would cause embarrassment and demolish her fantasy. But neither does she respond. She simply leaves her hand in his, as if it were something over which she has no control.

In the above example, the woman deceives herself about the reality of her situation. She also treats her hand as if it were a mere disconnected 'thing'. The truth is that she is free either to respond to the man's advances or to reject them. This freedom places on her a responsibility she would prefer not to have. So she engages in a form of self-deception.

Another illustration: the waiter

The waiter plays his part in an exaggerated, clichéd way, balancing his tray and pouring drinks as if he were merely a puppet playing the role of waiter.

This waiter, suggests Sartre, is also guilty of bad faith. The truth is he is free either to carry on being a waiter, or to throw down his towel and leave that instant, perhaps to travel the world or find love or pursue a very different career. But again, this freedom weighs heavily on his shoulders, and so the waiter deceives himself by acting as if he is a mere thing. He acts as if he were 'made' to be a waiter, much as an egg-timer is made to time eggs. He pretends that choice of what to make of himself is not one he faces. But of course, it is.

Existentialism and freedom

Sartre is one of the best-known existentialist philosophers. The existentialists place human freedom at the centre of their philosophy. For Sartre, that we are free is not just a, but *the*, fundamental truth about human beings. He expresses this point by saying that, for human beings, 'existence precedes essence'.

An obvious contrast here is with Aquinas (see page 65). Clearly, many things have a purpose, such as an egg-timer made to time eggs. For such objects, 'essence precedes existence'. They exist so that they can fulfil a particular role. According to Aquinas, *the same is true of human beings*. They too have a God-given purpose that it is their moral duty not to thwart.

Sartre rejects this view. He claims that human beings differ from mere objects in that, for humans, 'existence precedes essence'. We exist, but not for any particular purpose as in the way that egg-timers do. Nor do we possess an intrinsic nature that determines how we will behave, in the way that hearts or egg-timers do. What purpose we have, and how we act, must be *freely chosen by us.* This responsibility to choose is unavoidable. We are, at every moment, able to break free from our old habits and the roles society has handed us. You are able, right now, to choose different values, to find new goals, to forge yourself anew.

Of course, we don't choose the particular circumstances into which we are born. I might be born into a wealthy family, or I might find myself a slave. These circumstances will inevitably restrict what I am able to do. Nevertheless, says Sartre, I am free to choose how I *respond* to these circumstances. Even if I am born a slave, I can choose either to acquiesce or to disobey and face the consequences.

Sartre thinks that the fact that we have this freedom at each moment to break free from all our old habits and choices and forge ourselves anew is something of which we are all aware, at some level. But it is also something we can find hard to bear – we make our choices 'in anguish, abandonment, and despair'. Which is why we fall into bad faith – why we end up deceiving ourselves about this radical freedom.

Sartre confronts us with this unavoidable responsibility to choose, and exposes the deceptions we perpetrate on ourselves in order to try to avoid it.

But...

Sartre insists that we are free. But how can he be so sure? If human beings are physical objects then they are governed by the same laws of nature that govern all other physical objects. So then surely they are not free – they merely *think* they are.

Sartre's belief in our freedom appears to be based on our subjective awareness. It *feels* to us, from the inside, as if we are free. But this feeling may be deceptive. Philosophers have certainly struggled to explain how it is possible for human beings to be both free and also subject to the same laws of nature as other physical objects.

Biography

Born 1905 in Paris, Sartre's father died when he was very young. Sartre moved to his grandfather's house, where he immersed himself in the library. In 1929, after graduating from the École Normale Supérieure, Sartre worked as a secondary school teacher. He was called up for military service in 1939 and was captured by the Germans in 1940. Released in 1941, Sartre returned to Paris where he had some involvement with the French Resistance.

After the war, Sartre became increasingly political, describing himself as a Marxist. He was pro-communist, though he became disillusioned with the Communist Party after the Soviet suppression of the Hungarian revolution in 1956. He is as well known for his literary output as he is for his philosophy. In 1964 he was offered the Nobel prize for literature, but refused. Sartre died in Paris in 1980.

Major works

Being and Nothingness
Existentialism is a Humanism

Hannah Arendt

1906–75

The banality of evil

*'The sad truth is that most evil is done by people
who never make up their minds to be good or evil.'*

Arendt's work focuses on political theory and philosophy. A key
episode in her career was her attendance at the trial of the Nazi
war criminal, Adolf Eichmann, as a reporter for *New Yorker*
magazine. Eichmann had been a chief architect of Hitler's 'final
solution' to the 'Jewish problem'.

After the war Eichmann fled to Argentina, where he was finally captured in 1960 by undercover agents of the Israeli secret
service – Mossad. They smuggled him out of the country to
Jerusalem where he was put on trial for war crimes and crimes
against humanity. Eichmann was widely assumed to be a monster – a vicious psychopath motivated by his seething hatred of
the Jews – but, based on her observations at his trial, Arendt
drew a very different conclusion. In her book, *Eichmann in
Jerusalem: A Report on the Banality of Evil,* Arendt argues that
Eichmann was, in fact, a remarkably ordinary man. Yes, what he

did was monstrous, but Eichmann himself turned out to be, not the cruel and pitiless monster of popular belief, but an unimaginative, mild-mannered functionary.

Arendt thought that Eichmann saw himself simply as a man doing his duty by following orders. He approached the murder of millions of Jews as just another bureaucratic task assigned to him that he must accomplish to the best of his ability. He had no great antipathy towards Jews, but carried out his orders unquestioningly and relentlessly, as if he and his accomplices had been asked to exterminate vermin. The humanity of his victims simply wasn't his concern.

Arendt's conclusions were highly controversial. Her portrait of Eichmann almost entirely contradicted the image of him in the popular imagination. Her views outraged many, and came under vehement attack. Particularly controversial was Arendt's claim that Eichmann was not motivated by anti-Semitism – he simply followed orders. If Arendt is correct, had Eichmann been ordered to save Jews, he would have done that instead.

Eichmann's loss of moral autonomy

What was fundamentally wrong with Eichmann, from Arendt's point of view? Her diagnosis is that he had *given up his moral autonomy*. In particular, he did not *think or question*. He simply obeyed.

After the trial, Arendt became less interested in political action and rather more in what motivates it – in particular in the kind of thought and judgement that lies behind it.

Kant, Enlightenment and Eichmann

Eichmann and the Holocaust are sometimes linked to the Enlightenment – the intellectual movement spanning the 17th–19th centuries that placed particular emphasis on the autonomy of the individual and the role of reason. Kant (see page 102) is one of the greatest Enlightenment thinkers, and he provides the classic definition of what Enlightenment is:

> *Enlightenment is the emergence of man from his self-imposed infancy. Infancy is the inability to use one's reason without the guidance of another. It is self-imposed, when it depends on a deficiency, not of reason, but of the resolve and courage to use it without external guidance. Thus the watchword of enlightenment is:* Sapere aude! *Have the courage to use your own reason!*

The term 'Enlightenment' was of course intended to contrast the new age of reason with the relative darkness of the Middle Ages, which tended to be dominated by deference to authority – particularly religious authority. Prior to the Enlightenment, education largely took the form of the handing down of truths by received authorities. Individuals were expected to accept, more or less without question, their pronouncements. If Arendt is right, Eichmann could be described as a pre-Enlightenment figure. He failed to question or to think for himself and denied his own moral autonomy. His role, he thought, was to accept and follow orders uncritically.

And yet, interestingly, the Enlightenment stands accused of being one of the root causes of the Holocaust (particularly by post-modern thinkers such as Adorno and Lyotard). Indeed, Eichmann is sometimes quoted as supporting that view. At his trial, he claimed to be familiar with the work of Kant, describing himself as 'having lived his whole life according to Kant's moral precepts'. Is this not a powerful indictment of Kant's Enlightenment vision? Arendt would certainly disagree. She points out that Eichmann's claim is:

> ...outrageous, on the face of it, and also incomprehensible, since Kant's moral philosophy is so closely bound up with man's faculty of judgement, which rules out blind obedience.

Eichmann may indeed have been familiar with Kant's ethics, but he did not understand them. Arendt says, 'from the moment he was charged with carrying out the final solution he had ceased to live according to Kantian principles'.

That Eichmann seriously misunderstood Kant was made clear when he said that Kant's categorical imperative could be summarized as:

> Be loyal to the laws, be a disciplined person, live an orderly life, do not come into conflict with laws.

It's clear that Kant's notion of duty is not equivalent to that of following orders and obeying the law. Ironically, Eichmann thought Kant's philosophy was that the individual should accept and follow the instructions of authority uncritically. Eichmann certainly wasn't what Kant would call 'enlightened'.

Biography

Born 1906, in Linden, Germany. Although included in this book as a philosopher, Hannah Arendt preferred the title 'political theorist'. Born to secular Jewish parents in Linden (now part of Hanover) she was raised in Königsberg (now Kaliningrad in Russia) and Berlin. She went to the University of Marburg where she studied under the philosopher Martin Heidegger (see page 288). They became romantically involved and the relationship continued, on and off, for a long time. Arendt also studied under the philosopher Karl Jaspers at Heidelberg, and later moved to Berlin.

In 1933, in common with most other Jews, she was banned from teaching in Germany and fled to France. After the fall of France, she fled again, moving to the United States in 1941, where she was granted citizenship in 1950. Arendt was a scholar at several notable American universities and eventually became the first woman full fellow of Princeton University. Hannah Arendt died 1975, in New York City.

Major works

The Origins of Totalitarianism

The Human Condition

Eichmann in Jerusalem: A Report on the Banality of Evil

Simone de Beauvoir

1908–86

The otherness of women

'One is not born a woman, one becomes one.'

The Second Sex is de Beauvoir's greatest philosophical work. Published in 1949, it remains one of the seminal feminist works. The book was deeply controversial, provoking attacks from both the political left and right. The Vatican even placed *The Second Sex* on its Index of prohibited books.

Three categories of being

The Second Sex addresses the question, 'Why is woman other?' What does de Beauvoir mean by 'other'? It is a concept that she adopted from Sartre (see page 176), who distinguishes three distinct categories of being or existence.

First, there is *being-in-itself*, which is the kind of non-human being or existence a mere thing has – such as a mountain, tree, chair or animal.

Second, there is the kind of 'being' that humans possess – the being of *consciousness*. Sartre calls this sort of existence *being-for-itself*. It is characterized by a fundamental form of *freedom* – the freedom to choose, to change, to be other than what it is. A person is not determined to be or do anything in particular in the way that a mountain, tree, chair or animal is. We have no essential nature that makes particular forms of behaviour unavoidable. We can choose to live a new life and adopt new values.

Third, there is *being-for-others*. I am not merely a being-for-itself, I am also a being-for-others, for others who may view me, and define me, in different ways.

Women defined as *other*

When de Beauvoir suggests that women are *other*, she is drawing on Sartre's notion of being-for-others. Women are defined by men as other. They are typically viewed as something inferior and secondary to whatever man sees himself as being: for example, men view themselves as rational and intellectual, and women as emotional and animal.

Indeed, women are viewed by men as a kind of being-in-itself. Like a heart or a lion, a woman is supposed to possess an essential nature that determines what she is and what she will do. Men have supposed that women have a role that is both natural and unalterable.

The truth, insists de Beauvoir, is that women are not *born* women. They are *made* women. Women do not have an essential nature that determines how they must behave. They too are beings-in-themselves, able to choose a different life. Women are free to cast off their status as other, to become, if they wish, financially independent, creative and intellectual.

Of course, de Beauvoir is well aware that not all women will rush to liberate themselves from their role as other. She notes that a 'woman may be well-pleased with her role as the other'. By embracing the definition of herself that men provide – by playing her allotted role with enthusiasm as if she were 'made' to fulfil it (like a mechanical Stepford wife) – a woman may try to hide her freedom from herself. For, as Sartre points out, with this freedom also comes great anguish. (Compare Sartre's example of the waiter (see page 316) who, by totally immersing himself in his role as waiter and pretending he is a mere thing with an essential nature that determines what he does, tries to hide from himself his fundamental freedom to choose to be and do something else.)

Criticism of de Beauvoir

Some feminist critics of de Beauvoir have argued that what she recommends, in effect, is that women become *more like men* – childless, financially independent and professional. She does not, it is claimed, sufficiently value other qualities traditionally deemed female. But this may be to misunderstand de Beauvoir. She is not saying that these 'male' qualities are *better*; instead, she believes that it is only by becoming professional and financially independent that women will be liberated.

Biography

Born 1908, in Paris, Simone de Beauvoir was a highly influential 20th-century thinker. A philosopher and novelist, she was one of the most significant figures in the rise of the feminist movement.

The daughter of a conservative and atheistic civil servant father and a devoutly Roman Catholic mother, Simone was a bright child, and her father encouraged her to read and write from early childhood. She was educated at a private Catholic school for girls. Unsurprisingly, given her schooling and her mother's faith, Simone was a religious child. But at the age of 14, she lost her faith, never to regain it. At school she began an intense friendship with Elizabeth Mabille (Zaza), a fellow pupil who died, very young, in 1929 – a tragedy that Simone blamed on the French bourgeoisie's obsession with money and class. Zaza's parents were intent on an arranged marriage for their daughter, and forbade her to see the man she loved. Simone believed her friend died of a broken heart and Zaza's treatment by her family and her subsequent death troubled Simone for the rest of her life.

Despite her father's wishes, de Beauvoir decided not to marry, but to pursue a life of study instead. An exceptionally gifted student, she passed her philosophy *agrégation* at the Sorbonne at the age of just 21 to become the youngest philosophy tutor in France.

While at the Sorbonne, de Beauvoir met the philosopher Jean-Paul Sartre, who was a student at the École Normale Supérieure. De Beauvoir and Sartre became lovers and remained so until his death in 1980. They had an 'open' relationship that allowed them to pursue liaisons with others (they described their own relationship as 'essential' and their relationships with others as 'contingent').

De Beauvoir described herself as Sartre's philosophical disciple. But although her thinking remained within the existentialist framework developed by Sartre, she made significant philosophical contributions of her own.

Partly as a result of her relationship with Sartre, and partly because of her own work, de Beauvoir became a great intellectual celebrity. She was a prominent political activist, attending demonstrations and writing in support of equal rights for women. She died in Paris in 1986.

Major works

The Second Sex

Willard Van Orman Quine

1908–2000

The attack on analyticity

'...for all its a priori *reasonableness, a boundary between the analytic and synthetic statements simply has not been drawn. That there is such a distinction to be drawn at all is an unempirical dogma of empiricists, a metaphysical article of faith.'*

Many philosophers have drawn a distinction between two kinds of truth. Take these two sentences: 'All bachelors are unmarried males' and 'All vixens are female foxes'. Both are true. But why?

It's tempting to answer: because of what the words 'bachelor' and 'vixen' mean. These sentences are true in virtue of meaning. The expression 'bachelor' has the same meaning as 'unmarried male'. They are synonymous expressions. So, 'All bachelors are unmarried males' is guaranteed to be true simply by virtue of the meaning of the words that comprise the sentence – likewise, 'All vixens are female foxes'.

We might add that, because these sentences are true in virtue of meaning, so there is no possibility of them being falsified by experience. Philosophers call those truths that are true in virtue of meaning, *analytic* truths. They are contrasted with non-analytic, or *synthetic*, truths, such as:

All bachelors live in the vicinity of the Earth.

This sentence is also true, but not in virtue of meaning. Its truth, it's tempting to say, is of an entirely different sort. It is true because it correctly describes how things stand – as a matter of fact all bachelors do live in the vicinity of the Earth. Had they not, the sentence would have been false.

It seems, then, that there are two kinds of truth: analytic truth and synthetic truth.

Quine's attack on the analytic/synthetic distinction

The analytic/synthetic distinction has been one of the bread-and-butter distinctions of philosophy ever since Kant (see page 177) who introduced the terms, although similar distinctions can be found in Hume and Leibniz (see pages 158 and 137, respectively). While not all philosophers were convinced that all *a priori* necessary truths are analytic (Kant wasn't), there was, before the 1950s, a broad consensus that the analytic/synthetic distinction was a real one, and that there were, indeed, two categorically different kinds of truth.

So when Quine presented a powerful-looking argument that the analytic/synthetic distinction is, in effect, empty, and that no distinction can be made between those true statements that are true purely in virtue of meaning and those that are not, the effect on the philosophical community was electrifying. Indeed, as a result of Quine's work, many philosophers, particularly in the United States, are now convinced that there is no cogent notion of 'analyticity'.

How does Quine attack the distinction?

The web of belief

According to Quine, our beliefs about the world form a web. They face the test of experience not separately, but collectively:

Our statements about the external world face the tribunal of sense experience not individually, but only as a corporate body.

To illustrate, suppose I believe that the Earth is flat, but then I come to possess two pieces of evidence suggesting my belief is false: a sailor tells me that he has sailed around the world and returned to the same place; and someone else has drawn my attention to the fact that, when boats disappear over the horizon, they disappear from the bottom up, as if the surface of the sea curved downwards.

These two pieces of evidence might lead me to have doubts about the Earth being flat. However, they are far from conclusive. The sailor might be lying or he might be deluded about having sailed round the world. The observation about distant ships might be dismissed by supposing that light rays travelling close to the surface of the sea are somehow bent over a distance. Of course, as more evidence against my theory that the Earth is flat begins to pile up, I might be more inclined to abandon my theory. However, as long as I am prepared to make increasingly far-reaching adjustments to my other beliefs – about the reliability of the testimony of sailors, about light, and so on – any apparently recalcitrant evidence can always be dealt with.

According to Quine, those beliefs that philosophers are inclined to call 'analytic' are simply those that are particularly well entrenched in our web of belief. They are the beliefs that we will be slowest to give up, given recalcitrant evidence.

But, insists Quine, *no belief is absolutely immune to revision in the light of experience in the way that analytic truths are supposed to be.* Given that enough recalcitrant evidence mounted up, we might decide that, rather than making ever more complex and dramatic adjustments to the rest of our web of belief, the most satisfactory solution would simply be to abandon one of the supposedly analytic and/or necessary truths. (Interestingly, some have since suggested that developments in quantum mechanics require that we revise the laws of logic.)

No satisfactory definition of analytic

The other key component to Quine's attack on the notion of

analyticity is that *no satisfactory explanation of the notion can be given*. We can define analyticity in terms of meaning, of course, by saying that the analytic truths are those that are 'true in virtue of meaning'. But, says Quine, the philosophical notion of meaning is just as opaque as that of analyticity. We might also try to explain analyticity in terms of the notions of synonymy, definition and necessity. Indeed, each of these terms might be defined in terms of the others. The problem is that together they form a tight little circle of notions none of which is ever properly explained.

Here's an analogy. Suppose I define a wibble as a collection of woobles, a wooble as an adult doofer, and doofers as the things that, when fully-grown, go to make up wibbles. I have defined each of my terms but have left you none the wiser as to what, if anything, I mean by them.

Quine says that we are in a similar situation with 'analytic'. Yes, we can define the term using other terms, but not in such a way that we get any closer to understanding what it is supposed to mean.

If I were to point to a pod of whales and say, '*That* is a wibble', what I mean by 'wibble' suddenly becomes much clearer. Can't we similarly explain what 'analytic truth' means? Can't we explain by just providing some examples, such as, 'All bachelors are unmarried'?

No, says Quine. Why suppose that 'All bachelors are unmarried' *is* unrevisable in the light of experience? True, we might not easily envisage circumstances under which we would consider it false. But merely because we can't easily envisage such circumstances doesn't mean that they don't exist.

If Quine is right that our statements are answerable to experience not individually, but collectively, and that *any* statement is potentially revisable in the light of experience, then even those statements that philosophers have traditionally called 'analytic' are revisable. But then to use such statements as examples of what 'analytic' means would be to beg the question. If Quine is right, they are not analytic.

Since Quine's attack on the notion of analyticity, it has largely, though not totally, fallen out of philosophical favour.

Explaining *a priori* knowledge

Armed with the notion of analyticity, several empiricist philosophers have attempted to explain how *a priori* knowledge is possible.

A priori knowledge can be established *independently of the evidence provided by our five senses*. It seems that we can know *a priori*, for example, that all bachelors are unmarried. We don't need to go out into the world and examine lots of bachelors to check that all are unmarried. We know, even before we look, that they will be. For example, we can also know *a priori* that two plus two equals four and that every surface is extended (has length and breadth). According to St Anselm (see page 51), we can even know *a priori* that God exists.

You can see how we might try to explain how certain

truths can be known *a priori* by appealing to the notion of analyticity. How can I know, without examining any bachelors, that they are all unmarried? Because 'bachelor' *means* 'unmarried male', I need only understand the meaning of the words that make up the sentence to know that the sentence is true.

Armed with the notion of analyticity, we can also explain why every bachelor being an unmarried male is a *necessary* truth. Bachelor means 'unmarried male', so 'All bachelors are unmarried' says that all unmarried males are unmarried, which is a *logical* truth (denial would be a *logical contradiction*).

Of course, it is debatable whether all *a priori* necessary truths are analytic. But if they are, that would certainly explain why they are *a priori* and necessary. Hence many philosophers have been drawn to the idea that all *a priori* necessary truths are analytic.

Biography

Born 1908, in Akron, Ohio, Willard Van Orman Quine ('Van' to his friends) was one of the most influential philosophers of the 20th century. Quine studied mathematics and logic at Oberlin College before winning a scholarship to Harvard University, where he spent his entire teaching career, holding the Edgar Pierce Chair of Philosophy from 1956 to 2000. During the Second World War he worked for US military intelligence. He died in Boston, Mass. in 2000.

Major works

The Ways of Paradox

Mathematical Logic

Set Theory and Its Logic

Quiddities

Word and Object

A. J. Ayer

1910–89

Meta-ethics

'We say that a sentence is factually significant to any given person, if, and only if, he knows how to verify the proposition it purports to express – that is, he knows what observations would lead him, under certain conditions, to accept the proposition as being true or reject it as being false.'

Meta-ethical theories focus on the nature of moral judgements. One question they address is: what we are doing when we describe things as being morally 'right' or 'wrong'? In *Language, Truth and Logic*, Ayer offers one of the most famous, and controversial, answers to this question.

Killing is wrong

On the face of it, when we say, 'Killing is wrong', we *seem* to be attributing to acts of killing a certain *property* – the *moral* property of it being wrong. Presumably, what we say will then be *true* or *false* depending on whether or not acts of killing possess that property.

However, if Ayer is correct, this appearance is deceptive. True, 'Killing is wrong' looks superficially similar to, 'Unicycling is easy', or, 'Running is healthy', but if Ayer is correct, while these last two sentences are indeed used to make claims (and so might be true or false), 'Killing is wrong' is *not used to make a claim at all*. Rather, when we say:

Killing is wrong,

we *express* our *attitude* towards killing. Compare it with:

Hoorah for the Red Sox!

This sentence is not used to make any sort of claim. Instead it is used to express approval of and support for a particular team. Because no claim is made, there is no possibility of the statement being either true or false.

In Ayer's view, the sentence, 'Killing is wrong', is used in a similar way, to express our disapproval of killing. Similarly, 'Repaying one's debts is right' is used to express our approval of debt repayment. Because, in each case, no claim is made, then *neither sentence is true or false*.

Ayer acknowledges that ethical terms can be included in statements of fact. But, as he here explains, their inclusion in such a statement adds nothing to its factual content:

If I say to someone, 'You acted wrongly in stealing that money', I am not stating anything more than if I had simply said, 'You stole that money'. In adding that this action is wrong I am not making any further statement about it. I am simply evincing my moral disapproval of it. It is as if I had said, 'You stole that money', in a peculiar tone of horror, or written it with the addition of some special exclamation marks.

Contrast with subjectivism

Ayer's theory is usually referred to as *emotivism* (and sometimes, for obvious reasons, the *boo-hoorah theory*). It is easily confused with a rather different meta-ethical theory called *subjectivism*.

Subjectivism says that when I say, 'Killing is wrong', I *claim* that I disapprove of killing. So a claim is made – but it is only a claim about my own subjective attitudes. What I say may be true or false.

Ayer's theory, on the other hand, says that 'Killing is wrong' is used *expressively*. That is why the sentence can be neither true nor false.

Of course, most of us *think* we use 'Killing is wrong' to make a claim, one that we suppose is true. But if Ayer is correct, we are simply mistaken.

Why emotivism?

What leads Ayer to emotivism? Two key thoughts drive Ayer in this direction. The first is his adherence to the positivist view that *a sentence can have factual significance only if it is possible empirically to verify it.* The second is his acceptance of Hume's claim that *moral sentences such as 'Killing is wrong' are not empirically verifiable.* It follows, then, that 'Killing is wrong' lacks factual significance.

But then how is 'Killing is wrong' used, if not to state a fact? This is the question that Ayer's emotivism is designed to answer. Emotivism allows statements such as 'Killing is wrong' to have a kind of meaning, even though they lack factual significance.

A criticism of emotivism

Emotivism faces a number of well-known objections, many of which are powerful. Here is just one example.

Emotivism rules out *the possibility of error* when it comes to moral judgements. If Ayer is correct that 'Killing is wrong' can't be true or false, then I can't be mistaken when I say, 'Killing is wrong'. Nor can I be mistaken if I say, 'Killing is right'.

But of course, we do acknowledge the possibility of error in moral judgements. We suppose, for example, that we were mistaken when we thought slavery was morally acceptable.

Emotivism, at the very least, has a hard time explaining why we acknowledge the possibility of error in such moral judgements if it is a possibility that doesn't actually exist.

Biography

Born 1910, in London, Alfred Jules ('A.J.') Ayer was a precocious child. He attended a boarding school in Eastbourne before winning first a scholarship to Eton, and then a classics
scholarship to Christ Church, Oxford. Although, as a philosopher, Ayer led a rich and eventful life, he once said that he
would have preferred to be a tap dancer.

Ayer's great work *Language, Truth and Logic,* was published
in 1936, when he was just 26. In this book he applies the
positivist thesis that a sentence is factually significant if, and
only if, it is empirically verifiable to derive a number of dramatic conclusions, including the conclusions that (i) all metaphysical theories are meaningless, and (ii) in describing things
as being morally 'good' or 'bad', we are really just expressing
our own attitudes. He died in London in 1989.

Major works

Language, Truth and Logic
The Problem of Knowledge
The Central Questions of Philosophy

Peter Strawson

1919–2006

Russell's theory of descriptions

'To refer is not to assert, though you refer in order to go on to assert.'

Strawson was a great respecter of the subtleties of ordinary linguistic usage, and he was suspicious of the tendency of the philosophers of his day to want to put everything into logical notation. When Paul Grice, Strawson's former tutor, said to him, 'If you can't put it in symbols, it's not worth saying', Strawson replied, 'If you can put it in symbols, it's not worth saying.'

Strawson made his name in philosophy in 1950 with the publication in *Mind* of his paper 'On Referring', which is critical of Russell's theory of descriptions (see Russell, page 258). Strawson argues that Russell's analysis of definite descriptions is insufficiently sensitive to the way in which they are ordinarily used.

Russell on descriptions

Definite descriptions typically have the form 'the so-and-so'. So, for example, the following sentences all contain definite descriptions:

The woman I met on the bus *is Spanish.*
The dog *ate my homework.*
The queen of Sweden *lives in Stockholm.*

In order to solve several thorny puzzles involving definite descriptions (one of which is outlined on pages 266), Russell offers an analysis of sentences containing them (an analysis being a clarification of the underlying logical structure of what is said).

For example, Russell would analyse, 'The queen of Sweden lives in Stockholm' in this way:

1. At least one thing is a queen of Sweden, and

2. At most one thing is a queen of Sweden, and

3. Whatever is a queen of Sweden lives in Stockholm.

So, if Russell is correct, the sentence, 'The queen of Sweden lives in Stockholm', actually makes *three distinct claims.*

Happily, in Russell's analysis, 'The queen of Sweden lives in Stockholm' comes out as true, just as it should, since each of the three claims contained in his analysis is true: there is exactly one queen of Sweden and she does live in Stockholm.

If Russell is correct then *definite descriptions are not used to refer*. When I say, 'The queen of Sweden lives in Stockholm,' I do not refer to someone – the queen of Sweden – and then claim about *that particular individual* that *she* lives in Stockholm. Rather, I talk *quantities*. I say that the number of individuals who are queen of Sweden is *exactly one*, and that for *all* individuals, if they are a queen of Sweden, then they live in Stockholm.

The king of France case

Strawson famously criticizes Russell's theory of descriptions. One of Strawson's objections is that Russell's analysis produces some very counter-intuitive results. Take a look at this sentence, for example:

The king of France is bald.

Is this sentence true, false, or neither? Obviously, it isn't true – there is no king of France. But then neither, I imagine you'll say, is it false. How can it be false if there is no king of France? Surely, as there is no such king, what we say is neither true nor false.

The problem for Russell's theory is this. In Russell's analysis, the sentence says:

1. At least one thing is a king of France, and

2. At most one thing is a king of France, and

3. Whatever is a king of France is bald.

According to Russell, the sentence asserts that there is exactly one king of France. However, since France is a republic and has no king, the first claim is false, so the analysed sentence *comes out as false*.

But, as we just said the sentence is *neither true nor false*, Russell's analysis gives the *wrong result*.

Strawson: descriptions refer

So what has gone wrong here? Strawson argues that definite descriptions *are* used to refer. When we use the description 'the queen of Sweden', for example, we use it to refer to a particular person. We do not, as Russell believes, *assert* that there is exactly one queen of Sweden. Instead, our use of the description *presupposes* or takes for granted that there is exactly one queen of Sweden for us to refer to.

Similarly, the use of, 'The king of France is bald' *presupposes* that there is exactly one king of France. As there are no kings of France for us to refer to, this presupposition is false. Because of this failure of reference, the sentence itself fails to say something true or false.

So, to sum up, Russell's analysis makes 'The king of France is bald' come out as false. Strawson has it come out as neither true nor false. As, intuitively, the sentence is neither true nor false, *it seems Strawson is right*.

Defending Russell's theory

The criticism of Russell's theory outlined here is far from decisive. Many philosophers defend his theory in the following way:

True, it feels uncomfortable to describe as false, 'The king of France is bald', but Strawson's explanation for this feeling of discomfort is that it isn't false. Perhaps our discomfort is due to the fact that, though the sentence is false, it would be *misleading* to say it is false.

A defender of Russell can point out that *usually*, when a sentence of the form 'The F is G' is false, it is false because although it is true that at least one thing is F and at most one thing is G, it is false that whatever is F is G. So, for example, 'The queen of Sweden lives in Swindon' is false because, although it is true that there is exactly one queen of Sweden, she doesn't live in Swindon.

We might then add that the reason we feel uncomfortable about 'The king of France is bald' being described as false is that the sentence is *false in an unusual way*. It is false not because the third of the three claims that make up Russell's analysis is false (whatever is a king of France is bald), but because the first is (there is in fact no king of France). And so while it would be correct to use the description of false, it would be misleading. If we say, 'That's false', our audience is likely

348

to conclude wrongly that there is exactly one king of France, but that he isn't bald.

So the mere fact that we feel uncomfortable about saying, 'That's false' does *not* show that Russell's analysis of 'The king of France is bald' is incorrect.

Currently, the philosophical consensus is that Strawson's objection, though ingenious, is not decisive.

Biography

Peter Strawson was born in the west London suburb of Ealing in 1919. His parents were both teachers and the family moved to Finchley, in north London, when his father was appointed headmaster of a local school. Peter attended Christ's College school, Finchley. He won a state scholarship and went up to St John's College, Oxford.

Disappointed with his second class degree in PPE (Philosophy, Politics and Economics), Strawson left Oxford in 1940 to join the military where he spent most of his war working on radar. After the war, he taught briefly at University College of North Wales, Bangor, before returning to Oxford where he had an illustrious career, first at University College (1948–68) and then at Magdalen College until his retirement in 1987. Strawson was made a fellow of the British Academy in 1960 and was Waynflete Professor of Metaphysics from 1968 to 1987. He was knighted in 1977. His son, Galen Strawson, is also a philosopher. He died in Oxford in 2006.

Major works
Individuals
The Bounds of Sense
Logico-Linguistic Papers
Freedom and Resentment
On Referring

Judith Jarvis Thomson

1929–

In defence of abortion

'You wake up in the morning and find yourself back-to-back in bed with an unconscious violinist...'

Is abortion morally wrong? Many argue that it is. Thomson constructs an ingenious thought-experiment, which she believes shows that it is, after all, morally permissible. As Thomson points out at the beginning of *A Defense of Abortion,* most opponents of abortion rely on the premise that a foetus is a human being – indeed, a person.

Armed with that premise, they might then argue as follows: A foetus is a person ... Every person has a right to life ... Therefore a foetus has a right to life.

Of course, we should acknowledge that a woman also has a right over her own body. But surely the right to life of the foetus trumps that right? A woman has a right to choose whether or not to have her ears pierced, but not whether or not to kill the person living inside her. And so, conclude some opponents of abortion, it is always wrong to kill a foetus.

Thomson suggests the first premise of this argument is questionable. She concedes that a foetus becomes a person sometime before birth. However, she thinks, the foetus is not a person at the moment of conception. It has the potential to become a person of course, as a planted acorn has the potential to become an oak tree. But for Thomson a newly fertilized ovum is not a person any more than an acorn is an oak tree. But let's suppose that a human foetus – *even at the very earliest stages of pregnancy* – is indeed a person. What, asks Thomson, follows from that? Not, she suggests, the conclusion that anti-abortionists draw. In order to argue her case, Thomson develops an analogy – the case of the violinist.

The violinist counter-example

Thomson outlines a hypothetical case that, she believes, is analogous to that of abortion:

> You wake up in the morning and find yourself back-to-back in bed with an unconscious violinist, a famous violinist, who has a fatal kidney ailment. You alone have the right blood type to help and so you have been kidnapped and plugged into the violinist's circulatory system, so that your kidneys can be used to extract poisons from his blood as well as your own. You are told that if you disconnect him he will die. But if you allow him to remain

plugged into you for nine months, he will be cured and survive.

Is it, asks Thomson, morally incumbent upon you to accede to this situation? Clearly not. It would be very nice if you were to agree to lie there for nine months until the violinist is cured. But you are not morally obliged to leave him plugged in. You have the right to disconnect yourself, if you wish. Yet if the violinist has a 'right to life', a right that trumps your right to do with your own body as you wish, then you *are* morally obliged to leave him connected.

Thomson thinks this demonstrates that there is something wrong with the 'right to life' argument. She suggests that if I believe I have a right to disconnect myself from this violinist, even though doing so will kill him, then I must concede that a woman has a right to abort a foetus, even if aborting that foetus will result in its death.

Thomson concedes people may have a right to life. But that does not mean they can never be killed, only that they should not be killed unjustly. There would be no injustice in disconnecting the violinist and thereby killing him. Thomson concludes that there is similarly no injustice in removing an unwanted foetus.

Objections

Thomson anticipates many replies to this line of argument, including the following:

353

The violinist is attached to you *against your will.* The unborn child growing within you, by contrast, was conceived through an act in which you engaged *freely*. This difference explains why it is morally acceptable for you to disconnect the violinist but not the foetus.

Thomson points out that, even if correct, this would still allow women who become pregnant through rape to abort (an act many anti-abortionists would oppose). Thomson also questions whether the fact that a pregnancy resulting from an act that you knew carried a slight risk of pregnancy means that you have no right to terminate. Suppose, says Thomson, that 'people seeds' drift about in the air like pollen. Open your windows and one might take root in your carpets or soft furnishings. You don't want children, so you erect mesh screens at every door and window to keep the seeds out. Unfortunately one of the screens has a tiny hole through which a seed passes to take root and grow in your home. Does this 'person plant' now have a right to the use of your home?

Surely not, suggests Thomson. It makes no difference that you freely and knowingly took the risk of a seed taking root in your house by having soft furnishings. Yes, you could have furnished your home with hard chairs and bare boards, but the fact that you took this slight risk does not entail that you are not within your rights to remove the rooted 'person plant'. The same then would appear to be true of a woman who engaged in sex using a condom that, unluckily, was defective. The fact that this woman knowingly took a small risk does not entail her not being within her rights to remove the 'person plant' that has now lodged inside her.

Opponents of abortion have questioned Thomson's analogies. But she is surely correct that, to show that abortion is immoral, it is not enough simply to show that a foetus is a person.

Biography

Born 1929, in New York City, Judith Jarvis Thomson was educated at Hunter College in New York. She is now Professor of Philosophy at the Department of Linguistics and Philosophy at the Massachusetts Institute of Technology (MIT). Although Thomson's philosophical interests cover a range of topics in ethics and metaphysics, she is probably still best known for her paper *A Defense of Abortion*, published in 1971. It is on that paper that we have focused here.

Major works

A Defense of Abortion
Rights, Restitution, and Risk
The Realm of Rights
Goodness and Advice

Saul Kripke

1940–

Against the description theory of names

'Proper names are rigid designators.'

Many philosophers have been drawn to the view that ordinary *proper names,* such as 'Elvis Presley', 'Aristotle' and 'Paris', have the same meaning as *definite descriptions* (roughly speaking, expressions of the form 'the so-and-so').

Take the name 'Aristotle'. If someone asks me who Aristotle is, I might well use a definite description to explain. For example, I might say:

> By 'Aristotle' I mean *the pupil of Plato and the teacher of Alexander.*

So, yes, we use descriptions to explain the meaning of names. But do names have the *same meaning* as descriptions? For example, is 'Aristotle' actually *synonymous* with the description 'the pupil of Plato and the teacher of Alexander'?

Let's call the theory that proper names are synonymous with definite descriptions *the description theory of names.*

How do names designate?

If the description theory of names is correct, it might explain how names are able to designate or refer. Again, consider the name 'Aristotle'. I am able to use this name to reach instantly across thousands of years and miles to locate a particular historical individual. How is that possible?

The description theory of names provides an answer. The designation of the name is whoever fits the relevant description. So, for example, if 'Aristotle' is synonymous with 'the pupil of Plato and the teacher of Alexander', then the name designates whoever, if anyone, fits this description. Designation is achieved by way of descriptive 'fit'.

Kripke's Gödel/Schmidt argument

Many philosophers now reject the description theory of names, and do so because they have been persuaded by Kripke's arguments. Here we look at just one of them.

Kripke asks us to imagine a hypothetical situation. The mathematician Gödel is credited with inventing the incompleteness theorem. For many people, the description 'the inventor of the incompleteness theorem' is the only description they associate with the name 'Gödel'. The day may even come when this is the only description that *anyone* associates with that name. Suppose this is actually the case. If the description theory is correct, 'Gödel' will, under these circumstances, presumably be synonymous with the description of 'the inventor of the incompleteness theorem'.

But notice that, if Gödel has the same meaning as that description, it should be *impossible* for Gödel to turn out *not* actually to be the inventor of the incompleteness theorem. To suppose it might turn out that Gödel didn't invent the incompleteness theorem would be to suppose it might emerge that the inventor of the incompleteness theorem did not invent the incompleteness theorem. But that involves a straightforward contradiction.

Yet, we *can* envisage such a situation. Suppose, for example, that a man called Schmidt invented the theorem. Before showing it to anyone else, Schmidt showed it to Gödel, who, in a fit of jealous rage, shot Schmidt and claimed the theorem for himself, which is why Gödel now ends up credited as the inventor of the incompleteness theorem. But Gödel did not invent it. Schmidt did.

If the description theory of names were correct, the name 'Gödel' would, under these circumstances, designate Schmidt (as he is the one who fits the description). But of course it doesn't. It remains attached to Gödel, despite the fact that Gödel turns out not to be the inventor of the theorem.

The conclusion drawn by Kripke from this and other arguments is that, though we may indeed use descriptions in order to explain 'whom we mean', a proper name is never *synonymous* with any such description. It could turn out that the bearer of the name does not fit the particular description or descriptions that we associate with a name, and that someone else (in the above example, Schmidt) does.

Similarly, it could turn out that Aristotle did few if any of the things we believe he did. Aristotle might yet turn out to be a habitual liar and fantasist who concocted a fictional life for himself, claiming the credit for writing and doing things that were actually written and done by several different people.

In which case, there is no guarantee that any one of the descriptions we currently associate with the name 'Aristotle' actually fits Aristotle. But then the name cannot be synonymous with any of those descriptions.

The causal theory of reference

How do names refer, if not by virtue of their bearers fitting a certain description or descriptions? Kripke sketches out an alternative theory often referred to as the *causal theory of reference.*

A baby is born and baptized 'Aristotle'. The name is then passed on to friends and relatives, who pass it on to others, who pass it on to still others. Eventually, after the name has been passed down many generations, it finally reaches me. The reason I refer to the person originally baptized 'Aristotle' is that each person who received the name used it to refer to whoever they got the name from used it to refer to. The reference to 'Aristotle' is thus preserved by a *causal chain* running from me all the way back to ancient Greece. It is this chain that secures the reference, not any descriptions I might happen to associate with the name.

Biography

Born 1940, in Omaha, Nebraska, USA. Saul Kripke is currently Emeritus Professor of Philosophy at City University of New York (CUNY). He is one of the most significant philosophers of language of the 20th century.

Kripke was prodigiously gifted and precocious. He wrote an essay on the semantics of modal logic at the age of 16 and was able to teach graduate level courses in logic at the Massachusetts Institute of Technology (MIT) during his second undergraduate year at Harvard. He went on to teach at Harvard itself, the Rockefeller University in New York, Cornell and Princeton, before moving to CUNY in 2002.

Major works

Naming and Necessity

Wittgenstein on Rules and Private Language

Peter Singer

1946–

Speciesism

'Most human beings are speciesist.'

Each year about five billion animals are slaughtered in the United States. They are killed to satisfy the American taste for meat. The vast majority of us consider this sort of treatment of other species morally acceptable (or at least not particularly unacceptable). But is it?

After all, we know, do we not, that animals suffer? They are also, to differing degrees, capable of enjoying pleasurable experiences as well. Why then are we morally permitted to treat the members of other species so very differently to our own?

In *Animal Liberation* (1975), Peter Singer presents us with precisely this challenge: to morally justify the way in which we discriminate between our own species and others. His conclusion, shocking to many, is that this discrimination cannot, in fact, be morally justified. Indeed, Singer believes that the vast majority of human beings are currently guilty of what Singer terms 'speciesism' (an expression first coined by the British animal rights campaigner Richard Ryder) – a form of bigotry against other species comparable with sexism and racism.

Of course, no one has ever suggested we shouldn't be able to discriminate between conscious beings, or that we are not often morally justified in doing so. For example, we discriminate between children and adults. We give adults the rights to vote, to drive and to live their lives more or less as they see fit, while withholding all these rights from children. But this discrimination is morally justified. Children are not yet mature enough to be able to exercise the right to vote responsibly or to drive a vehicle safely. Here is a difference that does indeed morally justify our discriminating in the way we do.

On the other hand, withholding the right to vote on the grounds of sex or skin colour is morally unjustified, as they are irrelevant when it comes to the ability to exercise the right to vote. Refusing such rights to people on these grounds therefore constitutes a form of bigotry. We would be guilty of sexism and racism.

So the difficulty the vast majority of us face, if we are not to find ourselves guilty of a similar form of bigotry, is to justify the way in which we discriminate between human beings and other species.

Mental sophistication

Perhaps the most obvious suggestion to make is to point out that humans are far more mentally sophisticated than other species. We are more intelligent. We possess a shared language. We have a sense of right and wrong. Don't these differences between humans on the one hand and cows, pigs, apes and sheep on the other justify the difference in treatment?

Singer doesn't deny that our superior mental powers *can*, under certain circumstances, be morally relevant. Suppose we want to test a product on live subjects in a way that causes great pain and sometimes death. One option would be to abduct adult humans and test it on them. Another would be to use animals instead.

Singer reminds us that testing on captive humans might well result in greater suffering than testing on animals. If we start abducting and performing experiments on a group of humans, those that remain will soon figure out the danger and anticipate a similar fate. Far more stress and anxiety may be caused than if we simply test on animals that have no knowledge of the experiments and therefore will not experience any such anticipatory fear. In this case, perhaps we can make a slightly better case (if not a good case) for testing on animals than we can for testing on humans.

But, as Singer points out, sometimes our superior intellect means that we will suffer rather *less* than would an animal subjected to similar treatment. We can explain to prisoners of war that they will eventually be safely released, whereas wild animals incarcerated for a similar period of time cannot be given that knowledge, and so may suffer rather more than humans who have been similarly incarcerated.

The mentally impaired
Perhaps the most obvious difficulty presented by this appeal to

mental sophistication to justify the way in which we discriminate against other species is that *some humans are no more mentally sophisticated than are some animals*. Human babies, in fact, are far less cerebral than mature primates. And of course there are many unfortunate mature humans who, either through an accident of birth, disease or physical damage, are no smarter or more mentally sophisticated than the average ape. If certain forms of mental sophistication are our criteria for determining who is deserving of full moral consideration and who is not, then *the boundary between those who are deserving and those who are undeserving will not coincide with the boundary between our species and others*. It seems we will have to say that, if it is morally acceptable to experiment upon or kill for meat the smarter animals, then it is morally acceptable to treat babies and the mentally impaired in a similar way. Or, if we continue to insist that it is morally wrong to treat the less cerebral humans in this way, then we will have to say that it's equally wrong to treat the smarter animals in this way too. What we cannot do is continue to draw the boundary between those who deserve our full moral concern and those who do not where we do – between our species and the rest.

A new attitude towards other species?

So Singer believes that we can be morally justified in discriminating between sentient beings. He agrees it would be more wrong to kill a normal adult human than it would be to kill, say, a mouse (in *Practical Ethics*, Singer suggests this is because a human, as a self-conscious being, can, and typically does, have a preference to go on living, whereas a mouse can have no such preference).

However, Singer argues that there is no moral justification for the way in which we currently discriminate. Discriminating solely on the basis of species is no more justified than discriminating on the basis of sex or race. So far as justifying our current practices is concerned, whether or not sentient beings have feathers or fur, a beak or teeth, two legs or four, is simply irrelevant – as irrelevant as skin colour or gender.

When we now look back a few hundred years to how white people discriminated against black, and men discriminated against women, many of us are shocked. With hindsight, it can be difficult to understand how those who were engaged in these practices were unable to recognize that what they were doing was wrong. 'How could they not see?' we ask.

The day may come when the human race looks back on the way we currently treat other species – raising and slaughtering five billion animals a year, in many cases under the most horrific conditions, simply to satisfy our taste for their flesh – and asks that same question. If that day comes, it will be, in large part, Peter Singer's legacy.

How *not* to avoid the charge of speciesism

Singer has many critics. Many criticisms focus on his utilitarianism. For an overview of some of the main criticisms of utilitarianism, see the chapters on Mill (see page 205) and Bentham (see page 188). However, even if we reject utilitarianism, the challenge Singer sets us – to point to the morally relevant difference between humans and other species that justifies our current discriminatory practices – remains. If we cannot meet that challenge, it is difficult to see how we can avoid the charge of speciesism, whether we're utilitarians or not.

Unfortunately, many people are under the misapprehension that if they can offer some cogent objection to utilitarianism, that is enough to fend off Singer's charge of bigotry. That is not the case.

Biography

Born 1946, in Melbourne, Australia. In 1938 Singer's parents, Viennese Jews, fled to Australia where Singer was born eight years later. After graduating from the University of Melbourne, he travelled to England to study at Oxford before taking on a teaching post at the University of New York for a short time. He then returned to Melbourne where he worked at the universities of La Trobe, Monash and then Melbourne. Singer is currently the Ira DeCamp Professor of Bioethics at Princeton University in the United States

Singer works in the field of practical ethics – his focus is on specific questions about how we should live. His ideas are controversial and outrage many.

Major works

Animal Liberation

Practical Ethics

How Are We To Live?

Index